Behind
the
Phantom's
Mask

A SERIAL BY

ROGER

EBERT

Illustrations by Victor Juhasz

ANDREWS
AND McMEEL

A Universal Press Syndicate Company

Kansas City

FOR CHAZ

Library of Congress Cataloging-in-Publication Data

Ebert, Roger.
Behind the Phantom's mask : a serial / by Roger Ebert ;
illustrations by Victor Juhasz.
p.   cm.
ISBN: 0-8362-8021-0
I. Title.
PS355.B52B4   1993
813'.54—dc20   93-13227
CIP

Fiction
Ebert, Roger.
Behind the Phantom's mask

**DO NOT REMOVE
CARDS FROM POCKET**

Also by Roger Ebert

An Illini Century

A Kiss Is Still a Kiss

Roger Ebert's
Movie Home Companion

The Perfect London Walk
(with Daniel Curley)

Two Weeks in the Midday Sun:
A Cannes Notebook

The Future of the Movies:
Interviews with Martin Scorsese,
Steven Spielberg, and George Lucas
(with Gene Siskel)

PART ONE

London

SHEILA CHESHAM cursed herself for her stupidity. She was trapped inside the stage machinery for *Phantom of the Opera*, and the performance was scheduled to begin in two hours. She was reluctant to scream out for help, because she had no business deep inside the bowels of the old theater—no business interfering with the first break Mason had received in long, grim years, his chance to play the Phantom before a London audience.

SHEILA CHESHAM

By wedging her arm beneath her, she was able to twist on her side and look up through the fearsome gears and pulleys toward the underside of the stage of Her Majesty's Theater. There was no way out except for the way she had come in, through an unmarked door in the corridor beneath the stage.

She had chosen her moment carefully, waiting until Leverance, the ancient stage manager, began the ritual of relighting his pipe, then slipping behind him and into the darkness. Her plan had been to creep out through the orchestra pit and mingle with the arriving audience. Then she could see

1

Mason's performance even though Leverance would swear she had not entered the theater.

Mason Devereaux was a superstitious twit, the kind of man who could command a stage in front of hundreds of total strangers, and yet seize up with panic at the thought that a single friend might be in the audience. He had turned pale when Sheila asked to attend his first performance as the Phantom: "Unthinkable, old girl. I'd go bone dry the moment I thought of you out there beyond the footlights." She had lied to Mason, telling him she would wait for news in the Coach and Horses after the show, and then she had slipped past old Leverance and tried to climb through the machinery.

Sheila tried again to free her long chestnut hair, which was caught inside the fierce brass wheels. She heard a rustling in the darkness. Of all of her nightmares, this was the worst: Trapped in the teeth of a giant machine with inquisitive rats.

A few days earlier, Billy (Silver Dollar) Baxter settled into his booth at the Polo Lounge of the Beverly Hills Hotel and searched the room for the faces of friends. No luck. The cocktail hour has gone to hell in this joint, he thought. Nothing but people like me.

"*Irving!*" he shouted. "*Brang 'em on!*"

Billy Baxter practiced the theory that all waiters everywhere would answer to the name of "Irving," if it were called out loudly enough. He was usually right. Waiters hovered over him, hoping to intercept his order before he bellowed for attention.

"Johnnie Walker!" he told Irving. "Black Label. No soda. No ice. In a clean glass. And wipe off the table and bring me some nice little cashews—none of that trail mix crap. I just got in off the trail. And a twist of lemon. Run it right around the rim."

In thirty years as a Broadway press agent, Baxter hadn't even bothered to maintain an office; he worked out of his briefcase and the phone booths of Broadway bars and delicatessens, feeding items to columnists. But now the columns had gone to hell. Instead of a quick plug for a club date, they contained dense paragraphs about psychiatric and gynecological emergencies. Nobody gave a damn about your client un-

BILLY (SILVER DOLLAR) BAXTER

RAVEN CHARLES

less it was bad news. The press agents these days got paid for keeping their clients out of the columns, and although Billy thought there was money in that—as long as nothing appeared, who could prove you weren't working?—it was against his principles. Robert Altman had once given him some good advice: "Fiddle on the corner where the quarters are." Billy had abandoned the Great White Way and got on the bus for Los Angeles.

"Billy Baxter."

It was not a question. It was a statement, made by a tall black woman who was towering over Baxter's table. Billy stood up so quickly he had to grab his drink to save it. Raven Charles was one good-looking lady. He liked the way she dressed. Lots of class. She looked like she belonged in one of those fashion ads where the models wore business suits and big horn-rim glasses, and had their hair pulled back in a bun, and tickled their cute little chins with the erasers of yellow Ticonderogas. And they always forgot and left one extra button open on their starched white shirts.

"Irving!" Billy cried. "Whatever Miss Charles will have! And whatever I'm having!"

Raven Charles glided into the booth and extended her hand. Billy liked her long manicured red nails. They were like the smell of napalm in the morning. The waiter covered the surface of their table with glasses and peanut bowls, ash trays and napkins, and Billy slipped him a silver dollar.

"Are you still handing out those silver dollars, Billy?"

"Economy move," Billy said. "They think it's a real tip. How often do you see a silver dollar these days? A lot of people, they think there's silver in it. Remember that time at the Cannes Film Festival? I brought a suitcase full. I had a hell of a time getting them through customs."

"How's it going, Billy?"

"As you can see," Billy said, spreading his hands. "Don't look too hard."

"I'm going to say two words to you," Raven said. "Mason Devereaux."

"Yeah, I knew him," Billy said. "The British actor. He had a brilliant youth, but that was back when he was still young. I met him during *My Fair Lady* on Broadway. He played Freddy, the kid. He was always doing those little acting workshops where they talk about regaining control of their instruments. Like they were pilots. He had a lot of promise. Then he got to be a lush. What do you want to know about him?"

"Do you think he could play the Phantom of the Opera?"

"Stage, screen, or TV? Because what I hear is, these days he's not the kind of guy you want to depend on for tonight at eight."

"It's for the film version," Raven Charles said. "The studio wants Sir Bradleigh Court, who's playing the lead in London, but I need someone else in the wings, as a negotiating ploy. This is all in perfect confidence."

"Yeah," Baxter said. "Mason could make a movie. If John Belushi could, Mason could. Just schedule all his key scenes for that little window between after he gets over the hangover and before he starts cheering up too much."

"Where you come in," the woman said, "would be like this. Realistic Pictures would hire you on a free-lance basis. You go over to London and talk to Devereaux, get to know him again, see what condition he's in. You could hint about a Hollywood role. Be our man on the ground over there. Keep an eye on his drinking. See if he can be taken seriously."

"You want some peanuts?" Billy asked. "Irving!"

MASON DEVEREAUX

"GIVE me a break, old man," Mason Devereaux implored Fontaine Eady. They were in the back bar of the Red Lion Pub, seven minutes' walk from Her Majesty's Theater. "Sheila is a good friend. But don't write any nonsense about romance. There's the age difference, for one thing. It's not seemly."

"May-December?" asked Eady, who had started out as an editorial

FONTAINE EADY

writer for a Murdoch tabloid, and worked his way up to the gossip column.

"June-October," Devereaux said stiffly.

"Are you quite sure there's only friendship involved?" Eady asked pleasantly, raising a finger for another round. He was good at his job. He had a cosmic indifference to the true nature of Mason's relationship with Sheila, even though he was a cousin of the Cheshams. On the other hand, it represented two inches of copy, which focused his attention wonderfully.

Devereaux glanced at his watch. "Ninety-three minutes to curtain," he said. "I should be at the theater. Who can say? I might be discovered even at this advanced age."

"You were born to play the Phantom," Eady told him. Devereaux looked at him sharply. It was only possibly a compliment.

"You know, when it comes to casting the *film*," Mason said, "my own physical makeup is a good deal more appropriate than Bradleigh Court's."

"Court is . . . too robust?" Eady asked.

"One could virtually call him fat. Not lean and colorfully gaunt like me—and, one might say, distinguished."

Mason took the drink Fontaine Eady had ordered, and allowed the smoky cognac to trickle down slowly, turning into courage. To get the film job would even his score with Bradleigh Court, who only had to look at Mason to make him feel a failure. Court had been his great rival for twenty-five years, since they had alternated in the roles of Othello and Iago at Stratford. "I play Iago every other night," Court had roared, "and Mason plays him every night."

Mason had gone on to play a Hamlet who was said, in certain circles anyway, to be the best in a generation. But then his triumphs had started to come in smaller and smaller venues, in obscure festivals and theater workshops, while Court had soared. In the years since they worked together, Court had become a star, while Mason brooded resentfully in the corners of theatrical pubs.

For Devereaux to miss this last great chance would be a sentence of failure, a return to the endless round of comic villains and provincial extra men that had become his career. But just now Eady was handing him another large brandy, and to tell the truth a bracer was appealing, before the ordeal ahead.

"Why does anyone give a faint damn about my love life, anyway?" Devereaux asked the newspaperman. A sense of well-being was stealing through his system. It was pleasant, sitting here, looking at his image reflected back from the crystal mirrors on every wall, engaging in wordplay with a scoundrel he had known for years. It was actually rather pleasant to be the subject of Eady's curiosity; it was not often that any item involving Mason Devereaux was newsworthy enough for Fontaine's page in the *Sketch*. "Let's assume for one moment that I am having an affair with Sheila Chesham. Who cares about the romantic aspirations of an obscure middle-aged actor?"

"No one, Mason," Eady replied pleasantly. "In fact, on your own merits, the only significant story you could generate right now would be your obituary. Brilliant start, failed promise. Brief mention of your success in Shakespeare, years and years ago. Colorful Soho pub character. Lifelong struggle with drink, blah, blah."

"Assuming I don't drop dead simply to amuse you," Mason said, returning his empty glass to the bar, "why would my love life be of the slightest interest?"

"Not yours, old boy," Eady explained. "Sheila's. She's young and she's pretty. And she has a title, which would make her seem all the more deliciously tarnished by any association with you. She will someday be one of the richest women in the United Kingdom, unless Labour takes her daddy's money away. The story lies entirely in the fact that she would find interest in a decrepit specimen such as yourself."

"Decrepit?" asked Devereaux, focusing on the end of the sentence that was nearest to him. "I admit I am closer to fifty than forty."

"So is the Queen."

T HE two men finished their drinks and walked out into the sunshine of the April afternoon. They parted at Jermyn Street, Devereaux walking toward Lower Regent Street and Her Majesty's. Alongside the theater he passed the ragged line of *Phantom* fans camped out on the pavement. They were prepared to squat day and night through freezing hailstones to get tickets to the bloody *Phantom,* Mason thought, and yet here he was—Mason Devereaux, today's Phantom, alive and in person—walking past them totally ignored. He turned in at the stage entrance and the ancient Leverance took his hat.

"No sign of Miss Chesham?" he asked the old man.

"She hasn't come in by the stage door, your honor," said the old man, who having played a bailiff on "Rumpole" had never surrendered the role.

HAROLD GASPER

"There you are, Devereaux! I was just asking myself—where can he be?"

Mason peered into the backstage gloom. It was Harold Gasper, one of the investors in the show. Eady's column always described him as the West End's impresario of last choice.

"Held up a bit in traffic," Devereaux said, popping a Rolo mint into his mouth. "Wretched road-works."

"We're trying something new this afternoon," Gasper said. "Can you hear that music?"

Devereaux did indeed hear mournful music leaking into the backstage area from the speakers out front.

"My idea," Gasper said proudly. "I have girls stationed in the theater, flogging cassettes and compact discs. The music will stimulate the customers' appetites."

"Funny. I don't recall any screaming on the cast albums I've heard," said Devereaux.

"Screaming?"

"A woman's screaming. Can't you hear it?"

"Part of the effect," said Gasper. "Now for God's sake get up to your dressing room and get the mask on, old man. Curtain is in forty-five."

MASON examined his face in the mirror for signs of intoxication. He'd had a few too many with Eady. As the score of *Phantom of the Opera* came pounding through the walls of the shabby makeup room, he began to curse the columnist. Obviously Eady had plotted to get him stewed, so that he would go onstage and make a fool of himself. That would supply a paragraph for Eady's page in the *Sketch*, couched in the language of phony regret: *Pity about poor Mason Devereaux . . .*

Mason found that his mouth was dry. It was starting again now, his fear of the stage—the flop sweat, the hound that hunted him down in every dressing room in the world. With the logic of the practiced alcoholic, Devereaux cursed himself for two oversights: Drinking too much, and not drinking enough.

There was a knock on the door and Carrie Catto, the makeup artist, entered. She was a sweet thing from the Polytech who always seemed to regard him with pity. They stood side by side at the mirror and evaluated the face she was to transform into the hideous countenance of the Phantom. He saw a man in the bloom of middle age, attractive in a certain light, the marks of the decades concealed by the good humor of the smile. She saw an aging actor with fear in his eyes, brandy on his breath, and sweat on his upper lip. As the cool alcohol swab passed over his brow, Devereaux closed his eyes and stared into the darkness, realizing that he could not remember a single one of his lines, not even the few he would need for the opening scene.

LIKE every Hollywood executive, Raven Charles had given more thought to her office than to her home. She'd sent the designer away with a laserdisc of *Swing Time* and told him not to come back until he understood why it was her favorite film. The result was a room that intimidated visitors, while at the same time informing them that she was warm and caring, and loved the green growing plants of the earth. The furniture was early Museum of Modern Art. The trees were tended weekly by a man who always wore green jeans. The obligatory human touch was supplied by a framed two-sheet of *Stormy Weather*. The desk held only a legal pad, a Mont Blanc pen, a telephone, a life-size sterling silver replica of the Phantom's mask, and a Rolodex, which contained more fax numbers than friends. Like Ginger Rogers in the movie, she was a great dancer, but she needed a partner. Loneliness was dangerous on the fast track. You bought scripts because they were about relationships that were happier than your own.

Raven held the mask to her face, the silver cool against her skin. Some days she felt so close to the Phantom that it frightened her. Her own life was the same as his, unfolding backstage in the shadows, while others won the applause. When the show was over and everyone went home, that could be her voice, instead of the Phantom's, singing that she deserved love just like everyone else.

Everything depended on this film. Her career had been a series of calculated steps—up from the legal department to story development, and then into production and finally to what was essentially the vice presidency in charge of *Phantom of the Opera*. If the movie was a success, Hollywood would be at her feet. If it failed, she could hear them now, the white men in their boardrooms, sadly observing that they had been too generous in trusting their gilt-edged property to her.

"There's no way you can screw this up," Ivan Bloom, the studio head, had told her. "Millions of people all over the world have paid a fortune to see this musical. Every single one of them and their five best friends will want to see the movie. Unless you give them a reason not to. Good luck."

She returned the mask to her desk. Bloom was the only man alive who could make the words "good luck" sound like a warning. But at least he'd given her the chance. Raven didn't need to be told how many ways she could screw up *Phantom of the Opera*. The obvious start in that direction would be the casting of Sir Bradleigh Court in the title role. He had arrived at that stage of his career when the only speech he could deliver convincingly was a toast to the Queen. His Phantom had ballooned into a parody of itself. Theater audiences liked it, because they were forty rows away from it. On the screen, in close-up, chewing every word before he swallowed it, Bradleigh Court would turn the Phantom into a smirking toad.

Raven Charles had an idea so private she dared hardly express it even to herself. Ivan Bloom would implode if he heard it. She believed that an obscure actor like Mason Devereaux, so brilliant in his youth, so misused and misunderstood ever since, was born to portray the Phantom. The role could only be played, she believed, by a great man who sincerely believed he was a failure.

MASON stared in terror at his reflection in the mirror. This was it at last, public humiliation at the end of a long descending life in the theater. Why had he agreed to understudy the Phantom in the first place? He could always make enough money in advertising to pay for rooms, food, and drink, using his dependable voice to marvel at the wonders of Sainsbury's fish fingers and peas.

From the corridor outside, he could hear Harold Gasper calling for a cigarette. If he failed today, the blame belonged at Gasper's door. Mason on his own would never have conceived of such a mad scheme. He could have remained happily wedged into a corner of the Coach and Horses, solving a crossword.

IT seemed to Devereaux that Gasper had always been lurking somewhere about on the fringes of his life. They had dropped out of drama school at about the same time, and had spent some months in the sixties in a fringe group devoted to the repudiation of the commercial theater establishment. Gasper had split with the group over his conviction that larger audiences could be attracted if naked Windmill girls were added to the revues. Their paths had parted, Gasper taking offices above a porno store in Soho and booking provincial tours of revivals and pantomimes, while Devereaux dissipated the early promise of his Hamlet on television, where he specialized in weak men who let their women down.

After losing touch for years, they had met again in the basement quarters of the Academy Club, a hole-in-the-wall off Beak Street. Gasper stood a round, and confided that he was an investor in *Phantom of the Opera*.

"Devereaux," he had said, signaling the barman for another, "the moment you walked into this room, inspiration struck me. I've found my man. You're older now. There's character in your face. I want to put you to work in the *Phantom*."

Devereaux raised his eyebrows—not too high, as he desperately needed employment.

"I thought Bradleigh Court had the job."

"For the time, yes," Gasper said. "But Bradleigh will want out in a year or so—this is strictly between us, of course—and then we'll need the right man to step in. Good heavens, man, it's a godsend! I want you to learn the role, and then I'll slip you into a matinee and who knows what might develop."

"In other words," Mason had said carefully, "you want to hire me as the understudy, with the possibility that something may come of it?"

"That's one construction," Gasper agreed.

Devereaux had held out for two more drinks before agreeing that the idea held promise. He might take the job or he might not, but he intended to get dinner out of Gasper before deciding. The dim winter afternoon had already turned dark when they marched down to Wheeler's to continue negotiations over a piece of fresh fish and a decent bottle of white wine. At closing time they were at the Coach and Horses, where Gasper, a conspiratorial arm over Mason's shoulder, had explained exactly what he had in mind. The understudy job was only the icing on the cake. By taking a carefully calculated risk and stepping perhaps an inch or two outside of the strict construction of the law, they could resurrect both their careers with one sensational theatrical masterstroke. They might not even, strictly speaking, be doing anything criminal, and certainly no one would ever know a crime had been committed. It was more of a . . . more of a prank, a lark, a *coup de theatre* one could fairly say . . .

Devereaux placed his elbows on either side of his glass, and looked into its amber depths for revelation. Gasper's proposal was reckless and mad. It was also bold and defiant, a thumb in the eye of the West End which had ignored Mason for so long. Norman, behind the bar, called closing time and began to collect the glasses.

Mason considered that there was a song that applied to his situation. If he had nothing, he had nothing to lose.

Now the moment of truth had arrived. Curtain was in minutes. The makeup girl turned a strong light into Mason's face, to examine her work. He closed his eyes and scurried through the wilds of his memory, seeking the fugitive dialogue, cues, and stage directions. He had rehearsed for weeks, but could not remember the words to any of the songs. Or the melodies. He knew he would be saved if at least his opening speech would return to him. Once properly launched, a performance had a way of carrying itself through to the end. He groaned aloud.

"Are you quite all right?" asked Carrie.

"Rehearsing, dear girl," Mason said.

B ENEATH the stage, behind a door marked with a lightning bolt and the helpful information TEN THOUSANDS VOLTS, Sheila Chesham contemplated the possibility of her death. It could come quickly once the fearsome stage machinery for the *Phantom* was set in motion. She had cried for help until her voice broke, but her calls were masked by the mournful musical score on the big house speakers. Stagehands pounded back and forth above her head, wrestling sets into their opening positions. Rescue was so near that its footfalls sent a thin rain of dust falling into her eyes.

She began to realize seriously that she might actually die, crushed within the gears of the ingenious stage apparatus that was used to create the Phantom's ghostly lair. She was pinned above the steel tracks for the Phantom's grotesque gondola, and surrounded by the nozzles for the mist that would drift across the stage. This time when the Phantom sailed on the lonely river of his underworld, the cargo might indeed be death. Would her death stop the show? Sheila wondered. Or would be it years before her bones were discovered?

I N the Royal Box above the orchestra pit, Harold Gasper tossed his gloves into one chair and took the other as his own. He looked down with satisfaction at the crowd filling the theater, at the excited teenagers from Essex, the serious Japanese, the members of

American tour groups thrilled to see each other again after being separated ever since breakfast. Here was one more Saturday matinee audience that could now congratulate itself on seeing the one musical that was essential for every London visitor. It made no difference if they enjoyed it or not. They had seen it, and could tell the folks at home. The secret of wealth in the declining years of the twentieth century, Gasper reflected, was to create an Obligatory Sight in a major city, and own it yourself. Obligatory Sights such as the Tower and the Houses of Parliament were a waste of everyone's time, because they didn't pay. The *Phantom* paid well, and it would go right on paying if he had anything to say about it.

Of course Andrew Lloyd Webber and the other investors knew nothing of his scheme for assuring the long run of the show. That was essential to his plan. After he and Mason took their little stroll outside of the law, the others would be able to project ignorance with complete conviction. They would have to be totally believable—even to each other, even to themselves—and they would be. Sitting well back in the shadows and keeping his hands beneath the level of the railing, Gasper took a revolver from his briefcase and laid it in his lap. It was not more than twenty yards from his box to center stage.

MASON stood up to face his doom. The actor had been transformed into the Phantom of the Opera, a process that, in his case, actually involved adding some color to his complexion. With the mask obscuring his face, Mason now looked indistinguishable from Bradleigh Court and every other Phantom who had passed through the play in the course of its long run. But could he do the job? Mason had sent Carrie out front to buy a brandy, and now he made a drinking motion with his hand, and she handed him the glass. He sipped through a straw to prevent damage to her work. Leverance knocked on the door with the three-minute warning.

"Time, gentlemen, please," said Mason, trying to smile with lips that were twitching with fear.

"Break a leg!" Catto told him.

"I shall need to break more than that," he said.

Devereaux followed Leverance through a dim series of passage-ways to the foot of a ladder that led up into the flies. He would first be glimpsed by the audience while shrieking his defiance from far above the stage. This was no job for an actor, Mason thought gloomily—it was a stunt for a bloody acrobat. Devereaux was terri-fied of heights, but now he was too drunk to care, and he climbed hand over hand up the old wooden steps, keeping his eyes resolutely level and trying not to think about the fall to the stage far below.

T HERE was a banging at the stage door, and old Leverance opened it to see Sir Bradleigh Court standing in the street, impatiently waiting for change from a taxi driver. The actor was notorious for his temper. As the driver fumbled with the pound coins, Court swung his cane around to hammer on the theater door again, and caught the stage manager sharply on the sleeve of his cardigan.

"Good heavens, Leverance! What are you doing here?"

"Opening the door, Sir Bradleigh."

"In future, try to do so at less hazard to yourself. Is the makeup girl still here?"

"I think you'll find her somewhere backstage, sir," said Leverance. "She has finished with Mr. Devereaux and is standing by if needed."

"Blast her! And blast Devereaux! I'll put on my own makeup."

Leverance cleared his throat tactfully. "I hope you've remembered, your honor, that Mr. Devereaux is going on in your place this after-noon."

"How could I forget, Leverance, with that bloody confidence man Harold Gasper ringing me twice this morning to remind me? I'm here to have some photographs taken for the *Sunday Times.* I'll get into costume and wait in my dressing room while the performance is under way, and when Lord Snowden arrives, send him directly in to me."

Court, striding through the backstage area, looked up and could just glimpse Devereaux, clinging to the ladder. He struck his stick against the floor in annoyance. The man had been a halfway decent actor many years ago, but now—no chance. Drink had been his ruination. Probably have to bail him out. Bloody fool Gasper. It was against all the rules for an understudy to go on when the star was fit to perform. But if Court ever hoped to have even the briefest of holidays, Devereaux had to have a warm-up in front of a real audience. Thinking of the house in Provence he had not seen in more than a year, Court went more contentedly to his dressing room.

HIGH above the theater floor, Mason Devereaux gripped the scaffolding with both hands. He was perched on a catwalk behind the center of the proscenium arch, and would make his entrance from that position, startling the audience as he revealed himself to the characters on the stage.

From far below, he heard the end of the overture and then the silence as the first actors appeared on stage. They played ladies and gentlemen who were inspecting the premises of a decrepit Parisian opera house. Devereaux took the script from his pocket and propped it before him, where it would be out of sight of the audience. He could get through the first scene, at least, by cheating. Large drops of perspiration splashed down on the page.

I've never yet gone completely dry during a performance, Mason told himself. He had forgotten lines and even misplaced whole passages on occasion, but somehow he had managed to get back on the track one way or another, usually with the help of a fellow actor's pointed hints: "I say, old chap, weren't you going to tell me something about *your experiences in the war?*" He had gone through flop sweat before, too—it was a punctual visitor before every performance—but never until today had he been completely confident that he would forget every single line and lyric. Those damnable brandies with Fontaine Eady had derailed him. And of course there had been no chance to rehearse the changes that Harold Gasper had planned just for this performance.

The orchestra began its moaning prelude to the Phantom's entrance music. Mason struck his forehead, trying to jar loose the lines that were lodged inside. Some seventy feet below, Sheila Chesham used her clenched fists to bang against the pipes of the stage machinery. Couldn't they hear the noise onstage? Didn't they realize she was trapped inside the giant wheels that moved the Phantom's world?

Devereaux heard his musical cue with a start, and lurched forward into view, far above the heads of the audience, howling out the Phantom's famous entrance lines. At least his voice had never failed him—that instrument once described by the *Telegraph* as the sound of a bartender at closing time in hell. Using the hidden script, he blundered through the scene somehow, and began a tricky journey down the ladders and through the shadows. There was a time, he thought, when I could recite all of Shakespeare flawlessly. Now I can't ask the time of day without a prompt.

I N the Royal Box, Harold Gasper waited patiently. Once Devereaux appeared onstage, he planned to stand back well concealed in the shadows of his box, and fire the revolver. As panic broke out in the theater, who would be looking at a stage box now seemingly empty?

Devereaux arrived wheezing and trembling at his second entrance position. Carrie Catto looked at him with apprehension. She had sent a lot of actors onto the stage with a final puff of powder, and had never seen one who looked more fearful.

"In heaven's mercy, my girl, race round to the Stalls Bar and get me another large brandy," Mason told her. "And tell the prompter I shall be in need of his services."

Carrie slipped through the inside stage door and ran around the theater to the lobby. It was empty except for the ladies behind the refreshment counter, and Douglas Brown, the theater manager, who was rocking on his heels in the center of the rug, stirring the ice in a Perrier. She didn't like Brown; he was too eager to put his hands on the female staff. She was hurrying toward the bar when they both heard a shot from the auditorium.

"That's curious," said Brown. "There aren't any guns in the play at this point."

They walked quickly to the nearest doors, which led to the dress circle. From the back row all they could see was a confusion of patrons standing in the aisles and on their seats, trying to get a clear view of the stage. They pushed their way forward until they could see the stage, and then Carrie cried out, "Oh, my God!"

There were two Phantoms on the stage. One lay in a pool of blood. The other stood over him, holding a revolver. A screaming woman was swaying suspended helplessly by her hair, twenty feet above their heads.

D EAD?" said Raven Charles, looking at her speakerphone in
disbelief.

   "Shot dead as a doornail at center stage ten minutes into
the first act," Billy Baxter told her. "Then another guy dressed like
the Phantom jumps onstage holding the pistol. While he's standing

there looking at the body, a dynamite brunette materializes out of nowhere and is hanging in the air by her hair. She's screaming bloody murder. I never saw the show before, but I don't think she was in the original script. Mason is flat on his back. He doesn't move. What an exit. My advice? Forget the *Phantom*. Film the murder."

"Maybe he was only wounded," Raven said.

"I seriously doubt he was only wounded," Billy said, shouting into the pay phone in the lobby of Her Majesty's Theater. "First he's laid out on the stage for about fifteen minutes. Then the ambulance boys administer CPR. Then they bring on a bishop who reads him his rites. After that they cover him up with a sheet and carry him off on a stretcher. He was exhibiting all the signs of a corpse."

Raven bit her lip. "Poor Mason Devereaux," she said. "He never even knew I wanted him for the *Phantom*." She wrote Mason's name on a legal pad and then crossed it off with quick, angry strokes. "Thanks for calling, Billy. Spend a couple of days in London, see a few shows, attend the funeral, and send me the bill."

Billy Baxter hung up the phone and walked through the lobby. Hanging by the ticket window a sign was still displayed with the poignant message,

AT THIS PERFORMANCE
THE ROLE OF THE PHANTOM
WILL BE PLAYED BY
MR. MASON DEVEREAUX

Billy took it down and put it in his pocket. "Souvenir," he told an usher.

I would very greatly appreciate a small drink," Mason Devereaux said. "Something to steady my nerves."

"You've had enough to drink," Inspector Fredson Rowley said to the trembling actor.

"My advice would be to answer the inspector's questions and then get well away somewhere for a long rest," said Harold Gasper. He stood in the shadows by the door of the dressing room, smoking, his shoulders against the wall.

After the panic had been sorted out onstage and the body of Sir Bradleigh Court had been carried away by the silent medics of the St. John's Ambulance Brigade, they had all gathered in the dressing room. Devereaux sat with an arm around Sheila Chesham, who was still smudged with grease and dust from beneath the stage. Carrie Catto hid weeping quietly in a corner. Harold Gasper, who had rushed back-

INSPECTOR FREDSON ROWLEY

stage right after the shooting, had identified himself as the senior member of management present, and was guarding the door. Rowley, who was a senior man from Scotland Yard, had by coincidence been in the audience with his wife. When it became clear that a man lay dead on stage, he had taken charge of the investigation.

"If one does not feel one has had enough to drink," Mason said, "one cannot be said to have had enough to drink."

"Pour him a brandy, then," Rowley said. "A small one. Perhaps it will settle him. I am still confused, Mr. Devereaux, by what has happened here. The play begins with you in the lead. A shot rings out, but when the Phantom's mask is removed, the dead man is Sir Bradleigh Court. Then you rush onstage with a revolver. Can you be of any assistance to me?"

"I haven't the slightest clue what happened," Mason said. He took the brandy and drank it needfully. "I had started the performance and was preparing for my next entrance. I felt in need of a drink, and sent the makeup girl out front to bring me one from the Stalls Bar. Then I found myself feeling quite unwell. Leverance, the stage manager, brought me a chair. He told me Bradleigh Court was in the theater and already in costume. I warned Leverance that Bradleigh might be needed, as I did not feel capable of returning to the stage."

Leverance nodded eagerly. "Sir Bradleigh was in costume for some photographs to be took, your honor," he said. "I told him Mr. Devereaux had been overserved. Sir Bradleigh took one look at him and said he would go on in his place."

"I was not overserved," Devereaux said with a stern look at the stage manager, who had broken the backstage code of silence. "I had been drinking, as is occasionally my custom before a performance. I think actually I was struck down by the sudden onset of the flu."

"It's been going around," Rowley said dryly. "Now what did you do then?"

"Bradleigh made his entrance," Mason continued. "I walked downstairs toward the dressing room, and was astonished to hear a woman's screams from the passage beneath the stage. I opened a door and found Miss Chesham entangled in the machinery."

Sheila shuddered and took Mason's hand. She nodded. "Mason was trying to save me," she said.

"What in heaven's name were you doing trapped in the machinery?" Harold Gasper asked, tapping a cigarette against the side of his lighter. "How very bizarre."

"I slipped in when nobody was looking," Sheila said, holding back the tears in her voice. "I thought I could crawl out through the orchestra pit without being seen. This matinee was Mason's great opportunity and I didn't want to miss it. He was . . . he was . . . afraid he'd have an attack of nerves if he knew I was in the house."

She sniffed wetly, and Devereaux squeezed her hand.

"I was horrified to discover Sheila in such a desperate position," he said. "I tried to lift a pulley so she could work herself free, and then I'm damned if I know what happened next."

"Three things happened at once," Sheila said. "At least I think so. It's so hard to sort out. Something sounded like a gunshot. A revolver came crashing down from somewhere above us and struck Mason on the head. The pulley sprang back, and that set the machinery into motion. I felt myself being pulled straight up by my hair, which was caught in some manner. Before I knew what had happened, I was suspended above the stage. The lights were in my eyes. I tried to look down, and I saw blood spurting from a wound in the side of the Phantom's chest. Then I saw another Phantom run onto the stage holding a gun."

"That's how it must have happened," Devereaux said. "Sheila was pulled up out of sight. I grabbed the revolver, and ran upstairs and onto the stage to help her. That's when I saw Bradleigh Court lying shot to death in his own blood."

"Good God!" said Harold Gasper. "What an incredible turn of events!" He lit the cigarette.

"We called out for an ambulance, and Leverance brought a ladder to help Miss Chesham down," Devereaux said, an edge of relief creeping into his voice, like a lifeboat survivor who realizes it is again possible to make plans. Rowley sighed heavily and shifted on the edge of the dressing table, turning the pages of his notebook back and forth, as if looking for clues. Sheila Chesham reached out gently to Devereaux and began to pick off the latex scar that was still attached to his face. There was a discreet tap at the door. Gasper opened it and found Douglas Brown, the theater manager.

"Terribly sorry to interrupt you, sir," said Brown, "but the customers are asking about their tickets." He stepped into the room and looked around curiously.

"Tickets?"

"Yes, sir. As the performance was less than halfway over when the accident took place, they say they are entitled to tickets at a future performance."

"Of all the bloody cheek!" said Gasper. "They come to see the *Phantom of the Opera* and they see the bloody Phantom shot dead on the stage, an experience they can dine out on for the rest of their lives, and they demand a refund! Bloody Americans!"

"Canadians and Japanese as well, sir."

"That will be all, Brown."

Inspector Rowley looked at the murder weapon, which rested on a newspaper on the table.

"It struck you on the head?"

"Apparently so," said Devereaux.

"And then you carried it onstage?"

"Just as I said."

"If indeed it is even the same weapon that must have shot Sir Bradleigh," Gasper volunteered.

"Ballistics will answer that for us," Rowley said.

There was another tap at the door. Gasper opened it impatiently. "What is it this time, Brown?"

"Lord Snowden, sir. Here to take the photographs."

Gasper made a hollow laugh. "Tell Lord Snowden that he will find his model at the morgue."

I T was later that evening. Billy (Silver Dollar) Baxter stood at the end of the bar in the Coach and Horses, a pub in Soho known for the famous characters who drank there while becoming less famous. He used a little plastic straw to stir the lemon peel in his scotch. He was feeling depressed—not only for Mason Devereaux, whom he had seen shot dead on stage, but also for himself. Mason was dead and Silver Dollar Baxter was out of a job and God was in heaven, apparently lost in thought.

A tall man stepped next to him at the bar and ordered a brandy and soda. Billy moved slightly to one side. "Very kind of you," the man said, his voice deep and very tired. Billy sighed. The stranger sighed. Billy kept his eyes on his drink. He was in no mood for conversation.

"Make it a large one," the other man said.

"Right, Mr. Devereaux."

Billy stared straight ahead. He could feel the hairs on his neck crawling. He looked into the mirror behind the bar and could clearly see the unmistakable Mason Devereaux standing next to him. Mason, the man he had just seen shot dead. Billy did not believe in ghosts.

"Mason Devereaux?"

"Yes."

"Silver Dollar Baxter. Irving! This is on me."

IN the gloom of Her Majesty's Theater, a cigarette glowed and faded, and a cough sounded loud because the space was so empty and so still. Outside, the call of an ambulance siren rose and then trailed away. The theater had not been dark on Saturday night for years—not since the *Phantom*'s endless run had begun. A naked bulb stood on a pole in the middle of the stage, casting a pale glow toward the first dozen rows. Into its dim light strolled Fontaine Eady. He peered over the edge of the orchestra pit, and could see the sheets thrown over the percussion instruments below. It seemed unnatural that the theater was empty. But tonight there was no heart for staging the play, and, for that matter, no Phantom to play in it. The star, Sir Bradleigh Court, lay dead on a morgue slab, and his understudy, Mason Devereaux, was no doubt nearly as horizontal on one of the chairs along the wall of the Coach and Horses pub.

Eady tested the rail, as if considering a leap down into the pit, but then he turned and walked out through a side door, his way illuminated by the dim pink light of the exit sign. A door marked TO THE BOXES was on his left, and, opening it to complete darkness, he felt his way up the carpeted stairs and through the door of the Royal Box.

It was from here, he knew, that Harold Gasper had watched what little there was of Mason Devereaux's first performance as the Phantom, and Bradleigh Court's last. Eady had stepped into the back of the theater as the lights went down, to see how Mason would do in his matinee performance. Surveying the house, he had glimpsed Gasper up here, alone in the box. Gasper had looked tense and unhappy, but then Gasper always looked tense and unhappy. The overture had started, and poor Mason Devereaux had shouted his way mechanically through the opening lines of the play.

Eady had been prepared to leave. It was too sad, what Mason had done to his talent. But then the Phantom had made his second entrance, looking somehow more fit and ready, and Eady had paused just long enough to be a witness when a shot rang out and the Phantom fell dead.

Eady did not know how he knew it, but he knew without any doubt that the actor had been shot by Harold Gasper. The moment the man had fallen, Eady's eyes had snapped to the Royal Box, where he saw nothing. No Gasper, no confusion, no curiosity, just an empty black space. And the thought flashed into his mind: Gasper has shot Mason—the poor bastard!

It was only later, backstage, that Eady discovered the dead man was Bradleigh Court, not Mason Devereaux. A five pound note had purchased that information and the rest of the story, as it was dimly understood by Leverance. Later, as the police and the others finally made their way out the stage door and through a mob of photographers and the curious, Eady had fallen behind in the shadows of the auditorium. Now he silently examined the interior of the Royal Box. Eady believed Gasper had fired the shot from the box. But Leverance had said the murder weapon struck Mason below the stage. Eady, who did not believe in magic, knew there had to be a way from here to there.

N EWS of the murder had raced through Soho, and the Coach and Horses was jammed with those who knew there was a good chance Mason would repair there to talk about it. Devereaux formed the center of attention until it became clear he was too far gone to provide more entertainment. He was finally left with an audience of Sheila Chesham and Billy Baxter, who he could dimly recall bending an elbow with during a Broadway run of *My Fair Lady,* years ago.

"To consider that someone would think me worth murdering!" he told them, for the third or fourth time. "It's very nearly a compliment."

"Mason, it's time for you to go home," Sheila said. "Let me call you a cab."

"It is better to be drunk than to be dead," Billy said. "Old saying."

Devereaux's thoughts were elsewhere. He heard neither of them. "It is very odd indeed how life works out," he said, his voice a resonating hymn of drunken melancholy. "Look at us sitting here at this table in this pub. If you had asked me this morning where I would be at this hour, I would have told you I would be right here—celebrating after the performance. And yet how strangely it has all ended. There was no performance and there will be no celebration, even though not one but two actors were on premises and in costume. And now the snow falls on every part of the lonely churchyard on the hill where Bradleigh Court will soon lie buried."

Sheila knew the signs. When Mason started quoting Joyce, it wouldn't be long until he started to snuffle.

"It's April, Mason," she said. "No snow."

Mason lifted up his hand and displayed his empty glass to Norman the barman, who passed a fresh drink over to the table. Norman turned back to a television news program showing a more nearly vertical Mason Devereaux.

"I know, I know, oh, yes, I know, it's time to go home," Mason intoned. "But this is my wake for Bradleigh Court, and although finer people will mourn him, none can feel what I feel. Did you know we were in the Royal Shakespeare together?"

"Everybody knows that," Sheila said.

"He as Othello, I as Iago, and then we'd switch. But this afternoon, God rest his soul, Bradleigh switched one time too many."

"Could anyone have known it was Bradleigh in the costume, and not you?" asked Sheila.

"He coulda fooled me," Billy said.

"Everyone would have known soon enough," said Mason. "He hadn't my voice, you know."

"But he hadn't spoken a word when he was shot."

"Too true," said Mason. "So Bradleigh was an innocent victim. And the bullet must have been intended for me. There must be something here . . . something I haven't figured out. If only I could think . . ."

"But you haven't an enemy in the world!"

"I am forced to conclude," Mason said, "that in fact I have at least one."

"I'm taking you to the country," Sheila said suddenly. It was the only way to get Mason out of the pub and off to a place of safety. "Come on. We can call my car."

"If you could delay just a second," said Baxter. "I hate to allow a thing like business to intrude on our memorial observation here, but in the shock of discovering that you were still alive there was something I forgot to tell you. I represent Miss Raven Charles."

"Yes?" Mason, hoping to get another drink before Sheila carried him away, was impatient.

"She is the lady who is going to produce the movie of the *Phantom*."

A stillness settled at the table. Mason seemed newly alert.

"Yes, Mr. Baxter? Billy, if I may?"

"Miss Charles thought you might be a good choice to play the lead."

"But Bradleigh Court was far and away the front-runner."

"He ain't the front-runner no more."

FONTAINE EADY took a fifty-pence coin and dropped it through the grating of an air shaft in the Royal Box. He heard it bouncing all the way down, and nodded his head with satisfaction. The screams of the audience must have masked the noise of the falling gun. He was certain that if he looked beneath the stage, he would find the same coin at the same place where Mason Devereaux had been hit on the head with the murder weapon.

Eady went out the door and felt his way down the darkened corridor outside the Royal Box, his gloved hand resting lightly on the invisible brass railing. After several steps he found an obstruction on the railing. It was another hand.

Eady brought his brass-handled cane up sharply, for protection. "I find it quite unpleasant," he said, "to find I am not alone in a dark place. Something from my childhood, I suppose."

A cigarette lighter flared, and he could see the face of Douglas Brown, the theater manager. The flickering light from below gave Brown's features a satanic cast.

"Good lord, man," Eady said. "What do you mean by creeping about in the dark?"

"I could ask you the same question," Brown said. "I work here."

Eady smiled. "A good point." He knew everyone employed in the London theater, and had known most of them for far too long. Brown flipped on a light switch, and they stood regarding each other.

"Such a tragic loss," Eady said.

"The memorial service will not be held until next week," Brown said sardonically.

"Then I'll save my sympathy for the occasion," Eady said. "I suppose you know the way backstage?"

"You will find no one backstage just now," Brown said. "Certainly none of the stars."

"I'm not looking for a person," Eady said. "I'm looking for an object. A fifty-pence coin, in fact. I dropped it earlier." He paused. "From the Royal Box."

· Their eyes met, and Eady realized he had struck a nerve. If he had somehow known instantly where the shot came from, he could sense that Douglas Brown suspected the same thing.

F ORGET the *Phantom*. Make a movie out of the murder."
It was the advice Raven Charles had received yesterday
from Billy Baxter. Now she was passing it along to Ivan Bloom,
the studio chief who had made her producer of *Phantom of the Opera*.
The tall black woman sat on the deck of her Malibu beach house,
talking into a speakerphone.

"Raven, honey, we have millions tied up in the *Phantom*," Bloom
said. "We can't rip off our own production with a cheap exploitation
film."

"That's not what I had in mind," Raven said, paging through the
Sunday papers. All the headlines shouted the sensational story of
the *Phantom* murder case. "This is a made-for-TV movie, Ivan. It
could be a good one. Mason Devereaux plays himself, we make it for
a certain price, it comes out now, the real *Phantom* proceeds on
schedule, and the publicity can only help."

"Made for TV . . ." Bloom said unhappily. His voice faded, and
Raven guessed that he was talking from his car phone. "I don't like
made-for-TV. I spent ten years doing made-for-TV, but now I do
made-for-movie. Much nicer."

"This is a project that is going to be made by somebody," Raven
Charles said. "Six writers got out of bed this morning, looked at the
front page of the *L.A. Times,* and sat down at their computers. The
Phantom is our property, Ivan. If anybody is going to rip it off, it
ought to be us."

"You make a certain amount of sense," Bloom said.

PART TWO
———
Thorn Hill

E VERYONE knows that spiders have eight legs," Mason
Devereaux said, "but I'm damned if I knew they had eight
eyes."

"Four pairs of each," Lord Chesham said proudly.

"It's the sort of thing one would learn at a decent school," said
Mason. "That's the price I've paid for having gone on the stage at
such an early age."

"Eight eyes, eight legs," Lord Chesham said. "Can't sneak anything past them." He sounded like a man who had invented something useful.

"Ummm."

It was one of those rambling conversations in which strangers
arrive at harmonious agreement on completely inconsequential
topics. The two men were sitting in teakwood chairs, weathered to
a worn silver, on the lawn of Thorn Hill House, Lord Chesham's
country home. Everything here was weathered to a silvery gray,
including Lord Chesham. An oak tree shaded them. Before them
the landscape fell gently toward a stream and lake. In the distance
stood a ruined Gothic tower. Chesham's ancestor had built and
ruined it, believing that nothing improved a landscape like a ruin.
There were even engravings showing the old ninth earl smashing at
the walls himself, with a hammer.

Devereaux, desperately hung over, was grateful to his host, who
had rescued him from the breakfast room by suggesting a stroll on
the grounds. He wished a butler would materialize and suggest a
drink. It was still not clear how Sheila Chesham had gotten him
away from the Coach and Horses and into a car and out here into
the reassuring calm of her family's ancestral home. Hadn't there

been an American involved somehow? Some loud man from out of his past, Silver Dollar Something, who talked of hiring Mason for the movies?

Mason slumped lower in his chair, squinting out from under the brim of his Panama. He had not yet been able to bring himself to think clearly of the events on Her Majesty's stage, and of his own role in them. Everything had gone wrong, of that he was certain, but he was not sure what would have constituted everything having gone right. It was pleasant to sit on the lawn, but he had a premonition his lawn days were numbered. Mason's stomach filled with a large doughy lump of fear, like a man who in the midst of an exhilarating sky dive thinks to check for his parachute.

"I say, would you fancy having a look at my spider house?" asked Lord Chesham. His wife had read to him out of the *Telegraph* about Devereaux's brush with death, but if the fellow wasn't going to bring it up himself, Chesham thought the subject was best avoided.

"I sorry to say I can't help you with spiders," Mason said. "You might have one of those chaps come round with a flit gun."

Lord Chesham looked pained. "I do not think of them as pests," he explained, "but as marvelous examples of adaptive behavior. I confess to being an incurable arachnaphile."

"I see," said Mason.

"I've just received a shipment of several Ctenizidae," Chesham said, making them sound like a cheese from Paxton & Whitfield. "They're amusing little beggars when they start fabricating their traps."

"Is it dark and cool in the spider house?" asked Mason.

"Very pleasant," said Chesham.

"Then by all means," said Mason.

THE two men had just heaved themselves up from their chairs when the hooting of a car horn carried across the lawns. An automobile was speeding up the gravel drive toward the great house. Squinting into the sun, Mason saw Sheila Chesham spring from the house and approach the car, from which emerged . . . was it Eady? Yes, it was Eady, who seemed to be welcomed everywhere, and with him, a younger man.

The nerve of Eady, following him here to Thorn Hill. It did not occur to Mason that as a cousin of the Cheshams, Eady would have visited here more often than Devereaux. In some obscure way still to be sorted out, he thought, Eady was to blame for everything. It was Eady who got him drunk before the matinee. And if it hadn't been for that . . . But here Mason's reasoning broke down, because if it hadn't been for that, Mason would have been dead.

H AROLD GASPER is the murderer," Fontaine Eady announced five minutes later in the library of Thorn Hill House. He walked a fifty-pence coin across the backs of his fingers. "You were the intended target, Mason, and Sir Bradleigh Court is being buried on Tuesday at noon. The decent thing would be for you to attend the service, old man. After all, he took the bullet for you."

"Don't talk like a gangster," Devereaux told him. "Not everyone can pull it off." He had obtained a Pimm's Cup from the butler and was feeling slightly more capable.

"It's hard to believe Harold Gasper capable of such a crime," said Douglas Brown, the theater manager, who had arrived with Eady. "But Mr. Eady has convinced me that Gasper is guilty."

They had all gathered self-consciously on the cracked leather sofas and gigantic armchairs of the historic library, where ancient leather bindings protected sets of *Punch* and *Country Life*. It's like a bloody rehearsal for *The Mousetrap*, thought Mason. All that's needed is for Bradleigh Court to climb in through the French doors.

"What could possibly have been the motive?" asked Lord Chesham. He felt that some sort of statement was expected from him, and remembered from Agatha Christie's novels that the motive was always the sticker in these affairs. He stood with his back to the empty fireplace. "Without a motive," he added authoritatively, "one doesn't have a reason for the crime!"

"Too true," said Eady.

"Have you gone to the police?"

"With what?" asked Eady. "A hunch? And let every paper in town share my exclusive?"

Lord Chesham nodded as if Eady had a point, and moved toward the sideboard. He had been keeping an eye on Mason, and thought it was time the poor man had his drink refreshed. Eady perched on the arm of a leather sofa and lit a cigarette. Douglas Brown quietly left the room, and a moment later Sheila got up and followed him. He was waiting for her in the hallway.

"The spider house will be deserted at this hour," she said, running her finger down his cheek. "It's dark, and it's cool."

A T the same moment in London, Harold Gasper sat at a table for one in Le Caprice, a tony little restaurant tucked in behind the Ritz Hotel. He accepted a light for his cigarette from Jeremy, the owner. He watched with a joyless eye as his depleted gin-and-ice was replaced with a fresh one.

Gasper wondered gloomily how long he would have to wait for the knock on the door, the dawn visit from the police, his photograph in the papers as he was led into the arraignment. The *Telegraph* would play the story on page three: INVESTOR NAMED AS PHANTOM KILLER. The *Sun* would have more fun with it: PHANTOM'S LAST GASP-ER. And Eady in the *Sketch* would crucify him.

"Dining alone, Mr. Gasper?"

The voice in his ear was confidential. Gasper looked up to see Inspector Fredson Rowley of Scotland Yard. He recognized him from the postmortem in the dressing room. Rowley sat down opposite him at the table.

"Please join me," Gasper said dryly. Rowley did not smile.

"What I'm looking for," he said, "is a man who plays Russian roulette. Are you that man?"

"I don't understand."

"No, of course you don't. My apologies. I believe, Mr. Gasper, that Bradleigh Court was killed by a shot fired from the Royal Box of Her Majesty's Theater. I believe you were in the box when the shot was fired, and that you fired it. I assume you dropped the gun down an air shaft that led beneath the stage. Perhaps you panicked when you saw the blood spreading beneath Sir Bradleigh's cape."

"Continue." Gasper lit another cigarette.

"The blood would have been a surprise," Rowley said.

Gasper looked up at him sharply.

"I discovered a curious thing about the murder weapon when I examined it."

Gasper blew out smoke. "Yes," he said. "I know the surprise. The remaining rounds were all blanks."

"You are aware that anything you say may be held against you?"

Gasper laughed, a dry, mocking sound. "There is nothing I can say that should not be held against me."

"I wonder, Mr. Gasper. I don't think you went into that box intending to murder anybody. You thought the gun contained all blanks, didn't you? How unlucky for everyone that one chamber contained a real bullet."

"I should rather have said," Gasper said, "how unlucky for Bradleigh Court." He signaled the waiter. "Now then, Inspector, shall we have the menu?"

FOR Mason Devereaux, the rest of Sunday afternoon unfolded in a haze of green grassy lawns and Pimm's No. 2, brought to him on a silver tray by the Chesham's butler. After drinks and a light lunch of sandwiches on the veranda, he drifted away from the others and sat alone for a long time in the chair under the oak, running the events of the previous day through his mind over and again. At first the alcohol clarified his thinking, and he darted this way and that among his memories. Then the Pimm's slowed him down again into a gloomy expectation of impending disgrace.

The death of Bradleigh Court had been followed so quickly by the curious materialization of that little red-faced American publicist— what was his name? Billy? And something about a movie role. Bar talk. It was all rather muddled. Such bad news for Bradleigh, such good news for me, Mason thought. For years it had been the other way around. Yet even now, my triumph arrives accompanied by the elements of my destruction. A tear of self-pity could have trickled down his cheek, but Mason was too depressed to bother.

He drank. The afternoon gradually wound down toward evening, with Mason watching the shadows stretch themselves thin across the lawn of Thorn Hill. From where he sat, he had been able to watch the comings and goings at the big house like a spectator at a play. He had seen Fontaine Eady speed off alone down the driveway in his big American car. He had observed the young man Douglas Brown walking across the lawn with Sheila, in the direction of the spider house. Lord Chesham had been in and out of the spider house with the young people before joining Mason briefly for a cigar and a page through the Sunday papers. Chesham had patted him almost kindly on the shoulder before retiring for his nap. Mason had no idea what Chesham thought of the rumors about himself and Sheila, and of course he did not dare to ask. The fact was that their relationship was largely a creation of the gossip pages. Mason felt far too shy to press his case, and so he and Sheila had entered into an uneasy friendship in which neither spoke of serious feelings.

At some point toward evening, he watched with a twinge as Sheila and Brown strolled across the lawn hand in hand, deep in conversation. What a sad trick time plays, he thought. The more one learns about love, the less opportunities there are to put it into practice. Obviously Sheila felt attracted to this Brown fellow. So be it. Another man might fight for her hand, but Mason felt himself so deeply flawed that he had nothing, really, to offer the girl. Mason had suspected, from time to time, that he had a chance with Sheila—but perhaps what seemed to be a special sparkle in her eyes was simply a young woman's amusement at a Soho clown. Mason admitted to himself that he brightened at Sheila's chestnut hair and easy laugh, but he was a tired old drinker who would only make himself unhappy with thoughts of love.

As the young people walked away into the shadows of an elm grove, Devereaux shook himself from his lethargy, rose from his chair, pulled on the sweater that was knotted around his waist, and went for a walk on the grounds, quite drunk, reciting depressing passages from *Hamlet*. The parts about the rogue and peasant knave.

T builds a little trap door," Lord Chesham explained to Douglas Brown, when he discovered the young man with his daughter in the spider house. He was pleased she had taken him to see the spiders. "Most amusing—unless you are the prey!"

He lifted up the glass lid on one of the terrariums that lined the walls, and sprinkled some beetles into the now home of the Ctenizidae. Then he leaned over to peer through the window.

"The beetle goes this way . . . and then that way . . ." Chesham narrated, watching the drama unfolding before them. "This way again . . . and then, hello! What's this? Oh dear! Trap door! Beetle checks in, doesn't check out."

They walked out into the late afternoon, and Brown cleared his throat. "There is something . . . personal . . . that Sheila and I would like to mention to you, Lord Chesham," he said.

"You must mean that business in Fontaine Eady's column," Chesham said pleasantly. "My wife read it out to me. Some silly talk of romance between Sheila and poor Mason Devereaux. Quite absurd. I told Eady I really ought to sue. Because he's my second cousin, he never takes me seriously. Besides, he's quite close to my wife. Let it go. Forgotten in a fortnight. That's my advice."

"This is not to do with Mason," Sheila said. "It's about Douglas and me."

"Douglas?"

"I'm Douglas, sir," said Brown. "We met earlier. I arrived with Fontaine Eady."

"Are you the theater chap? Apologies. We met earlier, then? Strange. I never forget a spider."

"We wanted to tell you something," Sheila said. "We're engaged, Daddy. Not really. Sort of. Going together."

"Better to tell your mother, I suppose," Chesham said. "She keeps up with that sort of thing."

He walked off to where he had left Devereaux, drunk under a

tree. Funny thing about that Brown. Wouldn't trust him to peel a potato. First impression.

Sheila looked after him. "I know that Father loves me," she told Brown. "I had it explained to me by a shrink. He said it helps to understand English males of Daddy's class and age if you know they were sent away to school at the age of five and beaten once a week for ten years."

They strolled hand in hand toward the elm copse that had been Sheila's hiding place when she was a girl. She showed Douglas the tree house from her girlhood, and the place where mushrooms always grew. He wanted to kiss her, and she let him. She tried to lose herself in the kiss, but she could not. Douglas was so young and so handsome that if he could awaken feelings within her, then she would know she was saved. She could date him, and go to the dance clubs with him, and they could fly off to Portugal for a week, just like the other girls her age. And then if nothing finally came of Douglas there would be other boys her age, and someday . . .

"You don't open your eyes when you kiss me," Douglas said. "What are you thinking of?"

"You," she lied.

The shadows fell longer as they strolled through the wood and down to the lake. On a ridge opposite, she saw Mason walking by himself, his head bowed, his hands clasped behind. They followed a fence to the fruit orchard behind the main house, and then turned to climb the lawn again. They saw Jeffrey, the butler, marching toward them across the lawn as fast as his stick would lead him.

"You'd better come quickly," he told them.

"What's happened?" asked Sheila.

Jeffrey, breathless for a moment, could only turn and point. In the distance they could see the household staff and Lord Chesham hurrying toward the Gothic ruin that had guarded Thorn Hill House for two centuries.

"It's Mr. Devereaux! He's fallen down a well!"

IVAN BLOOM was a happy man. The studio chief sat in the state-of-the-art projection room of his Bel Air home and manipulated remote controls. Satellite images marched across the 144-inch screen of his giant front-projection television setup. He watched tennis from Costa Rica, socialists elected in Ontario, food prices rising in Mexico City. The room was also equipped with twin 35-mm movie projectors in a fireproof booth; home screenings were obligatory for Hollywood studio heads. But Bloom would rather play with his video equipment than watch a movie.

It all came down to a matter of control. When you watched a regular movie, the projectionist was in charge—some union guy sent over from the studio. You told him the focus was off, he told you to find yourself another projectionist. But with his giant-screen TV system, Bloom himself was masterfully in command. He worked his way through the remote controls: brightness, color, tint, sharpness, contrast, and then back around, again and again, in a blissful search for the perfect picture. Voices and laughter floated in from the patio, but he disregarded them. They were only guests, who had crept furtively from the room after an hour of impatiently watching Bloom experiment with the controls.

ASHLEY ST. IVES

On the patio, Raven Charles took a Perrier from a passing tray and listened to Ashley St. Ives, the agent who was Ivan Bloom's current squeeze. Raven knew their setup. Ashley and Ivan spent weekends together in Bel Air, but during the week Ashley lived in her Beverly Hills co-op. She believed separate addresses helped create an appearance of independence, since Ivan was often in competition with her other clients. Yet tonight, as on so many other nights, Ashley was acting as Ivan's hostess. The real message, Raven thought, was that, sure, Ashley was playing house with Ivan, but she'd double-cross him if the price was right.

"It's driving me crazy," Ashley was moaning. "Why can't he behave like any other executive and just show a goddamn movie on Sunday nights? Is that too much to ask? Ivan goes nuts over every new electronic gizmo that comes on the market. Honey, this is a man who has spent way too much time down in the dungeons with the dragons."

She lit a cigarette and jumped as an electronic squeal shot out of the media room. "Look at this party," she whispered to Raven. "A disaster. I invited some very important people over to see the new Oliver Stone, and what is he showing them? Connie Chung putting on her makeup. The man actually sent the projectionist home! And then when he shows a laserdisc, it's even worse. Three seconds of dialogue, and then Ivan jumps up and starts adjusting the sound. First Tom Cruise is in front of you. Then he's behind you. Then he's in the bowels of hell. With all the time Ivan screaming, 'Listen! Here's how Tom Cruise sounds on the THX disco setting!' He drives people out of the house."

Raven took a glass of white wine from a passing tray and handed it to Ashley. "At least he doesn't fool around."

"Fool around?" Ashley asked. "Give me a break. This is the kind of guy, he asks you up to see his etchings, at six in the morning you're still looking at his etchings."

Raven laughed. In a perverse way, she almost liked Ashley St. Ives, who reminded her of Joan Collins. What you saw was what you got. Of course, what you saw changed every week, but then so did what you got. They were always in synch. Ashley was easy to read. In a race against time, she was rotating through the basic Hollywood romantic strategies more quickly than was completely seemly. She was an experienced trophy wife who for twenty years had ascended the marital escalator, one marriage at a time, until she'd arrived at the top floor as the fiancée of Ivan Bloom, president of

Realistic Pictures. This was the time in her life when she should have been free to concentrate on her career, to marry a man who could make her one of the most powerful agents in town. Instead, she had a fiancé whose private Sunday night screenings were an industry joke. When she invited a powerful client over to the house, it was so he could see she was sleeping with a nerd.

Ashley looked around. Of the twenty-five people she'd invited, eight or nine were left. Three of them were actually huddled over a Sony Watchman in the pool house. Where was Ivan? She could hear him bragging that he was able to pick up a soccer game that had been blacked out in Salvador.

A telephone rang. Probably somebody who had left their diamonds behind in the haste to flee. Ashley took it at poolside. No, it was a call for Raven Charles, who looked astonished at what she heard, and went looking for Ivan Bloom. Ashley poured herself a thimbleful of vodka and watched Raven and Ivan talking urgently. They were framed in the big patio windows. She felt no jealousy because Raven would never be stupid enough to saddle herself with Ivan. Raven Charles might be a black woman who had worked her way up from the legal department, but at least if she ever got her hands on a studio she'd know what to do at a goddamn Sunday night screening. Maybe I'll go lesbo, Ashley thought. Women know how to behave in social settings.

DOWN a well?" said Ivan Bloom.

"About an hour ago," Raven told him. "Billy Baxter just called me from London. He saw it on the news."

"Was it on the BBC?" Ivan asked, brightening. "Maybe I can pick it up on my satellite!"

"Not right now, Ivan," Raven told him. She palmed the remote-control device and slipped it behind some cushions. "Think first. More than ever, I'm convinced there's a TV movie in this. I've never been more sure of anything in my life. It's Gothic humor, it's sex and violence, it's backstage drama, it's cross-promotion for the *Phantom* feature film."

"That's a lot of *it's*," Ivan said thoughtfully.

"Think of the story line. An understudy goes on stage as the Phantom of the Opera, gets drunk, is replaced by a knighted star who is shot dead onstage—and then, a day later, his life having been spared through an incredible coincidence, he falls down a well. Plus, he's sleeping with the Jane Seymour type."

"It's a touch anticlimactic," Bloom mused. "Could he sleep with Jane Seymour after he falls down the well?"

"We'll get a top writer on it," Raven said. "Ivan, let me have this one. I want to take the red-eye to New York and get on the Concorde tomorrow morning. I can sign a deal in two days."

"Okay, already," Bloom said. "Take it. Get on it. Buy it. Call me. Oh, and Raven?"

"Yes?"

"If he's dead down there at the bottom of the well, what do you do then?"

"I'm not the writer, Ivan. I'm the producer."

Ivan nodded. That made sense. He looked around for his satellite widget. If the BBC was feeding coverage of the story to the CBC in Vancouver, the bird should be right in position for his dish. Everybody would love to see it.

"And Ivan? Don't tell everybody about the story until I have the deal zipped up," Raven said.

"Oh," said Ivan.

R AVEN CHARLES boarded the overnight flight from Los Angeles just as dawn was creeping over the grounds of Thorn Hill House on Monday morning. The banks of emergency lights fell on a media circus. The hosts of the morning TV programs had been driven to Thorn Hill during the night, and now they reported breathlessly on the heroic struggle to save Mason Devereaux. Photographers dangled from hovering helicopters. As news, the tragedy of Mason Devereaux was inconsequential, but as a story, it was dynamite.

Lord Chesham had ordered a tent erected near the site. It had last been used at the celebration of his wedding anniversary, and sad white streamers still hung from the corner poles. He and his wife Beverly sat glassy-eyed on folding chairs with Sheila, as the household staff brought coffee and wholemeal toast from the kitchen. There had been comings and goings all night. Brown had left before dawn, returning to London where he was needed in the emergency process of casting a new Phantom. Fontaine Eady had just arrived at home in London when the news bulletin of Mason's fall flashed on the telly, and he had driven back to Thorn Hill, arriving at midnight. As a cousin of Lord Chesham he was allowed to share the tent, to the intense envy of the other journalists.

The rescue attempt was under the charge of a Special Forces colonel named Jack McHugh, who had arrived in costume for the role. He wore a beret and an olive sweater with leather gun patches on the shoulders, and had a smudge of clay across his forehead. His early hopes of a quick outcome had been disappointed.

"There is absolutely no indication of Mr. Devereaux," he told the group in the tent. "No sight, no sound."

Sheila closed her eyes and sat perfectly still. Her mother conducted the interview. "Have you thought about dropping a television camera down the shaft, Colonel McHugh?"

"Until your man Fitzroy arrives, we have no idea what that would lead to," McHugh said. "What if there's water down there, Lady Chesham? What if he's unconscious and we electrocute him? What if we drop the camera on his head and brain him? It wouldn't go down at all well if he were killed by the rescue effort. We've shouted at him with a loud-hailer, but there's been no response. Nothing."

"Here comes Fitzroy now," Lady Chesham said. A weathered gnome came hurrying up the rise toward the Gothic ruin, and doffed his cap in the direction of the Cheshams.

"Do as the colonel instructs, Fitzroy."

"Sir?"

"You've heard the situation," said McHugh. "A man has fallen down the well and we have no idea of his condition. How long has it been since you last inspected that well?"

"Inspected it?"

"You are the chief groundskeeper?"

"Indeed I am, sir. But I have never looked down that well. It's been boarded up since years before I was born. Most likely since the last century."

"The boards were rotted halfway through!" Sheila said.

"Yes, ma'am," Fitzroy said. "It is a sad day. Was the deceased a friend of yours?"

"He is not, so far as we know, deceased," Lady Chesham said firmly. "Go and help the men with their work, Fitzroy."

The gnome left gratefully. From their position on top of the rise, the Cheshams could see a back-up of vehicles on their private road. Mason Devereaux had become an overnight celebrity. If he were still alive, down there somewhere beneath the ground, here was his great break at last.

Lord Chesham looked around wearily. "Sandwiches for the new arrivals, Jeffrey," he told the butler.

W H E N Raven Charles emerged from customs at Heathrow's Concorde terminal, Billy (Silver Dollar) Baxter was waiting impatiently behind the barrier, a sheaf of the Monday papers under his arm.

"Look at this," he said. "They're goin' nuts."

Even the quality papers were using their larger typefaces to follow the saga of Mason Devereaux. The story possessed what newspeople like best, a human interest angle that was both tragic and funny. The previous night, a BBC newsreader had been forced to choke back laughter as he described how Mason Devereaux had escaped a fatal bullet onstage at Her Majesty's Theater, only to fall down a well.

"The car's waiting," Billy told Raven Charles. "I got us press credentials. Anybody asks, you're with Cable News. Too bad this guy died just when you were ready to talk turkey with him."

"Do you think he's dead?" Raven asked him.

"He's either dead, or he needs a drink real bad," Billy said. "I say lower a bottle down on a string, and if it comes up empty, send a guy in after him."

Raven looked at Billy curiously as the car nosed out of Heathrow and onto the motorway. He looked like a cross between Ted Koppel and the Pillsbury Dough Boy. She could imagine no one more different from herself than the red-faced Baxter, and yet she had liked him from the first time she'd met him, a few years ago at the Cannes Film Festival. She enjoyed Billy's compulsion to say exactly what was on his mind. After years of concealing her emotions, of telling people what they needed to hear, of massaging insecure egos, she knew why kings kept fools: To say out loud what everybody was really thinking.

"What's a classy broad like you doing making a personal appearance, anyway?" Billy asked. "I coulda handled this on the horn."

"It's a great story," Raven told him, looking out the window at the rolling green countryside. "It could make a great movie."

"It's none of my business," Billy said, "but are you thinking comedy? Or tragedy?"

I didn't realize you were with the news these days," Fontaine Eady said. "It's unusual when a studio executive leaves her job to become a TV reporter. Of course they're very well paid in the states . . ."

The columnist for the *Sketch* smiled blandly at Raven Charles, who held a china cup of tea between her hands and inhaled as if the aroma itself could revive her. She had traveled six thousand miles since yesterday. Eady had rescued her from the press tent and invited her into the conservatory at Thorn Hill. They had met at a dozen premieres.

"Come on, Fontaine," she said. "You know I'm still with the studio. Don't blow my cover."

"Yeah, Eady, give us a break," Billy Baxter said. He perched on one of the white wicker chairs with a pile of newspapers in his lap.

Eady chuckled with delight. "Mason would enjoy all of this so very much," he said. "Of course, there may be a great deal more than meets the eye. The murder is an enormous complication. On the other hand, if Mason had simply fallen down the well, without the murder, would there have been quite the same level of interest? There you have me."

Raven stood at the window and looked out to where the search for

Mason Devereaux was still under way. The afternoon light glanced coldly off the surface of the lake. The landscape looked to Raven as if it had been carefully arranged centuries ago; even the trees and hills seemed placed according to a plan.

"The Gothic ruin is what we call a folly," Eady said, joining her at the window. "It was built by one of the Chesham ancestors to grace the hill and lend interest to the view from the house. It was originally intended to double as a wellhead, but the well has been boarded over for decades. Then the weight of Mason's body opened it."

"This is a natural story," Raven said.

"I don't know if you have a story," Eady said, "but you certainly have a location."

COL. JACK MCHUGH tried the buckles on his leather harness and found them secure. He looped a flashlight around his neck, tested the walkie-talkie, and gave thumbs-up to the men on the winch. They began to lower him down into the well.

The TV crews crawled on each other's shoulders to shoot the rescue attempt. The Chesham's tent had been pressed into service as a command post. Chesham had ordered his Range Rover driven to the site, and he and his wife sat inside with the windows up and the doors locked, refusing interviews and listening on the radio to the reports of the BBC newsmen who were twenty paces away. Sheila stood as close as she dared to the side of the well and watched as McHugh was lowered out of sight.

"All that really remains is the recovery of the body," Chesham told his wife.

"You must pretend all is well for Sheila's sake," she told him. "She doesn't love Mason, but she's quite fond. It will be a painful blow."

"I gather she fancies this Brown chap."

"Douglas Brown? Passing," Lady Chesham said.

"Passing?"

"I give it a month. I had a talk with the young man. He has no depth. Our Sheila must have her depths to plumb, Peter."

The rope unwound slowly down into the gaping hole in the ground. Even the TV commentators fell silent.

"Which of your demented ancestors built this monstrosity?" Lady Chesham asked at last, looking at the Gothic tower that stood over the wellhead.

"Ninth earl. Follies were all the rage in his day. The notion was, you looked out over your land, and at just the right point in the distance you wanted to spy a suitably ruined castle or tower or some such. Added a touch of romance to the thing."

"The ninth earl?" his wife said. "The same one who tried to drown all those people?"

"The same. And bloody well would have, if the butler hadn't saved them." Chesham chuckled at his prankish ancestor. "He invited them all over for New Year's Eve. Had his hand on the hydraulic lever at the stroke of midnight, when the aged retainer struck him with the flat of a broadsword and saved their lives. Quite a story."

"That happened right around here?"

"So I vaguely recall. My father would have known. Listen!"

The BBC was broadcasting McHugh's voice live from the bottom of the well.

"How many feet?" McHugh was asking.

"You're close to the bottom, Jack," his surface crew told him.

"Can't see below me. Gear's in the way. Devereaux, are you there? Hello! No answer . . ."

"You've got to be almost down."

"That's it!" McHugh said. "Stop lowering. I'm standing on the bottom. It's muddy but it's firm. A little water."

"What about Devereaux?"

"There's no Devereaux."

The voice echoed into emptiness. The Cheshams stared at the dash radio in disbelief.

"Hold on!" McHugh's voice crackled with urgency. They could hear wet splashing noises over the hookup.

"Was he wearing a hat?" McHugh shouted.

"An old Panama," Sheila cried out to the man on the radio.

"Well then," said McHugh. "I've found his hat."

5 0

LATER that afternoon, Harold Gasper sat in his rooms in the Albany, in a cul-de-sac off Piccadilly, and talked on the telephone with the manager of his bank. They were discussing an overdraft of several thousand pounds. Gasper was trying to be encouraging.

"I haven't two pennies to rub together, old man," he said. "But hold fast another month and it will all come right."

The manager did not sound like holding fast. "You mentioned certain investments, Mr. Gasper."

"Yes. The *Phantom,* I can tell you, would seem to be coming to the end of its run. Not this year or next, but eventually. Lloyd Webber has too many other shows on the boards. It's yesterday's news. Let me tell you what I did. I approached some of the smaller investors in the play and bought up the remaining terms of their shares—the end of the run—for what looked to them like favorable terms. You see, I was gambling that the *Phantom* would run longer than they thought it would. And now, of course, even you can see that with the enormous publicity given to the tragedy of Bradleigh Court, it will run forever. It's exactly the sort of production that will benefit from such a macabre association."

He paused. "It goes without saying I had no idea Bradleigh would be murdered."

"Of course. But please be so kind as to explain to me, Mr. Gasper, how this affects your overdraft."

"My shares will double in value," Gasper said. "I'll sell. You'll have your money in a month."

The manager signed off doubtfully. Gasper hung up the telephone and stood looking out the window of his sitting room. Across the way, making no attempt at concealment, was an officer assigned by Scotland Yard to keep an eye on him. Gasper all but nodded to the man.

He had expected Fredson Rowley to arrest him after their conversation at the Caprice, but Rowley hadn't made his move. He is playing at cat and mouse, Gasper thought. Even if I could prove I thought the gun contained blanks, I should still be charged with reckless homicide. I confessed to him, in effect, and what did he do? Wished me a good day.

Gasper saw a figure walking toward his door.

"Well, now," he said to himself. "Our fine young murderer, right on schedule." He went to open the door.

J E F F R E Y, the arthritic butler, gave his arm to Lady Chesham as they entered the musty old library at Thorn Hill. She helped him to a chair. Her husband and daughter followed them into the room, where ancestors looked down from their portraits, except for the ninth earl, who was posed gazing intensely through a port-hole at three pop-eyed fish. The Cheshams were joined by McHugh and Fontaine Eady, who pointedly closed the door behind them. McHugh walked over to the big library table and centered a muddy Panama on it.

"His poor old hat!" cried Sheila, running over to the table and picking it up. "M.D.," she said, reading the letters Mason had neatly inked on the leather liner. "He bought it at Bates's. Downstairs from his rooms in Jermyn Street. The shop with the hat over the sidewalk. Every time we'd walk by there, he'd . . . he'd . . . tip it at their sign."

She was overcome by sobbing. Lady Chesham took her gently by the shoulders and guided her to an old leather couch in the center of the room. Lord Chesham cleared his throat with embarrassment and stood with his back to them, studying his shelf of books about spiders.

"Are you quite sure he wasn't down there somewhere, McHugh?" Eady asked.

"There wasn't room for more than me," the colonel replied stiffly.

"Then he must have dropped his hat down the well and wandered off into the woods. People don't simply disappear from the bottoms of wells. Not in my experience."

"He was seen to fall into the well by no less than two members of our household staff," Lady Chesham told him sharply.

"Oh, he went down the well, sure enough," McHugh said. "But he wasn't there when I went down after him."

"The Mystery of the Locked Well," Eady mused.

"It isn't a thing to be made light of, you dreadful person," Sheila said, looking up fiercely at the journalist. "You got him drunk on the day of the performance, and you printed all of those lies about Mason and myself, and now you stand here smirking and turn it all into a farce."

"That is certainly not my intention," Eady said calmly. "Just think. A man falls down a well. When you go to look for him, he isn't there. Did he climb out again? No. Then where is he? It's a classic detective formula, dear girl. I've read dozens of versions of it. The locked room with no way out. They all end the same way."

"How do they all end, sir?" asked McHugh.

"There's a way out," said Eady.

L ET'S put our cards flat on the table, shall we?" Harold Gasper said. He was standing in front of his fireplace, regarding Douglas Brown. The younger man sat facing him like a student before a headmaster.

"First," said Gasper. "What does Rowley know? He knows I had the gun, fired the gun, disposed of the gun. He thinks there's more to it than that, and until he finds out exactly what, he's having me watched."

"Is that the character outside?" asked Brown, looking uneasily toward the window.

"It is. To continue. Second, what do we know? Like Rowley, we know I had the gun, fired the gun, disposed of the gun. What only you and I know, Brown, is that you procured and loaded the gun."

He picked up a fireplace poker and slammed it down hard on the brass log bucket, causing Brown to jump on his chair. The younger man looked miserably at the silver-framed photographs on the table beside him, showing Gasper in the company of the rich and famous.

"Why haven't you simply named me to the police?" he said at last, almost inaudibly.

"I may. Information is money, Brown. I need money. That has been my motivation right from the very beginning. Until I am actually arrested and charged with the murder, I prefer to keep my information to myself."

"I feel wretched," Brown said.

"Murderers often do. Shakespeare is shot through with it."

"Don't call me a murderer, Gasper. It's true that I went into this thing with you, but I never intended for anyone to die. I didn't see how you could hit anything at that distance, let alone a skinny old fool like Devereaux."

"Heavens," Gasper said. "It's the plot for a splendid melodrama, isn't it? Whom shall we cast? You handed me the loaded revolver, but you hoped my aim was bad!"

"I don't know what I thought," Brown whispered miserably. "I was a fool. I wanted Devereaux dead, and yet I didn't want him dead. I was playing with fate."

"Of course we both thought Mason was standing in for Bradleigh Court at the matinee," Gasper said. "Damned bad luck for Bradleigh that he got in the way."

"If Mason knew what was going to happen," Brown said, "why didn't he tell you the switch had taken place? Then we could have pulled the stunt another day. Or we might have come to our senses and dropped it."

Gasper laughed, a hollow, mirthless sound. "With a drunk, who ever knows? How would you suggest Mason inform me he was no longer appearing in the play? Run round to the Royal Box in his Phantom's makeup?"

SHEILA CHESHAM still sat in the library at Thorn Hill with her mother, who held her hand and patted it from time to time. The others had left. It was evening, and a fine drizzle had started to fall. Jeffrey had been in to close the windows and offer them tea, which they declined.

"It helps to think of it as a disease, my dear," Lady Chesham said at last. "Men like Mason can't help themselves. They have all the best intentions in the world, but after they take the first drink they find there's no turning back. My brother Freddy was exactly the same."

"Is that why he fell off the Ferris wheel in Vienna?"

Lady Chesham nodded.

"I never knew," Sheila said.

"Families as a rule don't go into a great amount of detail about such things," Lady Chesham said.

"What hurt me the most," Sheila said, "was when Fontaine Eady wrote those horrible lies. There was nothing like that between Mason and myself. I thought of him like a father. He was witty and charming, and something fun was always happening when he was around. That was why I liked him."

"Did he feel about you like a daughter?" her mother asked quietly.

"We never discussed that sort of thing."

"Men have such an incredible gift of self-delusion, Sheila. Even after they're middle-aged and on the ropes as Mason was, they still believe themselves attractive to women. It's their personality that's irresistible, that's what they tell themselves."

"It *was* irresistible!"

"You were fond of him, weren't you, Sheila?"

"But I was . . . I was dating Douglas Brown."

"Did Mason know?"

Sheila studied the figure in the carpet. "Probably not," she said at last. "Do you think that if he saw us holding hands together yesterday he—threw himself down the well?"

"Hardly likely, I should say. For one thing, how could he have known there was a well there?"

Sheila nodded and leaned her head against her mother's shoulder.

"Poor unfortunate man," her mother said.

There was no noise in the room except for the quiet whisper of the rain outside. The day had grown dark quite early. The two women sat quietly on the sofa in front of the dying fire.

Quite suddenly, a loud creaking noise startled them. It came from one of the bookshelves. The women rose to their feet as a section of the wall began to rotate toward them. The mud-covered figure of Mason Devereaux fell forward into the room.

PART THREE

Ballroom

THE situation is fairly guarded at the moment," the duty doctor told a small group waiting in the hospital corridor. "Mr. Devereaux is dehydrated and suffering from exposure. He was possibly concussed in his original fall. And we are treating him for withdrawal from alcohol."

"But he'll be all right?" Sheila Chesham's face was pale in the fluorescent lights of early Wednesday morning.

"We'll know more in twenty-four hours. If you like, you can go in to see him. Five minutes."

Sheila was at Mason's bedside in a moment. The actor looked thinner and older, and for the first time she could see the possibility of mortality in his face. His tousled hair, which gave him a perennial youthfulness, was concealed beneath bandages. Ominous plastic tubes led beneath the sheets, and an IV device gurgled in the silence. His famous Panama hat, still splashed with mud, was parked on one of the bedposts, as if he had tossed it there.

"Thank God you're alive," she told him, taking his hand.

"Never thought I'd make it, old girl," he said weakly. "Totally lost. Splitting headache. Pitch black. Freezing cold. Not a drop to drink."

"The whole world was cheering for you," Sheila told him. "It was on all the news programs. There's a press conference tomorrow to retrace your steps through the hidden passages."

"You don't say!" He brightened slightly. "Was it on in the States, as well?"

The doctor materialized at her side and led her away. Mason could glimpse others through the open door of his room—Lady Chesham, perhaps, and an anxious Harold Gasper—but they were not permitted to enter. His head fell back on the pillow and he gave himself over to a reverie: Which of the nurses he had seen so far was the best candidate for popping across the road and fetching him a drink?

L ATER Wednesday afternoon, in the library at Thorn Hill House, Ashley St. Ives paged impatiently through the *Tatler*. It was filled with photographs of elegant women in expensive dresses at London parties, and the Hollywood agent suspected none of them would be much impressed by her own social triumphs on the Bel Air circuit. Ashley was haunted by the possibility that her victories were meaningful only to the small group of female rivals and ex-wives she had climbed over to achieve them. It was depressing when you were not on speaking terms with the only people who really appreciated your achievements.

St. Ives had arrived in Britain only hours earlier, on the trail of what she knew would be a major deal. When the Devereaux saga turned into a worldwide media circus, she had taken the red-eye from Los Angeles and hired a car to bring her directly to Thorn Hill House. She was not pleased to learn that Raven Charles had beaten her by a day. Now they were both waiting for a press conference that would explain Mason Devereaux's astonishing escape after falling into a well.

Lord Chesham had not been eager for his family home to remain in the spotlight; he was happiest when the public forgot entirely that he even existed. But when the Attenborough boy, who had found some sort of good job at the BBC, rang up to say the world wanted to see what Devereaux has gone through, Chesham had reluctantly agreed.

Now he had a house filled with strangers. He had stopped in the library for a second to find a book on the web patterns of the ill, and hurried out again in fear of the loud and brilliant types who had scattered themselves on his furniture.

A SHLEY, who was exhausted, was making her usual attempt to dominate the room. Her flaming red hair was pulled back tightly from arched eyebrows, her lips were a shocking crimson, her blouse was carelessly buttoned, and her shoes were four-inch stilettos. For many years she had dressed in the same way, in the style of a college boy's wet dreams, and the results had never disappointed her. Women of course considered her vulgar, but what women thought did not interest her. No man had ever complained that she looked like a tramp.

Now she looked across the room, where Raven Charles sat near an obnoxious New York press agent named Billy something. Billy had been introduced, but Ashley St. Ives made it her practice to remember only the names of the powerful. As for Raven, Ashley instinctively knew they were not on the same side of the Devereaux production. Too bad. She would rather have worked with Raven than with the thieves and parasites she usually found as her partners. Ashley suspected she couldn't count on Ivan Bloom. Even though she was the studio chief's mistress, she knew Ivan placed more trust in Raven. After all, he'd assigned her to produce the *Phantom* film version. For that matter, Raven had been first with the idea of a Mason made-for-TV movie. Details. If Ivan Bloom had to choose between them, Ashley decided, he would certainly favor his own mistress over a mere employee. Well, wouldn't he? She lit a cigarette and asked herself if she was looking at an ashtray, or a priceless Sumerian relic.

R AVEN CHARLES looked around the old room with awe. It was like a movie set for a library, with busts of Shakespeare and Milton peering down from the high shadows. If she possessed a library like this, she would live for the rest of her life with her books, curled up by the fire with a volume of Trollope in her lap and a brave old dog slumbering at her feet. She looked across at Ashley St. Ives, who had crossed her extravagant legs and was blowing out smoke. Raven, with her oversize horn-rim glasses and her conservative navy business suit over a white blouse, was not so much a contrast to St. Ives as a rebuke.

They were both obviously there with the same idea. *The Mason Devereaux Story* was begging to be filmed as a TV miniseries. It was a sensational property—and, Raven thought fiercely to herself, the perfect opportunity to leave the Realistic Pictures payroll and open her own production company. She would twist Ivan's arm until he gave her some of the overseas rights. She would put Devereaux under personal contract. The public, having fallen in love with him on the miniseries, would demand Devereaux as the lead in the movie *Phantom,* and then Raven would use his contract as leverage to negotiate her own production deal. There was only one blemish in her plan. Ashley St. Ives was planning exactly the same scenario. And Ashley was sleeping with Ivan.

It wasn't fair, of course. Raven had staked out Mason Devereaux even before the bizarre events of the past few days. But life wasn't fair. Raven was sure she could outwit St. Ives in an even fight. But if Ivan Bloom had to choose between them, Raven thought to herself, who would he choose? The loyal associate who was first with the idea? Or his mistress? She smiled grimly to herself. It wouldn't even be close. Ivan's vote would be transmitted directly from his genitals to his intercom, bypassing his brain.

Raven had known for a long time how she could win that competition. She could take a man like Ivan Bloom away from an insecure, neurotic woman like Ashley St. Ives with almost pathetic ease. Powerful men, she had learned, were hypnotically attracted to power in women. Ivan would cave in like a teenage boy. The problem with that scenario, she thought, was that if you won, the prize was Ivan Bloom. Ivan with the light-footed social grace of a wrestling announcer. She would have to outwit St. Ives on the field of battle, before Ivan ever got the chance to choose between them. She would have to lock up Mason Devereaux.

While the two women plotted their strategies, they treated each other as if this were a routine social coincidence—a chance encounter in a British country home, six thousand miles from where they had last seen each other on Ivan's Malibu veranda.

"I didn't know you were a friend of Mason Devereaux's," Ashley said at last.

"I've been a fan of his for a long time—from afar," Raven Charles told her. "When I was in college I visited Stratford and saw him as Hamlet. I've never forgotten him."

"I never saw *Hamlet*," Billy Baxter said, "but I saw *Macbeth*, and it had a lot of the same words."

I T was a rotten, rotten shame, old man, and that's all there is to be said about it."

Harold Gasper was speaking quietly at the bedside of Mason Devereaux. It was Wednesday afternoon. The nurses had left them alone for the moment, and the door had been closed on the journalists camped outside.

"I blame myself for my immorality, my selfishness, my greed, and most of all my stupidity for ever having had anything to do with your damnable scheme," Mason declared, in a whisper that shook with anger. "You didn't even keep your promise to wait until the end of the play to shoot me, so that I could at least have gone down in triumph."

"I was too nervous, Mason. How would you have felt? I am a cheat and a confidence artist and I admit to that," Gasper told him pleasantly. "But I am not a murderer. The death of Bradleigh Court was an accident, a tragic accident. And for the next fifteen minutes, Mason, you are the most famous man in the world."

"Did you think to check the bullets, to make sure they were all blanks?" Mason asked. "Did that thought occur to you?"

"Not for a moment. I was entirely focused on our plan. It never occurred to me that Brown would have a plan of his own."

"I would like to take that sleek rodent in human form," Mason said, "and cast *him* down a well. What could he have been thinking of?

"He told me he 'sort of' wanted to kill you," Gasper said. "Those were his exact words. What an odd notion! To *sort of* want to kill someone. He wanted you dead, all right, but he lacked the nerve to take the responsibility. He left it all up to fate. He was playing Russian roulette with his gun but your head."

"But why kill me?" Mason asked. "Jealousy? He feared me as a rival for Sheila? Don't make me laugh."

"Money," Gasper told him. "It's always money in the end, isn't it, Mason?"

"But I haven't three pounds in my pocket."

"Not your pocket. Sheila's. That little idiot believed every word he read about your nonexistent romance in Fontaine Eady's column.

He wanted you to die so that Sheila and her fortune would fall into his arms."

"How can anyone so young be so despairing and devious?"

"It almost excuses us, doesn't it, Mason, that we were well into our middle age before we became villains."

"Don't make me laugh."

A nurse hurried in and ordered Gasper from the room. Beneath the sheets, Mason caressed the brandy miniatures that Gasper had smuggled to him, and when the nurse had departed he allowed one to trickle blissfully down his throat. He knew there was some connection he had to make, some realization that was eluding him . . . and then a snapshot of the Sunday landscape projected itself upon his memory, and as he saw Sheila and Douglas Brown in the middle distance, holding hands, he knew that if Brown would attempt murder, he was capable of anything. Mason knew what he had to do. He had to find Sheila and protect her.

REGAN BURKE, a researcher for the National Historical Trust, called the press conference to order. She stood in front of the celebrated library wall that had yielded Mason. With her were the Cheshams, including Sheila, who had returned from London. Douglas Brown stood by Sheila's side. His hand snaked out to take hers, but her fist was crumpled into a ball around a damp handkerchief. Flanking the Cheshams were McHugh, the rescue expert, who expanded in the limelight, and Fitzroy, the groundskeeper, who contracted.

Burke, a jolly brunette with a pageboy haircut, seemed amused by the way an architectural curiosity had thrust her into the limelight.

"The secret passage was really rather famous in the late eighteenth century," she explained. "Any number of diarists wrote about being led through it by the ninth earl, when they were invited to dance in his underwater ballroom. It was only in the last century or so that the Chesham family lost track of its existence."

"We knew vaguely that it was around somewhere," Lord Chesham volunteered, "but we had no idea exactly where."

"And no interest," his wife added.

"Underwater ballroom?" asked a reporter for Cable News.

"Doesn't the very notion bring back that whole delightful Age of Romance dottiness?" asked Burke. She was like a museum guide. "It was a time of Gothic novels and ghost stories, Frankenstein and Le Fanu, and the British aristocracy fancied itself as the subject of the books it read. It was all the rage to build bizarre Gothic country homes—the stranger the better."

"But the underwater ballroom?" the TV reporter repeated. "Can you explain it a little more clearly? Was it like synchronized swimming?"

Lord Chesham cleared his throat and stepped forward. "Perhaps I can help," he said. "It would appear that the ninth earl had a large artificial lake excavated on his land. It still exists. As a boy I fished in it. You drove past it on your way to this house. Before he filled it, the ninth constructed a ballroom to fit on its floor. Two huge steel quarterspheres were fabricated in Birmingham and brought to this district by rail, to be put into place on the bottom of the lake, with portholes in them—so the guests could look out at the fish, I imagine, or the fish could look in at them, for that matter."

"I say," said Fontaine Eady, "was that the famous earl who tried to drown an entire New Year's party?"

Chesham looked severely at his cousin, who knew perfectly well that it was.

"Exactly!" said Miss Burke helpfully. "His plan was to pull a hydraulic lever at the stroke of midnight and drown them all, while he escaped through a secret door into the well. Mason Devereaux made the same journey in reverse—from the well into the ballroom and up here to the library. It saved his life."

"Luckily, the ninth earl's insane plan was foiled by a servant," Lord Chesham said. "It goes without saying our family is a good deal less eccentric these days."

"Of course," said Fontaine Eady.

"Could you give us a nice sound bite, describing exactly how Devereaux escaped?" asked the American TV reporter.

"After Devereaux fell down the well," Burke said, "he stumbled against the old spring-loaded secret door. It opened, it closed behind him, and that's why Colonel McHugh found nothing but a hat when he was lowered down the well."

Raven Charles, standing near the rear of the room, could hardly refrain from hugging herself with delight. This was the opening sequence of her movie, already cast and written for her, with Bob Hoskins as McHugh, and Helena Bonham-Carter as that lovely little Sheila Chesham. But who would play Devereaux? Someone dissipated and yet oddly heroic, she thought, like Peter O'Toole . . .

"Devereaux must have been completely disoriented in the pitch darkness," said McHugh, "but he blundered out of the ballroom and into the passageway, and eventually he emerged right here." He swung aside the concealed panel, which gave onto a cobwebbed opening behind the bookcases. "All right, then. Shall we have a look? Who's game?"

Lord and Lady Chesham declined to make the inspection tour. McHugh led the strangely assorted party down into the old stone staircase, and for the first time bright lights flooded the mouldy passageway beneath the grounds of Thorn Hill House. Fake plaster pillars pretended to hold up the ceiling, and the ninth earl's tastes were reflected in fresco murals of frolicking nymphs, who could just be glimpsed beneath two centuries of mold and neglect. As the small party descended the steps, a hush fell upon them. They were conscious of trespassing on a world of long and unbroken silence.

J EFFREY, the butler, stood in the center of the rug of the old library at Thorn Hill House and could just hear the faraway echoes of the party descending into the passageway. He bowed to Lord and Lady Chesham as they left the room. Left alone, he coughed discreetly into his handkerchief, and moved creakingly over to the sideboard, where a rare Highland whiskey could be found. He was just lifting a glass to his lips when the telephone rang. He heard the voice of Mason Devereaux, demanding to talk with Sheila Chesham immediately.

Jeffrey looked at the opening of the passageway, and calculated the effort it would take him to descend the clammy stairs and catch up with the inspection party. Then he regarded his glass, warm and amber in the afternoon sunlight.

"I am very sorry, sir," he said, "but Miss Chesham is not here at the moment. She is touring the underwater ballroom with the party from the press."

"The press? Who else? Is Brown there?"

"I believe the answer is yes, sir."

I N London, Mason struck the sidebar of his bed in frustration. Douglas Brown was a madman capable of harming Sheila and anyone else who stood in his way. Sheila had to be warned. Gingerly, for he hated the sight of blood, Mason detached the tube running into his arm. He had to go to Sheila and save her.

But who would have imagined it could be such an ordeal to put on a pair of boots? He sat unsteadily on the chair next to his hospital bed and tried to tug at his boot without toppling over on the floor. He was weak and dizzy, and frightened that the duty nurse would burst in at any moment with more of her disgusting cheerfulness.

He took another sip from the miniature, and with a last desperate tug brought the boot onto his foot. He stood up shakily and walked to the door, peering both ways down the corridor. It was deserted for the moment. Mason was light-headed, and aware he was not thinking clearly. He dodged down a side passageway and found an unlocked fire escape door. A moment later he was in the Fulham Road, not far down from Finch's King's Arms—not a bad pub that, he thought, and then, feeling vertiginous, he knew he would require a proper drink before he could summon the strength to help Sheila.

He hailed a taxi and asked to be hurried to the Coach and Horses in Soho, where Norman the barman would give him a brandy and a telephone, and he would be cared for and understood. He was a sick man, he knew, but he had looked far more ill on other occasions, staggering into the Coach under sail. Half the regulars looked as if they were dying, anyway.

I say, Devereaux!" It was Harold Gasper, astonished to see him at the bar. Gasper had visited Mason only hours ago in the hospital, and now here the actor was again, rematerialized in his regular corner of the pub, his drink in front of him.

"Good God, man, what are you doing here? How did you get out of the hospital? What happened to all those tubes that were stuck into you?"

"I had to get away," Mason said, "to help Sheila. When you told me Brown had loaded the revolver, I knew she was in danger. So I came straight here for a drink to set me on my feet. I've got to get out to the country. No. Not enough time." His head was reeling. "Got to ring her. Give her a warning."

Gasper sat next to him at the bar, steadying his arm as he leaned away from curious ears. He watched as Mason took a deep draught from his glass. "Where is Sheila right now?"

"She is safe for the moment," Mason told him weakly. "She's on a tour of that underwater hellhole with the press. I'll warn her off Brown when she surfaces. It will be the last act of a ruined man. I'll save her, and then stand up to accept my punishment."

"Brace up, old man!" Gasper told him. "Try to see all the way round your situation. You've become the most famous man in Britain. Our little plan ended in disaster, it's true, but it was not your fault. You are not a murderer. I promised you publicity, and you have it."

"True enough, I'm on every front page," Mason said, rotating his glass, "but the moment it's discovered that we cooked up that whole bloody farce between ourselves, it's off to prison for both of us."

"Who knows?" Gasper asked him.

"Who knows what?"

"Who knows that you were involved?"

Devereaux thought. "You do," he said at last.

"Who else?" asked Gasper.

"Douglas Brown?"

"Is Brown likely to go to the police, Mason? Think for a moment."

Their eyes met, and Mason held out his glass automatically for a refill. He was beginning to catch Gasper's drift.

"Don't be too quick to call attention to Brown. Be careful what you say to Sheila. That whole area is fraught with complications."

"But if Sheila is in danger . . ."

"She is in more danger if Brown's role is known. Brown is desperately eager that it remain completely unknown." Gasper bent down more closely toward Mason. "Just run through this with me, Devereaux. The police know I fired the gun. The inspector, Rowley, had a conversation with me the other day. He had discovered that all of the rounds were blanks—except one. He assumed I didn't know about the real bullet. I could have named Douglas Brown as the person who inserted it in the weapon, but since Rowley didn't arrest me on the spot, I chose not to. Information is invaluable in a situation such as this. Rowley hasn't charged me with anything yet, but he's having me watched. There was one question he should have asked me, but he didn't. Can you guess what it was?"

"The entire subject is a mystery to me," Mason said.

"It was this. If the gun did contain blanks—then why on earth was I going to shoot you with them? Think, man, think!"

Mason stared at him helplessly. "Obviously, because we planned it together?" he said at last.

"No, Mason, no!" said Gasper. "Apart from Douglas Brown, nobody knows you were involved. Let's keep it that way, old man. Why should we both go to prison? You're on the brink of the first big break in a long and dismal career. I'll serve time no matter what happens. It's too late for me."

Gasper lit a cigarette and thought. Then he leaned intently toward Mason. "I'll take the rap. We have a new story now. Listen carefully. You didn't have the slightest idea that I was going to shoot blanks at you."

"Why not?" asked Mason.

"It was my own stupid publicity stunt, cooked up entirely by myself, to stage a fake shooting," Gasper explained, speaking urgently. "I wanted to get some publicity in the papers. I thought I could do it without being seen. Phantom gunman shoots at Phantom. I slipped you in as the understudy for one reason only—to save embarrassment for Bradleigh Court. I obtained the revolver from

Brown. He loaded the real bullet, for reasons which he can explain to the police at his leisure. That's our story, and it has the advantage of being very nearly the truth. Brown may believe you had advance knowledge, but he can't prove it."

Mason sipped his drink thoughtfully. "Do you think it will fly?"

"I'll put on a great performance for the police," Gasper said. "After all, I always was a better actor than you."

AFTER Gasper paid for the drinks and left, Mason remained for a time at the Coach and Horses. He telephoned the hospital and informed them he wouldn't be coming back. He accepted a drink or two from well-wishers. Benevolence began to creep into his mind. He felt gratitude toward Harold Gasper. Being granted his own deliverance somehow made Sheila's danger seem less, as well. Or perhaps it was the brandy. Mason was feeling reasonably better. Uncanny how, after two or three days off the booze, it regained its magic for you.

He walked to the telephone and placed another call to Thorn Hill, learning from Lady Chesham that her daughter was still with the press tour of the underwater ballroom. He left strict instructions for Sheila to phone him at the earliest opportunity, carefully neglecting to tell Lady Chesham that the number he left was the Coach, not the hospital room. Then he lifted a forefinger to Norman, the bartender, who brought another drink.

The Coach was quiet at this moment before the pre-theater crowd. He took his seat again at the end of the bar and spread the day's newspapers in front of him—the papers with their wonderful black headlines screaming out his name. MIRACLE MASON! cried the *Daily Mail.* And indeed there had been long hours when he knew it would take a miracle to save his life. They had come during the long night he had spent in the cold darkness of that terrifying labyrinth under the grounds of Thorn Hill House.

HIS first thought, after falling down the well, had been that he was dead. But he was not. Testing for broken bones in the darkness, he seemed intact, apart from a nasty bump on his head. He had been spared by the deep cushion of leaves and rot at the bottom of the well. He used his hands to explore the clammy invisible walls around him, only to lurch into utter blackness and silence so total that his breath roared in his ears.

He had passed out. Awakening, he felt the familiar unease of the man in need of a drink. He was covered by a thin cold sweat, the damp on his skin made worse by the space around him, a void that smelled like wet turtles. He reached out into the darkness, but the walls of the well had disappeared. He stumbled into the dark, calling for help until he was convinced it was futile, baffled by the things he found and touched in the blackness: Tables, chairs, statues that were dead cold to the hand. Where was he? What had happened to him? Had he landed at last in hell for his sins? Or were the Catholics right about purgatory, and was he condemned to linger for eons in this nonplace?

A long time later, after periods of sleep, wake, creeping, and dread—he had no sense of the passage of time—he followed the floor upward into a passage, using the clammy walls as a guide, testing each footstep fearfully as he envisioned a bottomless chasm before him. It grew slightly warmer, and he could feel the whisper of an air current against his face. Suddenly, miraculously, he heard Sheila's voice floating in the nothingness.

He had pushed forward desperately, crashed against a wooden surface, and then stumbled out into the library of Thorn Hill House, where in a second he was clutching a snifter of brandy and learning old family legends about an underwater ballroom. The stories held no charm for him. He knew all about the ballroom. He had been dancing there for an eternity with the ghost of the accursed ninth earl.

Mason stood up heavily, nodded to Norman, and made his way out into the streets of Soho. His feet knew the way home—down Shaftesbury to Piccadilly Circus, around past Boots, cross at the lights, and then down Eagle Place to Jermyn Street and his rooms in the Eyrie Mansion. He tipped his hat as usual at the topper hanging above Bates's Hat Shop.

MASON DEVEREAUX?"
Mason admitted that it was he.
"Ashley St. Ives."

Mason closed his eyes and allowed a deep and weary sigh to escape. It was late the same evening, and he had been dozing in front of the telly when the telephone rang. He had been expecting this call ever since Fontaine Eady had written in the *Sketch* that a Hollywood agent was in London to bid for his story. The gossip columnist had helpfully set the stage: That Ashley St. Ives was the mistress of Realistic Pictures chief Ivan Bloom, that Mason's story was the key to her burning ambition to move up from agent to producer, that her private life was so complex she was rumored to be the original for all seven of the women in the new Jackie Collins novel.

"How pleasant to hear from you."

With the telephone lodged between his ear and his shoulder, Mason walked over to the sideboard and refreshed his brandy. Then he settled down in a chair next to the window, and sent his famous voice coiling down the wire in an attempt to convince St. Ives she was listening to a great actor.

The ironies, Mason thought, were too many to contemplate. Still half-asleep, he thought back through a brandy haze to recall the details of the day. Success was calling him at last, and yet he shared with Harold Gasper an awful secret. Together they had plotted the publicity stunt that resulted in Bradleigh Court's death. True, Gasper said he would take the rap. But would the police believe Gasper's story? The whole grim and foolish business stood ready to be unmasked at any moment.

"I'm calling from the St. James Club, just down the street from you," Ashley told him. "I just checked in. I was down at Thorn Hill for today's tour of the underground ballroom. It was such a thrill to walk down your secret passageway!"

"Not my passageway, Miss St. Ives. I want nothing more to do with it."

That was the right note, Mason thought. Acerbic and a little amused. A touch of Michael Caine.

"Unless it's on a movie set, of course," said Ashley St. Ives.

"Now you have my attention."

"Here's the bottom line, Mr. Devereaux. I want to tell the story of your amazing experience. It can be a great motion picture. It deserves the best production team, and it deserves you in the lead. I'll fight for the best every step of the way. Great drama and high adventure."

"And just a touch of macabre humor," Mason murmured.

"Exactly! It has everything! And you're hot right now. There's money to be made. I'll have a screenplay written by one of the top writers in Hollywood. It'll be about an actor in the *Phantom* who gets caught in the middle of a web of danger and intrigue—and romance, of course. We're lucky that the original *Phantom* is out of copyright; we can do anything we want with the character."

"Most fortunate."

"When somebody becomes an overnight celebrity with docudrama possibilities," Ashley explained, "we usually get somebody else to play him. But you're an actor. That makes you the perfect person to star in your own story."

"Up until now, don't you think," asked Mason dryly, "that everything I have accomplished was rather negative? I was not shot dead, after which I fell down a well."

"There is an element of irony," St. Ives said evenly. "I'm not saying there isn't. It's a story for a Jonathan Demme, a Blake Edwards. Both close personal friends of mine. It's not for De Palma or Scorsese. Also good friends, of course. It's time to move on this, Mr. Devereaux. Timing is everything. I want you to meet me at the Majestic Hotel in Cannes on Friday. It's the opening weekend of the film festival. Pack your tuxedo."

"The Cannes festival?" said Mason. He formed a mental picture of himself walking up the great flight of red-carpeted stairs, nodding to Gerard Depardieu and Catherine Deneuve while the fans surged against police barricades. "But that's day after tomorrow! Everything is happening so quickly. Just at the present moment I don't even have an agent."

"I'm walking right down Jermyn Street with a contract," St. Ives said. "It's not too late, is it? I'd be happy to represent you."

R EMEMBER me?" said Billy (Silver Dollar) Baxter. It was the Thursday morning, and Mason stood in the doorway of his flat at the Eyrie Mansion. He did remember Billy, from long ago. They had met when Baxter was the press agent for *My Fair Lady* on Broadway, and Mason was the juvenile opposite Rex Harrison. But hadn't they met more recently? Mason's short-term memory was a little shaky. He searched his recent hangovers for clues. Hadn't Billy been in the Coach and Horses last Saturday night—late on the day when poor Bradleigh Court was shot dead? Mason had been drinking with Sheila, and then Baxter had walked in, and Mason had been drunk, and then something something something and then Sheila had taken him to Thorn Hill, where he had fallen down the well.

"I do remember something about our last meeting," Mason said evenly.

"Please make the acquaintanceship of Miss Raven Charles," Billy said, as if announcing a diplomat. He stood aside in the narrow corridor, and Mason found himself shaking hands with a tall black woman. He invited them into his flat. Raven Charles, he thought. The name was familiar. It was a little early to start drinking, but under the circumstances he poured himself a sherry. The pieces were beginning to fall into place.

"Aren't you the woman who is producing the film version of *Phantom of the Opera*?" he asked. "What an unexpected pleasure."

Raven sat down, declined Mason's offer of a drink, and went straight to the point. "I've admired you for a long time, Mr. Devereaux. Ever since I was a college student hitchhiking through England, and I saw your Hamlet at Stratford. I had a standing-room ticket. I could have stood there for days."

"Well," said Mason. He was touched.

"Even before all of these adventures befell you," she said, "I was already considering you for the Phantom. You, Mr. Devereaux. Not

Bradleigh Court. I sent Mr. Baxter over here to England talk with you, but he arrived just as this whole amazing scenario was unfolding."

"Yes," said Mason. He sipped his drink, trying to conceal the strange effects her words were having on him. He was . . . damn! He was actually quite moved. Could this woman have any conception of what it meant to him, to be spoken to in this way, to have his Stratford days recalled, to be discussed in terms of a leading role, after decades of insults and condescension?

"I'm pleased that you've enjoyed my work," he said.

"Now there are two films to be considered," Raven Charles said. The *Phantom*, of course. And *The Mason Devereaux Story.* I want to make both of them."

The sherry glowed within Mason, who liked the way she talked, directly and openly. And he liked the way she looked, businesslike, the curves of her figure held in deepest confidence by the classic lines of her Armani blazer. He liked her smile, so frank and friendly. He even liked the fact that she had employed Billy (Silver Dollar) Baxter to fly over and talk to him. Mason sensed, with an insight born of long years of drinking, that Billy was his soul mate: Another quixotic hero using a bar stool as a throne, a pub as a stage, a drink as an audience that never tired of his performance. For Raven Charles to pick Billy Baxter as her contact man showed some imagination, he reflected. Even a sense of humor.

But then a spear of alarm cut through Mason's heart. There had been a visitor last night. Here in the flat. He tried to focus through his hangover. St. Ives. He had been drinking, and the conversation remained a little unclear. Certainly St. Ives had said nothing about a film of the *Phantom*. She had been interested only in his ludicrous personal adventures. He remembered her arriving at his door with a contract, after he had spent the evening at the Coach and Horses.

Raven smiled. "I understand you don't have an agent at present."

His eye fell on a sheaf of legal paper on his desk, and he picked it up. "Oh, dear," he said. "I'm afraid I do. Funnily enough, I obtained an agent only yesterday evening." He picked up the document and read from it. "Her name is Ashley St. Ives."

The name struck Raven like a blow. Ashley was poaching. She had hurried back to London and come knocking on Mason's door, trying to snatch his story and even the *Phantom* film project out of Raven's hands. Billy began to say something, but she laid a restraining hand on his arm.

"Do you know her?" asked Mason.

"Oh yes," Raven said. "We've known each other for a very long time."

A F T E R the two had gone, Mason stood uncertainly in the middle of his flat. He should pack for Cannes, he knew, but he had no idea what to take along. His old seersucker jacket? His white tropical suit? With a sudden surge of guilt he realized he had still not talked to Sheila Chesham. But what could he tell her? To beware of Brown? That Brown had put the real bullet in the revolver? It would be the same thing as admitting that he, Mason, was part of the plot. And now that Gasper had promised to cover for him . . .

He broke his reverie with a start. Brown was a murderer and he had to be sure Sheila was safe. He moved to the telephone and then stopped at the sideboard for a drink. It was past noon, time to switch to brandy. Of course, Brown was not a *hardened* killer, he mused. He had put only one bullet in the revolver. It was sheer recklessness, of course, but it made Brown less of a killer than a criminal tempter of fate. Now he had learned his lesson.

He put through a call to Thorn Hill House. Sheila came to the phone breathless with concern.

"I just heard you checked out of the hospital . . ."

"I was really quite all right," he said, "and I detested those tubes they stuck into me. They said I was dehydrated. Me! Imagine!"

"Mason . . ." she said. He sensed a strange tone in her voice.

"Yes, dear girl?"

"There's something I have to tell you. Douglas Brown and I have become engaged."

"Engaged?" He did not quite register the word.

"Not officially. Kind of. But we might be going to be married. Someday. Not right away. That's what I wanted to say. Because . . ."

"Yes?" He had been prudent to pour himself a brandy.

"Because you know how much I care for you, dear Mason, and . . ." Her words came in a rush, but then they trailed off.

"Yes, dear girl? Well congratulations, of course, good heavens!"

". . . and I wanted you to know . . ."

"Yes. Of course." What should he say to her? His mind was a blank. "But there's one thing, Sheila. About Douglas Brown. Are you quite sure you know him well enough to take this step? Because it is a big step, you know."

"I hope so," she said. "I'm sure we'll get to know each other better. It's all sort of new . . ."

"Yet you don't sound . . . as happy as you should, dear girl."

"Oh, Mason!" She broke into tears and hung up the telephone. Mason sat down heavily in his armchair and held his head in his hands. He cursed himself for not being able to think more clearly. Of course he had no chance with Sheila. Never had. If he told her what he knew about Brown, he would condemn himself. If she told Brown, then Brown would trade the information to the police.

He lifted his head and sat staring out the window. He had found out something just now that he had always known but never quite admitted. He loved Sheila Chesham. This was the right time for another brandy.

PART FOUR

Cannes

FOR those who attend it every year, the Cannes Festival is not so much a trade fair as a way of life. Like a prison camp or an encounter group, the festival establishes its own reality. Its citizens do not measure success by the standards of the outside world, but by what they claim to have achieved during the festival. The trade magazines carry directories of the names and hotels of the heavy hitters, followed by a single word: Buying, or Selling. Those with lesser tasks, such as Making, or Reviewing, are not listed. Movie publicists arrive on the Riviera days before the festival begins, bribing desk clerks for a room with a view, convincing restaurant owners that an adequate buffet can be spread for less than $300 a head. From La Napoule on the east to Nice on the west, residents search in vain for taxicabs, which are all lined up outside the Aéroport Côte d'Azur, ready to prey on festival first-timers.

Billy (Silver Dollar) Baxter was not a first-timer. "Irving!" he shouted. "Taxi! On the double! With a wax job! Mercedes!"

His hawk eyes ran an inventory on the massed piles of Louis Vuitton luggage that had accompanied Raven Charles on their flight down from London, and paused affectionately on his own bright red three-suiter, constructed of a space-age fabric that had been advertised on a TV shopping network as all that stood between our brave astronauts and microasteroids from outer space.

Inside the terminal, Raven was telephoning the studio, thinking furiously, trying to prepare the best strategy for discussing the Mason Devereaux situation with Ivan Bloom. How much did he already know?

When Raven originally sent Billy Baxter out from Los Angeles, it had been on a simple assignment, to scout Devereaux as a possible

Phantom. Then Mason had fallen down the well, and Raven had flown over personally. The Devereaux case was already a sensational story, but when Mason stumbled to safety through the secret passageway, it became a career-making prize. And at that point the predatory Ashley St. Ives had materialized in England, determined to snatch the package out of Raven's hands.

How should Raven handle this with Ivan? The studio head obviously knew that both his producer and his mistress had flown to Europe. Did he know Ashley had signed Mason, and was positioning herself to snatch the *Phantom* film project away from Raven? With any other couple, Raven would assume that they shared information. She doubted if Ashley shared anything with Ivan beyond her opinion of what shirt he should put on for the evening.

Raven hated French telephone operators. They treated every call as an affront. She hadn't any change and was trying to call Ivan collect, ree-verse-eeeng les charges, and now the studio had her on hold, forcing her to listen to taped commercials for Realistic's forthcoming releases. The taped messages, she knew, came from an electronic gizmo Ivan had discovered at Radio Shack and hooked up himself. It was almost endearing, the way teams of high-priced publicity counselors massaged the studio's image, and then Ivan the home-brew electronics wizard undid their work with his bright ideas.

Her call was accepted. The sound of violent coughing came down the line, and she could picture Ivan igniting his cigar.

"Raven, honey, what's going on over there?" The studio chief's voice sounded worried. "Ashley told me you've promised the *Phantom* to this drunk. What's his name?"

So Ivan had talked to Ashley! But did he know Ashley had Mason under contract? Raven instructed herself to remain calm.

"His name is Mason Devereaux," she told him. "We discussed him, Ivan, you and I. Last Sunday. We said there was a made-for-TV movie in the *Phantom of the Opera* murder. That was even before he fell down the well. That's when I came over to sign him up."

"Did you?"

"Did I what?"

"Sign him up?"

"Not yet," Raven said. "He just got himself a new agent. The negotiations are probably going to take place here at Cannes. I personally think he has the potential to play the Phantom. Especially since Bradleigh Court's funeral was Tuesday."

"It's incredible, the vultures in this business," Ivan complained. "Here's a drunk who can't even get his garbage collected, and overnight he has an agent. Probably some ambulance chaser."

"It's Ashley St. Ives," Raven said. "Didn't she tell you?"

There was a silence at the other end. "So I'm negotiating against myself?" Ivan said at last.

"No. We are negotiating against her. She doesn't work for you, Ivan. I work for you. She's your girlfriend. I'm your producer."

"Why would she sign him up, knowing we were going after him? How could she do that to us?"

"She wants to be a producer."

"That makes sense," said Ivan. "How about you? Do you want to be my girlfriend?"

"Not funny."

"Only kidding."

"What should I do?" she asked him.

"See how things develop," he said.

"What does that mean?"

"How should I know what it means?" She could detect the beginnings of a whine in his voice, a tone that said women were ganging up on him and it wasn't fair. "I'm faced with a nasty case of divided loyalties here."

"That's right, Ivan. But they're your loyalties."

I RVING!"

The cry rang through the American Bar of the Majestic Hotel with the confidence of a foghorn. During most of the year, the elegant veranda room was a haven for the rich expatriates who had retired to Cannes with their dogs, jewels, and *Financial Times* subscriptions. During the festival, the bar was a zoo. A procrastinating elderly couple stood up and marched out of the bar at the first sound of Billy's voice. They had forgotten the festival began today.

"Irving! Brang 'em on!"

Behind the polished mahogany bar, Robert the bartender rolled his eyes at his staff. He recognized the voice without even needing to see the florid figure on the other side of the room.

"Oui, Monsieur Baxter! Tout de suite!" he said. He poured scotch in a glass and placed it on the tray of one of his young assistants, who slapped a freshly starched napkin over his arm and hurried to the corner where Billy (Silver Dollar) Baxter was holding court.

After they had arrived from the airport, Billy had escorted Raven Charles to the lobby elevator, ordered her luggage sent up to her suite, and headed straight for the bar with his three-suiter under his arm. The New York press agent was a fixture at the Majestic, where his method for dealing with the waiters was the same as everywhere else on earth.

"It's simplicity itself," he was explaining even now to his companion, a rat-faced little man with a pencil mustache who he had somehow picked up between the door and the table. "You shout at them. Then they can't ignore you. A guy could spend all night sitting in some bar clearing his throat and tapping his fingers and never get a drink. Watch this.

"Irving! Brang 'em on! Johnnie Walker! Black Label! Generous portion! Clean glass! *Pas de* soda! *Pas de* ice cubes! No olives, no little crackers. Hup! Hup!"

The waiter was already at his side, bearing a glass of whiskey. Baxter produced a stainless steel case from an inside coat pocket, unfolded it into a rubber stamp, and applied his signature to the bill.

"None genuine without this mark," he said. "Sometimes, late at night, your signature gets a little lazy. Any bum could forge it. So I had a rubber stamp made. No mistakes that way."

"But why," asked his listener, "do you call them Irving?"

"Every waiter everywhere in the world answers to the name of Irving," Baxter explained. "Try it yourself. Don't ask me why."

Rat-face was a good audience. He reminded Billy of the guy in *Casablanca* who got shot.

"You Buying or Selling?" Baxter asked. It was a safe opener.

"Maybe Buying, maybe Selling," the man said. "I am hoping to meet a British actor named Mason Devereaux. You recognize the name?"

"Yeah, the guy who fell down the well. What about him?"

"Can you arrange a rendezvous between us, Monsieur Baxter?" Rat-face handed Billy his card.

"Arrange?" Baxter paused with his glass halfway to his mouth. "Any time, day or night, you wanna meet Mason, all you gotta do is buy him a drink."

"In a proper way, arrange a meeting," the man said. "Not via le cocktail. Through his agent, politely."

"So, call his agent. Today, her name is Ashley St. Ives. Tomorrow, he might get lucky."

"Miss St. Ives has not returned my telephone calls," the little man said.

Billy glanced at the man's card. "With a name like Excaliber Pontoon," Baxter said, "she doesn't know it's you. She thinks it's a ship-supply store."

The little man looked pained. "My name was originally Romanian," he explained. "I have anglicized it. Does it offend you?"

"Anglicized it?" Baxter said. "You woulda done better throwing darts at the funny page. Irving! Brang Monsieur Pontoon a drink! Hup!"

"Perhaps you would like to hear my offer?" Pontoon asked him.

EXCALIBER PONTOON

"Not particularly."

"Then how can we proceed?"

"To separate destinations."

L I F E was good. Mason Devereaux sat in the beach restaurant of the Carlton Hotel and pretended not to notice that a dozen photographers were taking his picture. Overhead, an airplane towed an advertising banner down the length of the beach, proclaiming: THE DEVEREAUX SAGA. His new agent, Ashley St. Ives, was masterminding a bidding war for the rights even as he aired himself in the soothing Mediterranean breeze.

Mason's skin still held the sickly pallor of a London winter. He sat in the shade to protect it, but close enough to the sunshine so that he could observe the parade of beautiful women who tanned on the beach, their breasts carelessly exposed. They were ignored by everyone except Devereaux, who had never been closer to a beach than a Soho strip club.

Before him was a plate of antipasto, mostly made, it seemed, from eggplants and capers. To his hand, a magnum of chilled white Bordeaux stood ready. He toyed with the thought that perhaps one of the topless beauties would find it amusing to be introduced to the figure of intrigue in the new Panama. See that helicopter up there? That's me, my dear. *The Devereaux Saga?* My saga.

The thought of Sheila Chesham visited him for just a second, provoking a guilty revision of his daydream, and then Ashley St. Ives broke his reverie. She was seated across the table from him, punching buttons on her portable telephone, and now she grabbed a waiter.

"I want a real telephone at this table," she said. "Toot sweet."

"Oui, madame. It is the only kind we have at the Carlton."

He hurried away. How did these hotels have so many different waiters, Mason wondered, that after every one promised you something, you never saw him again?

Ashley lit a cigarette. "Now, Mason, about Little Denny Brennen."

"Remind me again, dear Ashley. Who is this person?"

"He's the hottest kid star on American television. He has a sitcom where he's best friends with a turtle whose mind is controlled by an ancient intelligence from another star. You mean you've never seen it?"

"I don't get to watch nearly as much telly as I'd like," Mason said. "Actor's hours, you know."

"Here's all you need to know. Denny Brennen is hot, and turtles are hot. They're spinning off a feature film where his turtle turns out to be a ninja godfather."

"Are those the little ones with the palm trees painted on their shells?"

"I'll explain everything, Mason. Here comes our boat now. Just be nice to Little Denny and his turtle and pose for the pictures. God, I hate turtles. Don't you?"

"I don't mind them in soup, with a nice sherry."

Mason drained his glass and looked with regret at the half-full magnum in the ice bucket. He rose to his feet. A powerboat was maneuvering close to the Carlton's pier, where the paparazzi had clustered like a herd of large smelly animals. Mason poured himself a glass of wine to take aboard the boat.

NOT far away, at a table in the shade of the restaurant bar, Raven Charles and Billy Baxter watched as Mason helped Ashley totter toward the boat in her high heels, which she insisted on wearing, even in the sand.

"The lamb goeth before the slaughter," said Billy, rotating his glass of Scotch whiskey. "That poor slob. Ashley has him bedazzled."

"I wonder about that," said Raven. "There's a quality every British actor seems to possess—even Mason. It may protect him against her."

As they watched, Ashley landed unsteadily on the deck of the powerboat, shrieked with delight, and careened into the arms of the skipper.

"What quality would that be?" Billy asked.

"An instinctive hostility against anyone who tries to steal their scenes."

A few miles offshore, opposite Cannes and just barely visible from its highest hotel windows, lies the island of St. Marguerite, known to every French schoolchild, where the Man in the Iron Mask was held captive three centuries ago. Although the true identity of the mysterious prisoner of Louis XIV has never been established, that fact does not discourage hordes of tourists, who visit the island to gawk through the medieval fortress where the prisoner was held.

The speedboat bearing the Devereaux party bypassed the tourist jetties and pulled up directly to the dock of the little Italian restaurant that nestles in the shadow of the prison. On shore, cameras were already set up for the press conference. Mason helped Ashley St. Ives tiptoe through the sand, as the agent whispered a briefing into his ear: "One of the ways you get publicity at this festival is to be seen socializing with the other stars. You're in luck because Little Denny is my client, and so we can all scratch each other's backs."

Mason was formulating a pointed reply when the paparazzi pack descended on them, led by a little boy wearing a silk Los Angeles Lakers jacket. His hair was tousled and his nose was freckled and there was a gap between his front teeth. Mason loathed him on sight.

"I hear you're a real drunk," said Little Denny Brennen.

"I beg your pardon?"

"That's what I hear. You got drunk and fell down a well and now you're so hot you're gonna save the CBS fall schedule."

Mason turned away. "Ashley? How much longer do we need to be here?"

"You grow up fast in tinseltown," Little Denny said, dancing around to face him. "In

LITTLE DENNY BRENNEN

show biz we all talk like this. Don't take it personally. I don't care if you drink. My nanny was a cokehead. She got fired. I'm eleven. I make around three million dollars a year. It's being invested for my education."

"I hope it will be sufficient," Mason said, sitting down on a restaurant chair. A second later he bolted to his feet with a stifled cry.

"He sat on Owanowa!" Little Denny screamed, while the cameramen elbowed for position.

"Good God, Mason, you've killed the turtle!" Ashley St. Ives said, smiling brilliantly as the TV cameras pointed toward her. She was able to talk without moving her teeth.

They looked down at the chair, where beady eyes peered out from deep inside a shell.

"Owanowa?" Mason said, pressing his handkerchief to the wound.

"The Ancient Oracle of Planet Owan," Little Denny Brennen told him. "He's a ninja godfather. Nobody knows that yet. We've won two Emmys."

"The turtle was supposed to be in his own silver bucket," Ashley St. Ives whispered ferociously to a French publicist. "Who put the goddamn thing on Mason's chair?"

"I wanted him to be able to see," said Little Denny Brennen.

Probing gently, Mason determined that the turtle had not broken his skin. He tried to remember what diseases were caused by turtle bite. He had read about one in the *Telegraph* where you grew lethargic and sat around all day, unwilling to do anything. He wondered what the symptoms were.

"Dennis? Did you deliberately place the turtle where you knew Mason would sit on it?" Ashley asked, trying to sound strict.

"What am I, psychic? How am I gonna know where Mason is gonna sit?"

"Mason," she said, "sit over here by me. Denny, maybe the turtle would like to play on the sand." She lit a cigarette. "Perhaps it's for the best," she whispered to Mason. "It's a famous turtle. First you escape being shot dead. Then you're saved from an underwater grave. Now you sit on the turtle."

"It doesn't build," Mason said.

"Nixon had six crises, Mason," said a familiar voice. "You've only given us two, and a turtle bite."

It was Fontaine Eady.

"Of course you'd be here," Mason told him, but he was relieved to see a familiar face.

"Oh, it's the biggest story at the festival," Eady said. "Come along, Mason, they're touring the fortress. Nothing can possibly happen to you there."

INSPECTOR FREDSON ROWLEY sat with Harold Gasper in an interrogation room at Scotland Yard. The air was blue with the smoke of Gasper's cigarettes. The two men had been talking for some time, but now they fell silent, regarding various possibilities they had discussed. Gasper sketched a likeness of the Phantom on an interrogation form.

"What am I going to do with you?" Rowley asked at last.

"Charge me with something," Gasper said helpfully. "What would it be? Reckless homicide, I imagine."

"When a man refuses to defend himself," Rowley said, "it's usually because he fears his defense will link him to a greater crime than the one he has been accused of. That's my theory."

"I pulled the trigger." Gasper shrugged. "It was a silly, stupid stunt and it went wrong. Bradleigh Court was a friend of mine. I'm quite prepared to take my medicine."

"Once again, Mr. Gasper. Will you tell me who put the real bullet in the revolver, if it was not you?"

"It was not me," Gasper said.

"Don't toy with me. I could as easily charge you with murder as pick up this pencil. I want to know the story of that gun. Where it came from, who loaded it, who you conspired with."

Gasper lit a cigarette. "Lock me up," he said. "I've confessed. You have the guilty party, Inspector. Case closed."

"God, you annoy me," said Fredson Rowley.

WHY aren't we at the Carlton bar right now?" Mason complained to Eady. "Why are we moping about in the bowels of a rat-infested French dungeon? What purpose is being served?" They had joined a party of demoralized journalists, who were being marched through a clammy stone passage by the cheerful Ashley St. Ives.

"Publicity, dear boy," said Eady. "This is what the festival is all about, isn't it? Enhancing the old image. They can't keep recycling yesterday's footage. On telly tonight you'll look dashing, exploring the cell of the Man in the Iron Mask."

The two men were reluctantly bringing up the rear of a media parade. Mason could see Little Denny Brennen up in the front, banging the faceplates on suits of armor.

"Why don't we quietly drop out and meet the others later?" Eady asked him, a note of concern creeping into his voice. "You've only been out of the hospital a few days."

"What, and let Little Denny snatch all the press clippings? You're right, Eady. This may be my only opportunity to be photographed in the tomb, or the bed-sitting room, or whatever the bloody hell it is, of the Man in the Iron Mask."

"I wonder if the Man has anything to drink," Eady said.

"Strictly *entre nous*, I'm astonished that the Man was a real historical personage at all. I had the impression he was from a comic book."

"I wouldn't mention that to the press if I were you," Eady advised him.

"Mason!" shrieked Ashley St. Ives. "Come up here where everybody can see you! I want you and Little Denny Brennen in the same pictures!"

"That is the most ill-mannered child on the planet," Mason growled to Eady. "If he were to appear as Oliver Twist, pleading for more gruel, the audience would rise up and shout, 'Starve the little bastard!'"

Mason shouldered his way to the front of the mob, where Little Denny was standing in front of a case displaying the historic Iron Mask.

"Who was this Iron Mask guy, anyway?" Little Denny was asking. "What did he do? Kill a major bunch of people?"

"There are many different theories about the identity of the Man in the Iron Mask," a museum guide informed him. "But to this very day, his true name remains a mystery."

"Jeez, why didn't somebody just ask the guy? You frogs got it coming to you!"

D O W N by the old yacht harbor at Cannes there is a restaurant with the forthright name of La Pizza, and it was here that Billy (Silver Dollar) Baxter sought relief from the mysteries of a French menu, with Raven Charles keeping him company.

"The names the French give this stuff, it takes you longer to say it than it does to eat it," Billy complained to Raven. "It's got nine syllables and the waiter treats you like a retard if you try to pronounce it. Then when it comes it's a squidge of midget meal in the center of an empty plate, garnished with a carrot embryo. That's why I like it at Italian joints. You want pizza, you say pizza, you get pizza. No controversy." He twirled a gooey thread of cheese on his fork.

"But pizza is an Italian word," Raven told him.

"The way I got it figured," Billy said, "you got 60 million Italians saying pizza, but you got 260 million Americans saying pizza. So it's an American word."

"I feel like this is my last meal," Raven sighed. Even her clothes seemed to express her resignation. Her power wardrobe was in the closet at the Majestic, and she had changed into jeans and a *She's Gotta Have It* T-shirt. The afternoon sun cast a golden glow across the harbor to the festival palace, but she was not here for the architecture. She was here to sign Mason Devereaux to a contract, and had not even spoken to him since his arrival at the festival.

She stabbed a lettuce leaf in anger. That hustling witch Ashley St. Ives had hijacked him and was no doubt dazzling poor Mason with all the cheap trappings of the festival. When an actor has labored in obscurity for long sad years, she thought, all you have to do is surround him with photographers and he thinks justice has been done at last. How was Mason to know that the photographers at Cannes were the lowest form of paparazzi, waiting patiently for him to split his pants for the supermarket scandal rags? Half of the photos taken at Cannes ended up in the *Star,* showing women with their boobs falling out and breadsticks in their ears.

On the sidewalk in front of La Pizza, the festival's tide ebbed and flowed. There were tourists and fishermen, housewives and retired

Swedish bankers, hookers and hitchhiking students and little gypsy girls selling roses. Raven's eyes passed idly over their faces.

"Billy?"

"Yeah, sweetie pie?"

"Why is he looking so strangely at us?"

She had singled out a rat-faced little man whose black polyester suit and bright green tie made him stand out from the crowd.

"That guy's name," said Billy, "is Excaliber Pontoon. That's all I know about him, and even that's gotta be wrong. He talks like a broken dictionary."

"I don't like him," Raven said. "There's something unwholesome about him."

"He smells like damp basements," Billy said helpfully.

MASON DEVEREAUX was perspiring furiously. He and Little Denny Brennen were seated side by side in a flood of television lights outside the cell of the Man in the Iron Mask, while Little Denny fielded the questions of the world's press and Mason's lips were frozen in a ghastly smile. He felt like he could use a drink.

"I guess you haven't seen my show," the child star was saying to an Australian interviewer.

"It's not on down under."

"Then come on up and join the real world," Little Denny said. "It's a show about how I bring this turtle home, see, and before long I notice he's using his beak to trace out words in the sand on the bottom of his bowl. The turtle tells me his mind is controlled by an ancient intelligence from another solar system, and I have been chosen to deliver his message to the ninja turtles on earth."

"And what role does Mr. Devereaux play?" asked the interviewer.

"None," Mason smiled grimly. "Nor will I in future."

"Have you even seen the show?"

"Never."

"Then why are you part of this press conference?"

"I can answer that one," volunteered Little Denny Brennen. "Mr. Devereaux is here because he got drunk and fell down a well. We have the same agent, and she thinks maybe he can pick up some free publicity by hanging around me. So far, she's right. Earlier today he got bit on the ass by the turtle."

Mason shot to his feet, determined to endure Little Denny Brennen's insults no longer. He took the child by the collar of his basketball jacket.

"You are the most ill-mannered child I have ever met," Mason told him, his nose an inch from the squirming little celebrity. "Has no one the nerve to teach you your manners?"

Ashley St. Ives hurried around the table and tried to pull Mason loose from Little Denny. The press surged forward and a TV cameraman was thrown to the ground. His light exploded. Little Denny jumped on top of the table and grabbed the Iron Mask from its display case. Ashley screamed.

Mason's whole world went black. At first he thought he had been struck on the head. There was a loud ringing noise in his ears. Then he saw the leering grin of Little Denny Brennen, close and yet somehow far away, as if glimpsed through a slit in the fabric of space.

"Has-been! Has-been! Teach you to mess with me!" he heard Little Denny taunting.

Ashley St. Ives swam into view. "Mason!" she screamed. "How in God's name did you get into the Iron Mask?"

HERE'S my plan," said Excaliber Pontoon, moving his head closer to Billy Baxter's and lowering his voice. "I want to produce a movie that will star Mason Devereaux and Elvira as the leaders of a plot to seize control of Club Med and run it as a vampire colony."

It was later on the Saturday afternoon, and Billy had once again been cornered by the insistent rat-faced producer, who had followed them as they walked back to the hotel from La Pizza. He knew it was imprudent to hold discussions about Mason without including Raven Charles, but Raven had gone upstairs to make calls, the Majestic bar was cool and friendly, and Rat-face was paying for the drinks. Besides, it wasn't every day you got to talk with a malfunctioning thesaurus.

"Where you gonna get Elvira?" Baxter asked, trying to sound intrigued.

"That's my problem," said Pontoon, looking around as if he might have forgotten the actress behind one of the chairs. "The film will be shot on location on the world's most exclusive beaches, caressed by flagrant breezes, where beautiful young women will be victimized by their scheme." He sounded as if he had memorized the entire pitch. "Devereaux and Elvira will be joined in an unholy intrigue to turn those nubile young innocents into surfing vampires. There will also be six rock-and-roll melodies. Here is my screenplay."

Billy regarded a dog-eared typescript with red wine stains on the cover. "You don't see many carbon-paper screenplays these days," he observed mildly. "Usually they're run off down at Kinko's Copies."

"In my country—ah, company—we prefer the ancient methods," Rat-face said. "Can you read this quickly?"

"I don't read screenplays," Baxter said. "I only read deals. They're better written, and they got a lot more twists and turns."

"Delay could be fatal," Pontoon warned. "Mason Devereaux is hot at the second, but the world will have forgotten him by the time this woman named Ashley St. Ives finds a script for him. My project is ready to roll. The sexy girls are waiting. It can be in theaters by September. Get me to Devereaux and I will convince him of this."

"What's in it for me?" asked Baxter.

"Ten percent."

"Ten percent of what?"

"That we can negotiate."

MASON DEVEREAUX felt as if he were living inside a telephone handset. His head was still trapped in the Iron Mask, which muffled some sounds while amplifying others into painful clanging reverberations. Through a cruel acoustic trick, the voice of Ashley St. Ives was particularly magnified by the mask.

"Stand back!" she was shrieking at the television cameramen, who were crawling onto tables to get shots of Mason's head encased in the Iron Mask. "Give him air! Call an ambulance!"

"He's fine. He's having a fun time." Mason recognized the voice of Little Denny Brennen. "All I gotta do," Little Denny said, "is just pull the mask off again and we're back to square one."

Mason took the mask in both of his own hands and began to tug, but his chin prevented the mask from slipping over his head. He felt claustrophobic inside the dark prison, which provided only a narrow slit through which he could glimpse Ashley's waving arms, Little Denny's triumphant smirk, and Fontaine Eady, dictating into a tape recorder.

"What has happened?" His voice rang painfully loud inside the iron shell, and he repeated again, in a whisper: "Ashley! What happened?"

"Little Denny grabbed the Iron Mask out of the display case and clapped it onto your head before anyone could stop him," the agent told him.

"I need a drink," he said.

"I know, Mason—but how? There's only that narrow slit for your eyes."

Mason felt for a chair and sat down heavily. He could dimly see guards pushing the photographers back into another chamber of the dungeons.

"How did the damnable original Man in the Iron Mask have a drink? I suppose brandy was not entirely unknown in his time?"

By turning his neck stiffly, he could scan the faces around him, as if through a narrow camera lens. Ashley leaned forward until he could smell Binaca through the slit.

"This is actually fabulous, darling," she murmured. "Think of the publicity! Nobody will believe I didn't plan it."

"I have an idea," Mason told her. "Why don't we celebrate with a drink?"

"Mason!" Now it was Fontaine Eady, swimming into sight. The view from inside the helmet was like a medieval channel-changer. "Mason! Can you hear me in there?"

"Perfectly well."

"The *Sketch* will pay you fifteen thousand pounds for the exclusive rights to your story."

"Make it twenty-five thousand and we have a deal," Ashley St. Ives said.

They were already talking about him as if he were far away, Mason thought. And indeed the outer world seemed more distant to him by the moment, indistinct and unfocused. Eady's face swam upward out of view, and then a loud crash filled Mason's head.

"Good Lord!" Eady said. "He's fallen right over."

"He's fainted," said Ashley. "Mason! Can you breathe?"

There was no answer from inside the Mask.

T HE first thing you gotta know," Billy (Silver Dollar) Baxter told Excaliber Pontoon, "is that this place is crawling with snake oil artists. One year I met a guy who wanted to sell me movies by the pound. Compared to you, he was on the level. Anyone that needs an agent to get an agent has a problem. What are your resources? You got any cash?"

"Let me be frank," said Pontoon, putting two books of the Majestic Hotel's matches into his pocket. "I represent some people who would like to commission productions without calling undue attention to themselves. All totally respectable executives, of course."

"Of course," said Baxter.

"But low profile."

"Below ground level," Baxter said.

"Do not make my task more difficult, Mr. Baxter. As you may know, there has been turmoil in Eastern Europe. Governments are in a process of transition. Currencies are gone tomorrow. It is complicated to off-load assets."

"Yeah," Baxter said. "All their money is tied up in cash. I got it. You wanna make some of your Romanian pals into movie producers, so they can run a laundry with the budget?"

Pontoon was about to reply when they heard a siren approaching up the circular drive beyond the Majestic terrace. Billy got up to have a look and saw Ashley St. Ives directing an ambulance that was backing toward the hotel's entrance.

"Put it on hold," he told Pontoon. "I gotta check this out."

He pushed his way down to the front of a gathering crowd, shouldered through the paparazzi, and saw a figure emerge from the am-

bulance and rise unsteadily to its feet. The figure had the body of Mason Devereaux and the head of an iron mask.

"Leave me alone!" the figure called out, its voice muffled and tinny. "Take your hands off!" Billy recognized Mason's voice and moved to his side.

"Mason, it's me—Silver Dollar Baxter," he said into the slit. "I know just how you feel. *Irving!* Double brandy for Monsieur Devereaux! And a straw."

IVAN BLOOM was unhappy. The studio boss hated overseas telephone calls in the first place, because they implied foreign deals, foreign money, foreign exchange rates, and, worst of all, foreign languages. He also hated the fact that he could barely hear the party at the other end over his speakerphone. That meant actually using a hand to hold a receiver to his ear, which left only one hand for his cigar and no hand at all for using the channel-changer on his television sets. And now he was even unhappier, because Raven Charles had left him holding the phone.

"Ivan?" She was back again. "Ivan, something terrible has happened! Mason Devereaux has caught his head inside an antique iron mask!"

"A what? Speak up, Raven!"

"It happened at some sort of press conference. Billy Baxter is with him now, trying to help out. Somebody put a famous old iron mask on his head and now they can't get it off again!"

"But they will," Bloom said. "The French will never let him out of the country with their national treasure. They have strict laws."

"Don't make jokes, Ivan. We're talking about a human being here. A man named Mason Devereaux."

"Lighten up, sweetie," Ivan told her. "In the final analysis, who isn't a human being?"

SHEILA CHESHAM heard about what had happened to Mason from a BBC camera crew that landed in a helicopter on the lawn of Thorn Hill House. They wanted a statement on the series of bizarre accidents that had befallen the unfortunate actor, and when Sheila expressed her sympathy, the reporter asked if it wasn't perhaps all a series of publicity stunts. Sheila slammed the door on them all and ran up the stairs to her room.

Douglas Brown was somewhere on the premises, but she had no desire to speak to him. She wanted to be alone, she thought, but the moment she was safe in her room she realized that what she actually wanted was to be with Mason.

It was strange about Douglas Brown. She wondered if she had started going out with him in the first place only to get someone's attention. Someone like Mason. There was something subtly wrong with Brown, she realized. Something flawed and underhanded. Did he have some strange power over her, that caused her to agree even when her whole being wanted to walk away?

There was a knock on the door, and Brown entered without being asked.

"I want to be by myself, Douglas," she told him.

"Have you heard the news? Your pal Mason has made a spectacle of himself at the Cannes Film Festival."

"I've heard that he's had another misfortune," she said.

"Trapped his head inside an iron mask," Brown said, almost snickering. He walked to the window and stood looking over the lawns of Thorn Hill.

"It was placed on his head by some child," Sheila said. She knew she had to speak plainly or she would burst out in tears. "Mason was simply standing there."

"Yeah, he does a lot of standing," Brown said. "Like he was just standing there when Bradleigh Court got shot."

"In point of fact, he was under the stage, trying to free me."

"It's almost like he knew something was going to happen," Brown said.

"Get out! Get out of my room!" Sheila cried. She rang for the butler. "Mason is a dear good friend of mine and you have no right to talk about him in that tone of voice."

"I am a dear good friend of yours as well, Sheila," said Brown.

Jeffrey the butler knocked and then opened the door with a quizzical expression.

"See Mr. Brown to his car," she told him. "Then pack a bag. I'm flying to France."

"Yes, madam," said Jeffrey. It was one of his bad arthritis days. "Could you possibly take it down from the shelf for me?"

"I was just going," said Douglas. "Good day, Jeffrey."

"Sir."

Brown was gone. Jeffrey measured the situation and disappeared. Sheila sat in a chair by the window and buried her head in her hands. Douglas had seemed so different the first time she met him. That had been months ago, around the time her theater friends first took her breathless with laughter through Soho to the Coach and Horses. She had, she remembered, met Douglas at about the same time she met Mason, and both of them had seemed part of a half-secret and slightly raffish fraternity.

The whole world of the theater was miles apart from the world she had occupied as a schoolgirl, growing up at Thorn Hill House, visiting at similar mouldy piles, meeting young men who assumed (as their parents assumed about them) that they would go to Oxbridge and then enter some well-paid profession where it was understood that a gentlemen had occasionally to be absent, in order to shoot and ski. Such specimens, brought forward for her consideration as possible husbands, seemed hardly more advanced than their originals in Trollope. They saw themselves primarily as the ideal managers for her fortune. In six of them combined there was not the wit to survive in Brighton without a credit card.

Douglas Brown, she knew instantly, was not like that. He lived by his wits, he looked for the angles, and had a clear idea of the money he hoped to make and the success he hoped to capture by the time he was thirty. She found him entertaining.

What it had finally came around to, was: One night her friends had tired of slumming in the Coach and Horses, and had announced they were off to Tramp. She had said she would stay. She felt more at home in that smoky, conspiratorial company than in a club where she could only hope to meet the same boring boys she already knew from the country, perhaps slightly improved by drink and poor lighting. She had met Mason several times before, and now, sitting next to him without distractions from her loud friends, she began to appreciate the peculiar quality of his charm. She liked his weariness and flashes of brilliance, his air of having met everyone, been everywhere, played every role, and forgotten as much as he could.

It was one of his favorite pastimes to sit in a corner of a theatrical pub and explain the denizens to her, one by one—that one, who was reduced to using his wife's money to produce his fringe musicals, or that one, whose career had never recovered from a disastrous experiment in making a British version of "Car 54."

But Mason had never quite made a move. She knew, because a woman could always sense such things, that he cared for her. But he never said so. Their meetings were always at her initiative, and on her terms. Because Douglas had been about her age and had actively courted her, and because Mason had been twenty-five years older and kept a certain distance, it had somehow become the accepted thing that she was dating Brown. That had been all right as long as it never amounted to anything, but Brown's mistake, she realized, had been to propose marriage. She might have continued to go about with him for months or years, but once she found herself engaged to him, she discovered that he did not fit, that instead of feeling good when she looked at him, she felt pain when she looked at Mason.

She climbed up on a chair and brought down the bag for Jeffrey.

PART FIVE

Sea Cave

THE first problem was crowd control. The entrapment of Mason Devereaux's head had become the biggest story at the Cannes Film Festival, upstaging even the documentary about Madonna's underwear. The Majestic Hotel brought in busloads of Riviera police to barricade its doors against paparazzi. Paying guests complained they couldn't get to their rooms.

Ashley St. Ives, faced with her first crisis as Mason's manager, was issuing instructions at the top of her voice.

"We'll fly him to the Mayo Clinic!" she cried. "We'll charter a Gulfstream!"

Billy Baxter, who had attached himself to Mason's side, shook his head. "For what? Surgery? This guy doesn't need a doctor, he needs a sheet-metal worker."

A conference room had been turned into the emergency center, with Mason at the center of it. He sat in a chair by the window, where the wind from the sea was fresher, but his breathing came with an alarming gasping noise, like a malfunctioning air conditioner. Two doctors visited the room and left again, shaking their heads, and a chiropractor attempted to wrench the mask from Mason's head, without success. It still remained, a large, dull, metallic fact.

"The doctors say it is . . . impossible," Ashley moaned softly.

"That's pronounced *im-poss-EEE-blah*," Billy said. "Don't take it too seriously. It's the only word the French use with Americans."

Ashley would have preferred Baxter out of the room; she saw him as an agent of her enemy, Raven. But Mason clung to the press agent as a link with the real world, and as a reliable source of drink.

"How you doin' in there?" Billy asked him solicitously.

"I feel as if I have loudspeakers stuck in my ears," Mason said piteously. "My face has never itched before, but now every inch of it wants to be scratched."

"*Irving!*" Billy called out to a waiter. "*Le Q-teeps, immediately-mont!*"

"And I need to use the facilities."

"Irving! *Ooo* is *le toilet?*"

"Monsieur! I have only two hands!"

Ashley turned up the sound on the television. "Look!" she said. "It's Jack Lang—the minister of culture!"

Lang was addressing a press conference at the Palais de Festivals.

"We express our grave concern," he said. "We are devoting our full attention to this crisis. The government of France will do everything in its power to protect the priceless national heirloom of the Iron Mask."

"What about Mason Devereaux?" a reporter shouted.

"No further questions," Lang said, waving at the cameras as his aides hurried him off the stage.

I N the hours after midnight the curious crowds in front of the hotel had finally gone home. Offers of aid were pouring in from all over the world, from people who claimed to be experts in removing iron masks, but Ashley decided most of them were cranks, and took the telephone off the hook.

"In the morning," she said, "we will take X rays."

"To do what?" asked Billy. "To see if he's still in there?"

Raven Charles had joined Billy for a visit to Mason's chairside, until Ashley coolly informed them she would like to be alone with her client. Then Raven went up to her room to call Ivan Bloom with an update, and Billy walked sadly by the water's edge. Although he glanced once or twice in the direction of cafés, he had no taste for a drink.

"Monsieur Billy!" Baxter saw a rat-faced little man emerge from the shadows. It was Excaliber Pontoon. Billy nodded, grateful for any company, and the two men walked in silence along the jetty near a pirate ship that had been built for a movie and anchored at Cannes for three or four years. Behind them on the shore, the lights of Cannes twinkled with invitations to casinos and midnight screenings, but out here the ancient splash of the Mediterranean was a reminder of an earlier time.

"This sea, she is the mother of invention," Pontoon said philosophically. "From the civilizations of her many shores came the birthplace of cradles."

"How you moving on your screenplay?" Billy asked.

"Very well. This ship, it is old?"

"Naw. About five years," Billy said. "It was built for a movie. Polanski lost a bundle on it. You've heard about movies that don't make money? His movie didn't even pay for the boat."

"What was the film called?" asked Pontoon.

"Something like *Pirate*. It starred Walter Matthau. Swell guy, wrong film. A guy like Matthau, he may be a great actor, but put him in a three-cornered hat and pantaloons, and he looks like drag night at the Bar Association."

"How do you *appell* it? Math-how?" Pontoon said.

"Accent on the Math."

"*Math*-how. *Math*-how," Pontoon repeated to himself.

"You get that one right, we'll work on Schwarzenegger," Baxter promised.

"Monsieur Billy, what can I do to help with your friend, Mason?"

"Nothing. They're doing X rays in the morning. That'll cost a bundle. I predict they'll discover that his head is trapped in the mask. The only answer is, get a can-opener. But the French won't stand for that. They say it's a priceless national heirloom."

"But so is Monsieur Devereaux!" said Pontoon.

"Yeah, but he ain't their treasure. Look out there," Billy said. He was pointing at a large silhouette on the horizon. "That yacht musta cost millions. Where do people get the money to float around like this?"

Pontoon looked out over the sea to where a massive form was outlined in running lights. "That is a United States aircraft carrier," he answered. "Part of the fleet will be calling here for a few days, I believe."

Billy stood looking at the vast, distant form. "You know what they have on those tubs?" he said at last. "A ship's surgery. Where they deal with shrapnel and things like that. A U.S. Navy surgeon wouldn't give a shit about priceless national heirlooms. How can we contact those guys?"

"Please, if you will permit me," Pontoon said. "I have my yacht awaiting here in the waters. We can use the marine radio to call them."

"Your yacht? I thought you lived in the hotel bar."

"We can take him to the ship's surgery."

Billy looked at the little man forgivingly and decided he was not so rat-faced after all. Even Peter Lorre was good-looking until he put on the weight.

DMIRAL JAMES RYAN was awakened with news of a strange call received in the radio room, and had it patched through to his cabin. He listened with amazement to the voice of a man who described himself as William Makepeace Baxter of Realistic Pictures:

"The life of an American citizen is at stake here, skipper. The French are gonna leave him in this mask until they can chip his skull out with a screwdriver. Devereaux is in lousy health to begin with, after two days of dancing in the underwater ballroom. Here's my plan. I got a pal here with a yacht. We sneak Mason out to you in international waters—cover of night. Then your surgeons do the right thing."

Ryan, who had been under fire in the Gulf War, was not inclined to split hairs when it came to a choice between a man's life and a French antique. "Sounds good to me," he said.

HAT was it that Hemingway had said? Or Fitzgerald? Something about how at three o'clock in the morning, it was always the dark night of the soul? It was the sort of quotation that only came to Mason in the middle of dark nights. He turned on his bed in the Majestic Hotel and groaned. The suite was billed at a thousand dollars a night, and last night the bed had felt incomparably luxurious, but tonight there was no position where the cruel mask did not dig into his neck.

He had a new admiration now for the original Man in the Iron Mask. Trapped in the same claustrophobic space, he imagined he could sense the other man's aroma, the smell of fear. Mason had left the light on in his room, but the eye-slit in the mask blocked out most of it, and here, in the darkness, he felt a kinship with the prisoner of Louis XIV. He tried to look on the bright side: He was the only other human in history to wear the mask. That would get him a mention in *Guinness*.

He twisted his wrist to look at his watch, but could not line up the numbers to see them. An image of Sheila came flashing into his brain, and he remembered her call, a few hours ago: She would be on the first morning flight from London. She would be a welcome island of calm, after the shrieks and hysterics of Ashley St. Ives, the agent he hardly knew.

He struck the mattress in frustration, and then got out of bed, barking his shin on a chair. Where was the blasted minibar? By crooking his neck sideways, he was just able to see the tiny refrigerator under the desk. He got down awkwardly on his hands and knees, and his head lurched forward, banging the mask on the furniture. He saw stars, and had to steady himself. Using his fingers to find the way, he turned the little key in the lock. There were rows of midget bottles inside, and he took a miniature of Remy Martin and screwed the top off. But how to drink it? Perhaps, Mason thought, if he laid flat on his back and poured it into the eye slit, he could slurp it on the way past . . .

"How about trying a straw?"

The sudden voice broke the spell of the night, and Mason jerked around to find its source. It took him a moment to aim his mask in the right direction—it was like using binoculars—and then Billy Baxter swam into focus, with a rat-faced little man nodding encouragingly over his shoulder.

"The rescue party is here," Billy said.

RAVEN CHARLES was on the phone to the coast, where it was still early evening, when she heard an unmistakable shout drift in through the open window. Carrying the telephone with her, she walked onto the balcony of her fifth-floor room and looked down to the Majestic's circular drive. Billy (Silver Dollar) Baxter was loudly hailing a taxi with cries of "Irving!" With him was the little rat-faced man who smelled of basements, and another man who had covered his head with a tuxedo jacket, probably to avoid the paparazzi.

Drinking made strange friendships, she reflected. Billy had been annoyed with rat-face only this afternoon, and now, after closing the Majestic bar, they were off together—probably to La Petite Carlton, the all-night bar on the rue d'Antibes where the party never ended. But who was the shy celebrity?

NOBODY recognized Sheila Chesham when she walked into the lobby of the Majestic a little after ten o'clock on Sunday morning. It was jammed with press, but she assumed it always was. She had taken the dawn flight to Nice and driven directly to the hotel in a taxi, without telling anyone she was coming, and now she hesitated before ringing Mason's room. Would she awaken him? He was a late sleeper, but she realized that under the circumstances he would probably be surrounded by doctors, agents, and room service.

She let the telephone ring a dozen times before hanging it up. Mason had probably been taken to a hospital, she realized. She rang Ashley St. Ives and again got no answer. Then, on a guess, she called Raven Charles. If she were in Cannes, she reasoned, maybe she'd be at this hotel. She was.

WHEN Raven opened the door of her room, Sheila could see at once that something was terribly wrong. Over her shoulder, she could glimpse six or seven people, including one in a military uniform. Raven stepped aside, let her in, looked both ways down the corridor, and closed the door quickly.

"Mason and Billy are missing," she told Sheila, taking her by the arm. "They left the hotel together in the middle of the night, with a man that Billy thought owned a yacht. The man in uniform is a U.S. Navy admiral. Billy telephoned him with some goofball plan to bring Mason out to an aircraft carrier, where the ship's surgeon could remove the iron mask. At about three o'clock this morning I heard noises out in front of the hotel and saw Billy and the so-called yacht owner, with someone who had his coat over his head. That was probably Mason. They were pretending to be drunk. Maybe they were drunk. Anyway, nobody has seen them since. Maybe they got in the yacht and couldn't find the aircraft carrier."

Sheila looked out the window at the horizon. "How could anyone not find the aircraft carrier?" she asked. "There it is right there."

"If they were as drunk as they seemed, God knows where they headed."

"Perhaps they had an accident. They may be floating around in life preservers. The mask could pull Mason to the bottom." She looked out at the limitless horizon, hysteria creeping into her voice.

"There's an air-sea search going on right now," Raven said quietly. "But do you know how many yachts there are on the French Riviera?"

F O R the third time, Billy (Silver Dollar) Baxter tried the door to the stateroom, and for the third time found it locked. He looked over to the narrow ship's bunk where Mason Devereaux lay quietly on his back, his hands clasped behind his mask, looking up at what little could be seen of the ceiling through his narrow slit.

"It's locked, and it will stay locked until Pontoon, whoever he is, gets whatever he wants from us," Devereaux said, his voice hollow inside the sounding chamber.

"You ask me, his name's not Pontoon and everything else about him is also fishier than a mermaid's lunch," Baxter said. It was oddly disturbing, talking to a man in an iron mask. You could never tell what he was thinking, and his voice seemed like it was coming from inside a coffee can. "How you feeling?"

"Not bad, considering," Devereaux said. "I have a ravenous appetite."

"Maybe I can get some olives and push them into the slit in your mask," Baxter said. "You could try to catch them as they roll past your mouth."

It was sometime Sunday morning. Billy could tell it was day from the sunlight that leaked around the cardboard taped outside their portholes. His wristwatch had been taken away from him, and he had little interest in the passage of time. His mind was occupied instead by treachery.

Rat-face had been filled with oily charm as they walked on board the yacht, which was skippered by a large man with a gold tooth. Pontoon had spoken quietly with him in an unfamiliar language that reminded Billy of subtitled foreign films about fascists on bicycles. Then the little man had shown his guests below to a stateroom, handed them a bottle of cheap Hungarian cognac, announced that he was going in search of soda, and locked them inside. A moment later they had heard the marine engines roar to life. And that was that.

At first the Iron Mask had proven a barrier to the cognac, but Billy had crimped the end of one straw and forced it into another, creating a crude plastic lifeline for Devereaux, who spilled more than he drank, and complained that the fumes made his eyes water. The rest of the night had been restless. Mason had been awakened several times by the reverberation of his own snores.

GOLD TOOTH

In the morning, Gold Tooth brought them coffee and croissants, leaving the tray outside the door and then covering Billy with an automatic while the food was taken inside.

"I feel guilty eating this breakfast while you're starving," Billy said, "but the smell must be driving you crazy, and at least if I eat it you won't be able to smell it anymore."

"Very kind," Devereaux said dryly. And then: "It must be you they're after, old man. I'm not of the slightest use to anyone."

"This rat-faced guy thinks you're the hottest property at the Cannes Film Festival," Baxter said. "Just ask me. I'm the guy that Monsieur Pontoon was talking to yesterday, when he was gonna spend big bucks just to get me to introduce him to your Miss St. Ives."

"But who is this man?"

"Says he wants to produce a movie. He wanted me to read a screenplay."

"Did you read it? Was there a decent role for me?"

"The inside I didn't get to," Billy said. "The cover looked like a tablecloth from a cheap Greek restaurant."

"Is it at all possible," Mason asked, "that this is a publicity stunt? Something dreamed up by the St. Ives woman?"

"Don't look now," Billy said, "but I think we're being kidnapped. But who's gonna go ransom? Nobody will pay a dime for me. I'm so broke, I cash my paycheck on the bus. How about you? Know any millionaires?"

"No," said Mason, and then he remembered that he did, after all, know one of the richest girls in England.

HAROLD GASPER watched the news bulletin on the BBC until the final montage of Mason Devereaux photographs: Mason in costume as the Phantom, Mason covered with mud, Mason in his youth, Mason in his cups. Then he switched off the set and stood next to it, drumming his fingers on a table. The silence in his rooms at the Albany was oppressive. So were his thoughts.

He lit a cigarette. If Mason was missing at sea, Gasper reasoned, he was either the victim of yet another freak accident, or someone had taken him captive. Neither scenario seemed likely. No one man could have that many accidents. Yet who cared enough to kidnap an alcoholic has-been with a bank overdraft?

"Douglas Brown!" Gasper said aloud. His voice sounded frightened in the silence of the flat. "And if Mason, then me, too. If we were both out of the way, there would be no one to testify against him . . ."

He walked to the window and looked outside for the reassuring presence of the man from Scotland Yard, who had been monitoring his movements for days. The man usually stood just across the way, in the shade of a tree, but just now he was not there. Probably gone for cigarettes, Gasper thought. Or to ring his boss. Funny, I rather miss him.

THE nose of the speed yacht was pointed like an arrow toward Cap d'Antibes, the little finger of land that ventures out into the Mediterranean between Cannes and Nice. On the bridge, the man who called himself Excaliber Pontoon stood next to a larger man who was expensively dressed in the costume of a yachts-man.

"We'll anchor offshore," he told the other man. "Then you drive back into town and pick up the Chesham woman. What an incredible piece of luck, that she followed Devereaux to Cannes."

"Egg salad," the other man said in a thick accent. It was his way of pronouncing *excellent*. When he spoke, a gold tooth flashed in the sun.

"Baxter and Devereaux are locked in the front cabin."

"Egg salad."

"Baxter we don't need, but we'll keep him for a few days just in case."

"Very egg salad."

E ARLY on the Monday morning, Sheila Chesham sat quietly at a table in a café on one of the back streets of Cannes. With Mason having disappeared into thin air, she had nowhere to go and nothing to do. She could only wait. Strange, she thought, that only a few blocks away from the sea, the film festival is irrelevant and Cannes is just another town in France. Across from her in a street market, housewives marched up and down with wicker baskets over their arms, looking accusingly at the fresh asparagus. The waiter brought Sheila an espresso, and she thanked him, her thoughts in another place.

Douglas Brown she now considered to be a stupid case of self-deception on her part, an attempt to pretend that her real emotions did not exist. She could no more marry him than Reggie Kray. Mason Devereaux was another story. She had liked Mason from the first moment she laid eyes on him in the Coach and Horses. To the theater friends who had brought her to the pub, he had been a has-been with all of his openings behind him. But she detected a doggedness that ventured upon courage, a sense of humor that was founded on the fundamental absurdity of life. Mason was worth knowing and even worth cherishing.

They became friends, on his terms, which had meant that he never made the slightest move that could be interpreted as romantic. It was up to her to search him out, at the Coach or in his digs in Jermyn Street, for a walk or a drink and a long talk. She was aware that their relationship seemed curious. They had become friends, and yet the gossip columnists like Fontaine Eady insisted on painting their friendship with a smirk. She was twenty-two, they kept writing, and the heir of one of the oldest and richest families in England. Mason, who was somewhere in his late forties, made a meager living recording commercials and working as an understudy.

"At this point in my career," he had explained to her, "I am faced with the choice of being onstage every night in a small and demeaning role—or being onstage once every three months in the leading role. It's no choice. I would much rather play the Phantom four times a year than carry a spear eight times a week."

Sheila smiled at her memory, and then her eyes filled with tears. She looked again at the morning edition of *Nice Matin,* the local paper, with its color photographs of Mason next to an old black-and-white shot of Billy Baxter. PERDU! read the headline. Lost!

In her heart Sheila suspected that Mason was more than simply *perdu.* She feared he was *mort.* Yachts did not simply disappear from the face of the sea—not in Riviera waters, which were as busy as a parking lot. And if that were so, and he were dead, then poor Mason had deserved a better fate. She stirred her coffee and then sat staring at it. There was no reason for her to stay in Cannes, she realized, but no place else she wanted to go. Perhaps she would sit at this table for the rest of her life.

"Miss Chesham? Miss Sheila Chesham?"

She looked up. A large round-faced man with a gold tooth was smiling ingratiatingly at her.

"Yes," she said, angry with herself for not denying it.

"Egg salad," he said. "Allow me to present this card."

"I'm very sorry," Sheila said, "but I have a great many things on my mind right now and I have no interest in meeting anyone."

"Please read the card," said the man.

She looked at it and gasped. It was Mason Devereaux's card.

At first she was too stunned to speak. "Then Mason isn't dead?" she asked finally, a whisper of hope in her voice.

"He was alive when I saw him late last night," said Gold Tooth.
"But he's missing at sea—isn't he?"
"Apparently not, Miss Chesham."
"But what could possibly have happened?"
"Why don't you ask him yourself?" Gold Tooth said soothingly. "I have a car right here, which can take you directly to Mr. Devereaux. He is considering an attractive deal, and wanted to get out of town."

I N the galley on board the yacht, Pontoon hummed an old Romanian folk song as he used a blender to prepare a mixture for Devereaux to sip through a straw. It was powdered Slim-Fast, and if Mason drank enough of it, he thought, it would keep him alive. He put the tumbler on a tray with sandwiches for the other man, and marched down the hallway to a locked stateroom door. Billy Baxter jumped up and then fell back when he saw the gun stuck into Rat-face's belt.

"Lunchtime!" Pontoon said. Devereaux lifted his heavy head in interest, but it fell back with the weight of the mask.

"My pal Mason here and me, we're being held against our will," Billy told Pontoon. "This don't feel like a screenplay negotiation."

Pontoon ignored him. "*Ici*, Monsieur Devereaux, try this. Strawberry flavored."

He put the tray down on a table near the door, and then stood wide of it, his hand on the gun.

"Are you located in New York, Monsieur Baxter?"
"The last time I looked."
"Do you know David Letterman?"
"We're like this."

L A T E R in the day Fontaine Eady returned from the Cannes waterfront with a grave face.
"They've called off the air and sea search," he said, walking into the American Pavilion, in the shadow of the Palais. "There is no sign of the yacht."

"Perhaps there was an explosion or a fire at sea," said Raven

Charles, who had taken over an office at the Pavilion. Ashley St. Ives was sitting in a free chair, sipping an Evian. Now that Mason had disappeared their rivalry had lost its point, and they were back on the terms of their long-standing truce. There was nothing at the festival to interest either one of them, but they lingered anyway, reluctant to leave this place where Mason and Billy had last been seen.

"If they were close to an island, could they swim to it?" Ashley asked.

"Unlikely," said Eady. "The Iron Mask weighed at least ten pounds. That would be like having a brick tied to your neck."

"Poor Mason," said Ashley St. Ives. "I only represented him for a few days, and yet, in that time . . ."

She searched for a thought to complete her sentence.

Raven Charles contemplated her rival wearily. St. Ives had elbowed her way into Devereaux's life and signed him to a personal contract, but Raven couldn't blame Mason. After decades of obscurity, the recognition must have been seductive.

"Was Mason survived?" asked Raven.

"No family," Fontaine Eady told her. "And he left no will that we know of. There was a memoir in the *Independent*, written by Harold Gasper. They showed remarkable restraint in not calling it an obituary."

"Gasper is the man connected to the original *Phantom* murder," Raven said. "I wonder if Mason really was mixed up in it?"

"Now we'll never know."

"Maybe he told his girlfriend," said a piping voice. They looked over to see Little Denny Brennen.

"Do you mean Sheila?" Ashley asked. "What do you know about her?"

"I saw her on television," Little Denny said.

"Funny enough," Raven said, "I called her hotel room just now and was told she hadn't been seen. I imagine she flew back to England without telling anyone."

"That's unlike her," Eady said. "I'll give a ring to her parents at

Thorn Hill and see if they've heard from her." He picked up the telephone.

"Wasn't he old enough to be her ancestor?" Little Denny said.

"Oh, for Christ's sake—shut up!" Ashley St. Ives told him.

"Strong words, coming from someone who's pulling down 15 percent of my salary," Little Denny said.

Ashley took a deep breath. "You're fired, Little Denny," she said. "Get yourself another agent. Life's too short to baby-sit."

Little Denny stuck out his tongue. "I'm gonna sue you for this!" he screamed.

"Have the turtle sue me, too."

"That's strange," said Fontaine Eady, replacing the receiver. "The Cheshams haven't heard from Sheila since this morning, when she telephoned to say she was going to have a cup of coffee and then join us down here at the beach."

L ET'S try it one more time," Billy Baxter was telling Mason Devereaux. He took a pill from a bottle that had been supplied by Gold Tooth.

"I never take medicine in any form. It's bad for my health," Mason said. His voice sounded stuffy now, as well as metallic.

"Close your eyes," Baxter said, "and when you feel it rolling down your face, stick out your tongue. Then I'll stick the straw up underneath and you can get a sip of orange juice here."

"But I . . . *wah, wah, wah . . . choo!*"

Mason's sneeze rang explosively through the slit in his helmet.

"Okay now, ready, set, go!" said Baxter. He popped an aspirin into the slit, only to see it roll out the bottom of the mask a moment later.

"You listening in there?" Baxter said.

"What's that? Speak up!"

Baxter tapped on the mask with his pinky ring. "Anybody home?"

"Sorry, old man," said Devereaux. "I was deafened by that sneeze. Now, then . . . *wah, wah, choo!*"

"They come in threes," Billy said.

"*Wah-choo!*"

"Okay, Mason, that's three!" Baxter announced into the slit. "All systems are go. Over and out!"

He slipped another aspirin into the slit, and when it did not roll out again he maneuvered the end of the straw up past Mason's neck. The mask moved awkwardly as Mason tried to find it.

Just then the steady throb of the yacht's powerful engines changed in pitch, after hours at open sea. Baxter looked up. They could hear footfalls on the deck above their heads, and the distant voice of the man called Excaliber Pontoon. Then the engines were cut off, and the silence seemed to ring uncannily in the small cabin.

"I have just a word of advice," Mason told him after a moment. "If you have anything at all to say about it, try not to get a nose cold whilst wearing an iron mask."

FREDSON ROWLEY of Scotland Yard read Harold Gasper's article about Mason Devereaux over lunch, which was a salt-beef sandwich at Sergio's, a little shop in Eagle Place. He had just been up for a look through Mason's rooms at the Eyrie Mansion, where he found nothing except deepening gloom. If it was possible to live in utter bachelorhood, Mason had made a good job of it. The miniature fridge held nothing but beer and tinned baked beans. The writing desk held only postcards supplied by the hotel. The bookshelves held Shakespeare, Shaw, Ibsen, Beckett, and the complete works of Peter O'Donnell.

Rowley finished his sandwich, lit a cigarette, and walked up to Piccadilly. It was one of those perfect days in May when London seems blessed with eternal spring. He crossed at the light, walked down past the Waterproofer shop, and kept on toward the Albany. He felt like a chat with Harold Gasper.

He reviewed the facts in his mind. Gasper had fired the shot that killed Bradleigh Court. On the other hand, Gasper thought the gun contained blanks—and he also thought it was Mason Devereaux onstage. Gasper was covering for somebody. In Rowley's experience, with these theatrical types, if you put a tail on them and left them to stew in their rooms, they talked more quickly than if you brought them in. They started composing speeches in their minds, and after a certain point they couldn't resist delivering them.

Turning in at the Albany, Rowley nodded to the man on duty.

"Any sign of our pigeon?"

"He hasn't been out all morning. No visitors."

Rowley nodded and rang Gasper's bell. There was no answer. He took his index finger and pushed at the door, which swung open easily. He walked inside and saw Harold Gasper staring at him with sightless eyes. The entrance wound, Rowley noted professionally, was small-caliber.

H E ' S gonna croak, and then all you're gonna have is a dead actor and ten pounds of scrap iron," Billy Baxter told Excaliber Pontoon. "Just listen to him."

In the silence of the locked stateroom, the sound of Mason Devereaux's breathing was painfully labored. It reminded Billy of one of those sleep machines that reproduced the sound of the tides. He and Pontoon looked down at Mason's form on the bunk.

"He has the flu bug," Pontoon said. "You would too, if you'd spent two days trapped in a well. He should drink lots of fluids and get plenty of bed rest." He sounded as if he were repeating instructions learned from a phrase book.

"What do you guys want with him anyway?" asked Baxter. "Ransom? Don't make me laugh."

"Do not call us kidnapplers!" Pontoon insisted, adding the *l* with precision. "Nobody has been kidnappled."

"Then put us both ashore, and it's case closed," said Baxter. "You take off, find a nice island somewhere, get a tan, and have a nice swim. I'll give you my recipe for rummy-yum-yums."

Just then there was the sound of running feet on the deck overhead. Pontoon slipped quickly out of the cabin and locked the door behind him.

"This is not the sort of deal where they want to have a lot of eyewitnesses walking around with a story to tell," Baxter whispered in

Mason's eye-slit. "Put it another way. We're all on the menu in the shark café."

O F course it's crazy, Ivan," Raven Charles was saying into the telephone. "What can I tell you? That I wish things had turned out differently?"

"This is very bad," Ivan Bloom whined. "You talk me into sending you to London to sign up some has-been actor for some cockamamy TV movie, and next thing I know you and Ashley are in a contest to run up expenses chasing this guy all over Europe, after which he disappears at sea—plus the French government is suing my ass because they say we're responsible for the loss of the priceless Iron Mask."

"I have a strange feeling that everything is connected," said the tall black woman, walking back and forth in front of her window at the Majestic Hotel.

"Oh, it's connected, all right," Ivan said. "The connection is, Devereaux and Baxter got drunk and jumped on a yacht and they're in Monte Carlo somewhere picking up babes in the casino."

"Not Mason," Raven said. "If he appeared anywhere in public, the mask would draw a crowd. Either he did drown, or somebody has him. And now Sheila Chesham is missing, as well. Where did she go? Is she gambling with Billy Baxter, too?"

"Meanwhile," said Ivan, "now that Devereaux is out of the running, what about Robert Mitchum for the lead in *The Mason Devereaux Story*? Only in the end he doesn't drown, of course—he's saved by the ghost of Elvis."

"Ivan, this is serious," Raven said.

"I'm perfectly serious," the studio chief said. "Don't think for a moment my idea wouldn't gross $200 million. Wayne Newton for the ghost."

The light on Raven's telephone was blinking. "I've got another call," she told him. She put him on hold.

"Miss Charles?" a voice said. "My name is Takeuchi. I want to talk to you about running a Hollywood studio for me."

WHAT have you done with Mason Devereaux?"
Sheila Chesham's voice was angry, but it betrayed her
fear. She stood uncertainly on board a yacht anchored off
Monte Carlo. On one side, she could see the condominiums of the
Rainier principality, mounting sternly up the mountainside like
mortgage payments. On the other side was the sea, empty except
for a few other pleasure ships, moving idly before the wind. Gold
Tooth's hand rested firmly on her arm—not squeezing, but with the
suggestion of great power—as she faced Excaliber Pontoon.

"Mr. Devereaux?" said Pontoon. "You will be seeing him shortly.
Also Mr. Baxter."

"They are in egg salad condition," said Gold Tooth.

"You're abducting them!" cried Sheila.

"They are our guests," said Pontoon.

She laughed defiantly. "Stop talking like a James Bond villain,"
she said. "Give yourself the name you deserve—kidnappers!"

Gold Tooth increased his pressure on her arm. "It is as Mr. Pontoon has explained," he said. "We are enjoying a little cruise. Come.
I will take you to them."

He led the way down the galley steps and into the narrow corridor that led to their stateroom. Pontoon produced a large brass key
and opened the door.

"Mason! You're alive!" cried Sheila, the moment she saw the
prone figure on the bed. Mason weakly attempted to raise his head,
but the effort was too much, and he fell back. She was at his side in
an instant, taking his hand.

"Mason! Can you hear me?"

"Hello, old girl," he said. "Afraid I've landed in a bit of a mess
here . . ."

"He doesn't sound well," Sheila said.

"He is egg salad," Gold Tooth said. "Just a small cold."

"What do you want from him? What's going on here?"

"Perhaps we should start with the first of those questions," Pontoon said smoothly. "It is not Mr. Devereaux we want something of,
Miss Chesham. It is you."

W E have the money, Miss Charles, but not the intimate knowledge of the American market," Takeuchi said. "That is where you come in."

It was evening. The handsome Japanese-American executive leaned forward and absentmindedly adjusted the flower arrangement on their table at the Moulin des Mougins, the most famous restaurant on the Riviera. Raven Charles, who sat opposite him in a backless Armani gown, smiled and kept her thoughts to herself.

"Running a studio can be a nightmare," she said. "It's more fun to be an independent producer, making the movies you like and leaving the financial problems to someone else."

"We would only want you to make the movies you liked," Takeuchi said. "That would be why we were hiring you."

Chef Roger Verge, his little white mustache bristling with drama, materialized at their table and supervised the delivery of several bite-sized birds, their little legs reaching pathetically for the ceiling. Microscopic but perfectly formed vegetables were arrayed around the tiny carcasses, as if the plate were being viewed through the wrong end of a telescope.

Raven had joined Takeuchi at the Moulin out of curiosity, and because she needed to think about something other than the disappearances of three people she cared for. She had learned about the murder of Harold Gasper on Cable News, while she was dressing in her hotel room. It was clear that all of these events were connected in some vague shadowy malevolence, but she could not guess its cause or purpose.

She had been intrigued by the opportunity to meet Takeuchi, a powerful press lord known only by a single name.

MR. TAKEUCHI

He was worth millions, she knew, and was said to be shopping for his own Hollywood studio. Now he seemed to want her to run it for him. It was a big job. A handful of women had run major studios in the past—Sherry Lansing, Dawn Steel—and Raven had often thought, during meetings with Ivan Bloom, that if Ivan could run a studio, anyone could.

She regarded the handsome Takeuchi and wondered what his story really was. An inch or two over six feet, he was one of those rare men taller than she was. His voice thrilled her down to her toes. It was like listening to Orson Welles with a Japanese accent. She fought the desire to lean forward and ask him to repeat, "We sell no wine before its time."

"Why me?" she asked.

"You show great promise," Takeuchi said. "We try to sign on with the right people just before they break out big. And you are known and respected at Realistic Pictures. People there would be happy to work with you."

"Realistic?" she said. Somehow it had never occurred to her that the studio they were talking about was Realistic. "But what about Ivan Bloom? He's already running Realistic."

Takeuchi's eyes were hard in the candlelight. "There is an old proverb, Miss Charles, that for every person who gets a job, someone else must lose one."

T HE next morning, the man who called himself Excaliber Pontoon sat on the deck of his yacht, his shoulders hunched over the keyboard of a laptop computer. He typed a final word and his hands flew up into the air like a concert pianist.

"Perfect!" he said. "The foolproof ransom note. It is delivered by fax from a phony electronic mailbox."

"What does it say?" asked Gold Tooth, standing by the railing with a revolver stuck into his belt. Pontoon's fingers flew once again over the keyboard. "Wait until I run the Spell-Checker on it," Pontoon said, "and then you can read it."

"What does it say regarding cash?" asked Gold Tooth. "That you can tell me now."

"Ten million pounds sterling, paid by electronic transfer to the central bank of Romania, to be credited to the government deficit," Pontoon said. "Brilliant! How can they trace a payment to a national debt?"

"And for us?"

"The same ten million pounds sterling, split sixty-forty," Pontoon said. "I'll hack into their system and transfer it out again before the Romanians even know they have it. They're running the whole country on an old Tandy 286."

"Egg salad," said Gold Tooth.

Y OU ask me, I don't know how much longer he can hold out," Billy Baxter said anxiously. He sat at Mason's bedside. Across from him, Sheila Chesham held Mason's hand. They were still locked into the stateroom.

Mason's breathing had grown increasingly labored. "Just a touch of the flu, old man," he said, his voice coming distantly from inside the Iron Mask.

"I think a touch of the fever, too," Billy said. He helped Mason sip orange juice through a straw.

"We've got to get off this ship!" Sheila whispered. "If they get the ransom money from my parents, they'll kill us and drop us overboard."

The ship shuddered and began to move. Billy looked up at the porthole, which was still taped over. All he could see was a diffusion of sunlight. Suddenly the light was cut off.

"What happened to the sun?" Sheila asked.

The room was pitch black, with not even a glimmer of daylight coming through the tape.

"It can only be one thing," Mason said, his voice hollow and weak. "They've taken the boat inside a coastal cave."

L ET him sniff all he wants," Ivan Bloom said, "but if he lifts a leg on my luggage, the dog dies."

The head of Realistic Pictures was standing unhappily in the customs area of the Nice airport. After listening to Ashley and

Raven taking turns with dire speculations over the phone, after the murder of Harold Gasper and the disappearances of Devereaux, Baxter, and Sheila Chesham, Ivan had grown too restless to remain in Hollywood and had booked himself through to the festival.

The police dog finished smelling his luggage, looked up at him, and wagged its tail. "Good doggy," Ivan said. The customs officer waved him through.

Ashley St. Ives, waiting on the other side of the crowd barrier, gave him a quick peck on each cheek. The red-haired agent was dressed in a white sailor suit and skyscraper gold shoes. "You aren't going to like it here, Ivan," she said. "There's a six month wait for a cellular telephone number."

"I brought a couple of walkie-talkies," said Ivan. "At least we can talk to each other."

"But we'll always be together."

"If we need to talk, we can always separate."

T H E curve of the bay at Cannes ends on the west with a steep hill that climbs above the city. It was here that a fort was placed centuries ago, its guns commanding the sea, and it was here that Raven Charles now sat on an old bench under a tree, looking down at the seafront below.

If she accepted Takeuchi's offer, she knew, this town would be at her feet. As the head of Realistic Pictures, she would have access to the most promising film projects, the top scripts and directors. She would be able to impose her personal vision on some of the films— a vision she was rarely allowed to exercise in the projects assigned to her by Ivan Bloom. As a black woman she was sick in her heart of films presenting her race in a violent and negative light. She knew a thousand positive stories, and she wanted to tell one or two of them in great movies. If she were honest, she also wanted power and fame and the other rewards of Hollywood success, of which the most elusive was happiness. Takeuchi was offering her a chance at all of those things.

But . . . what about Ivan? She stood up and began to walk slowly down a cobblestone path through the old town. What about the lovable goofball who had provided her first big break, who had spotted her in the ranks and had faith in her ability to produce? She had no great respect for Ivan's abilities as a studio chief, but she knew his heart was in the right place. Simply losing his job wouldn't really bother Ivan for long—after all, getting fired was the path of upward mobility in Hollywood. But losing it through the betrayal of Raven Charles! That would wound him deeply. She wondered if she was capable of such a decision. And she knew her whole career depended upon it.

PART SIX

Casino

MASON'S breathing had grown more labored. Sheila sat by the side of his cot and held his hand. If help did not arrive soon, she feared for his life. Billy Baxter sprawled glumly in a seat under the porthole. There was nothing to do but wait.

"They can't simply allow a man to die," Sheila said, her voice betraying a subtle undertone of fear. "They can't just stand there and do nothing."

"Be brave," Mason said, his voice hollow inside the Iron Mask. "Don't worry about me. I'll pull through."

He knew he was lying. He was drifting in and out of hallucinations now, restless sweating nightmares. The mask acted as a sensory deprivation device, cutting him off from reality, and his dreams expanded to fill the void. In one of them he was in a helicopter, being flown back to the peace of his suite at the Majestic Hotel. But something had gone wrong. He looked over and saw that the pilot was dead at the stick, his head hanging at an unnatural angle. The helicopter turned on its side and fell sickeningly from the sky. He tried to wrestle the controls, but they would not move. Ahead of him in the sky, he could see a banner being pulled by an airplane. It read: THE MASON DEVEREAUX SAGA. Then the blades of the copter had snagged the banner, and he was twisting down out of the sky.

"Until they get their money, we stay right here," Billy Baxter predicted grimly. "That's the moment when we gotta make a break for our lives. You ask me, nobody is supposed to get out of this alive. We've spent so much time with that rat-faced Pontoon we could pick him out of a lineup in the dark. They can't afford to put us back on the street."

1 2 2

Mason's breathing sounded more labored now, as if every breath were a struggle. "Falling . . . falling," he said. "Only way out . . ."

"We gotta have a plan," Billy said, almost to himself.

Just then the door slammed open and they were blinded by the overhead lights. "We have a better plan, Monsieur Baxter."

Excaliber Pontoon stood inside the door, covering them with a revolver. Gold Tooth stood behind him with a machine gun. "A very sensible plan. Miss Chesham's father will remit ten million pounds into the national treasury of Romania, and I will remit it out again, using my laptop computer and calling on my specialized knowledge of their accounting procedures."

"You're quite a computer whiz," Billy said, stalling for time.

"Thank you," said Pontoon, and Billy could swear he was almost blushing. "You were so cruel as to insult my name one day, Mr. Baxter. Now that we are about to part, I can reveal that Excaliber Pontoon is actually my CompuServe password."

Mason experienced a strong sense of déjà vu. The scene, he realized, was like in all Bond movies, where the villain had 007 at his mercy—but instead of killing him, wasted time explaining himself.

"Now, Monsieur Baxter," Pontoon said, "if you will handcuff your group to one another, yourself included. Single file."

DOUGLAS BROWN sat in the musty gloom of his flat in Covent Garden, and waited, as he had for two days, for a knock on the door, for the telephone to ring, for someone to make the connection between the deaths of Bradleigh Court and Harold Gasper, and the insignificant theater manager who had been linked with Sheila Chesham. He wondered how any intelligent investigator could fail to draw the obvious conclusion.

He had been sleepless all night, staring at a shelf filled with the manuscripts of plays—plays he dreamed of producing one day, when he was a West End impresario. Now that ambition was smashed, Brown thought bitterly. The whole game was over, and with it his hopes of marrying Sheila Chesham and using her money to establish himself in the theater.

He was a pathetic fool. A week before that botched matinee, he had been certain that Sheila Chesham would marry him. Then he had seen Eady's column in the *Sketch,* reporting that Sheila and the pathetic Mason Devereaux were an item. Even though Brown of all people should have known better, he was convinced the item was accurate. Blinded by the fear of losing Sheila, he lacked the confidence to ignore Eady's speculations. A nightmare picture formed in his imagination: Mason, drunk and unkempt, sitting in the Coach and Horses, one hand grasping a pint glass and the other Sheila's thigh, while the two of them plotted how to squander her fortune on a lifetime of drinks for Devereaux.

He had known Harold Gasper for two or three years, ever since the shadowy investor had first bought shares in the *Phantom.* He had suspected for at least half that time that the *Phantom* shares represented almost all of Gasper's assets—that other investments had failed, and that the quarterly checks from the London production

were all that stood between Gasper and ruin. Gasper's front was very nearly his entire essence.

Brown deliberately went drinking late one night in the Colony Club, an off-hours room upstairs over the Trattoria Otello in Dean Street. He had an idea he might find Gasper there, and he was right. They had talked until the sun came up, and then walked back to Gasper's rooms at the Albany and talked some more. When they had parted, they had a plan that would humiliate Brown's rival, and guarantee Gasper's financial standing for some years to come.

But I didn't think it through, Brown thought. Somehow I never really thought Gasper would go ahead with the whole insane scheme. It was an idea, not a reality. That's why I was able to put the real bullet in the revolver—because it was like a dream. Then when it all really happened and Bradleigh Court fell dead, there was only one person who knew I was responsible for the death. Harold Gasper. Would he go to the police? Not likely. To do that, Gasper would have had to implicate himself. But then Brown had been shocked to discover that Scotland Yard knew Gasper was involved. So it had been necessary to murder him.

Now Brown sat in the must and gloom and reflected that two men were dead, and what was the result? Sheila had thrown him out and flown off to Mason, and now both of them were missing. Maybe they were kidnap victims, as the papers thought. Or maybe they were in Ibiza, necking on the beach. What did it matter? There was no longer any hope of Brown getting his hands on the Chesham estate.

T A K E U C H I ' S private speedboat was waiting for Raven when she strolled through the fragrant evening out to the end of the Carlton Hotel pier. Behind her, the lights of Cannes sparkled in the early dusk, and along the Boulevard Croisette the men in their tuxedos and the women in their gowns and jewels were beginning the leisurely stroll down to the formal evening projections of the film festival.

She had attended the black-tie screenings before, and knew what she would be missing. The red carpet would be rolled out to curbside, and all the European TV networks would be there to record the arrivals of the stars, whose names would be breathlessly shouted by announcers: Alain Delon! Rosanna Arquette! Miss Catherine Deneuve! The crowds would surge forward against the police barricades as the stars mounted the long flight of outdoor steps to the Grand Auditorium, turning at the top for a slow wave at the camera—very slow, so that the designers who had supplied the women's gowns could get free TV exposure worth millions of francs.

The speedboat was captained by an efficient Frenchman dressed like a naval officer, and he helped Raven step down into the craft, which was already occupied by the ashen-faced Ivan Bloom and his mistress, Ashley St. Ives.

"If there's anything worse than a small plane, it's a small boat,"

Ivan complained, holding onto the railing with both hands. "Some guy wants to have dinner, let him make a reservation in a restaurant like everybody else. He thinks he's gonna impress me with his yacht, he's crazy."

He was wearing a tuxedo, with a walkie-talkie tucked into each of the breast pockets. He'd had a fight with Ashley back at the hotel over that. Ivan wanted her to carry her own phone. She told him her purse was too small. He said he would look ridiculous with a phone in both pockets. Only marginally more ridiculous, Ashley had reassured him, than with a phone in one pocket. He had not found that encouraging. Now he clung to the rail and wished himself elsewhere.

"This could be very good for you, Ivan," Ashley said. Her red hair was combed up under an outsize admiral's cap. "You know how these millionaires are. They rent these boats and they want to get the use out of them. Raven, darling!" She hardly paused to shift conversational gears. "I know you're still depressed by the disappearance of poor Mason. Well, we all are. Devastated."

"It's not simply Mason," Raven said, ignoring Ashley's tone of voice, and really directing her answer to Ivan. "What about Billy? And now Sheila Chesham?" She allowed the boatman to help her down to a leatherette seat. "And yesterday Harold Gasper was found in his London flat, shot through the head. There is some linkage here that we're all missing."

"There's not much mystery about Mason and Billy, you ask me," Ivan said. "You take the world's biggest drunk and put him in the hands of Silver Dollar Baxter. I ran a check on him. He's the world's second biggest drunk. Locked up inside the mask, Mason goes crazy for a drink. Billy finds a pal with a boat, they all get juiced up, and right now they're sleeping with the fishes."

Raven did not answer him. She was afraid he might be correct. The speedboat roared away from the pier and made a great arc in the sea, its wave forming a crescent that pointed toward the *Rashomon,* Takeuchi's famous yacht.

Raven looked at the ship growing larger across the water, and wondered if she had made the right decision after Takeuchi had offered her the top job at Realistic Pictures. At first she had been reluctant to take the job away from Ivan Bloom, who had given her an early break. Then she performed a cold and hard analysis, beginning with the fact that Takeuchi obviously wanted Ivan out of the job. If she didn't take it, someone else certainly would. It was a Hollywood fact of life that if you held open the door and let someone else go through first, you'd be left standing on the sidewalk. She had a good idea why Takeuchi had invited them all to dinner tonight. Ivan and Ashley obviously suspected nothing.

Takeuchi stood on the deck of the great ship, his tall figure silhouetted against the setting sun. His craft was a converted minesweeper that had once belonged to John Wayne and still boasted a helicopter landing pad along with its formal dining room and sleeping accommodations for twenty. A flight of steps was lowered for the arriving powerboat, and crew members helped hand them up to the press lord, who shook hands and asked them to join him on the sun deck for cocktails.

"The sea is so calm tonight," he said, "that I thought we could sail for Monte Carlo while we are having our dinner. The casinos are open until very late, and we can try our luck."

RAVEN CHARLES sat quietly and let the others talk: Ivan, who rattled on about the headaches of running a major film studio; Ashley, who dropped broad hints that with the right financial backing she could produce one hit after another; and Takeuchi—who, Raven observed, talked just as much as the others, but with the difference that he said nothing. All of his remarks were pleasantries, designed to kill time until he dropped his bombshell.

The dinner took the form of an elegant Japanese feast. Raven used ivory sticks to pick up tiny flowerlets carved from cucumber, and to dab a speck of hot mustard on the sushi. Ivan was more direct. He speared a piece of raw fish through the center with the end of his chopstick, and raised it to his nose for a suspicious sniff.

"It is all very fresh," Takeuchi assured him. "It was alive not ten minutes ago."

Raven knew that silences were an accepted part of a Japanese meal. Ivan did not. "I saw in a movie about some Japanese fish that has a poisonous organ," Ivan told Takeuchi. "The deal is, the rest of the fish tastes great, but one bite of the deadly wrong part, and it's curtains. You have to trust your chef with your life."

Takeuchi nodded silently and smiled. Ivan waited for him to say something, but he did not. Ivan looked thoughtfully at his sushi.

As Raven watched the famous press lord, she wondered what conversational entry Takeuchi would use when he got to the real subject of the evening. Would he break the bad news bluntly to Ivan Bloom? Or would he use that subtle Japanese skill of conversational indirection, employing euphemistic flattery so vaguely that it would take Ivan a week to realize he had been fired?

As the lights of the Riviera twinkled over his shoulder and the yacht sliced through the sea en route to Monte Carlo, Ivan, the home electronics addict, tried to convince Takeuchi to invest in the latest computer equipment: "With a Powerbook hooked into a cellular phone, you can use your laptop to tap into Dow Jones even when you're two hundred feet in the air—on a ski lift, for example!"

"Surely that would be the last place one would want to use a computer?" Takeuchi said politely.

"Oh yeah?" Ivan expanded with pride. "Just ask Ashley here. Wasn't I in touch with my broker from Telluride last year, baby?"

"That's right, Ivan," she said. "You never got off the lift. You just went around and around, up and down, typing on your laptop and telling everybody what you were doing."

"And what'd they think?"

"They thought you were crazy, Ivan. You should have at least worn your skis."

Their places were cleared and plates of strawberries and Italian ice cream were set before them. Coffee and brandy materialized, and a servant opened a mahogany chest to offer Ivan a Havana cigar. Ashley stopped the steward and took a cigar for herself. Raven shuddered. Women who smoked cigars were trying to tell you something about themselves that you didn't want to know.

"Now this is living!" Ivan said. "Cruising in a yacht off of Cannes, France. Pleasant company, top cuisine, a breeze in your hair and beautiful women to complete the picture. Take it from me, Tak, the motion picture business will break your heart, but it has its rewards."

"I know very well, Mr. Bloom," Takeuchi said.

"You in the business?" Ivan asked. "I didn't realize. I thought you were in print."

"Motion pictures too, Mr. Bloom. As of noon today, I own Realistic Pictures."

"But that's my studio!"

"Was."

FONTAINE EADY was bored. When his limousine arrived at the casino at Monte Carlo, he could barely be bothered to dislodge himself from the leather cushions and walk up the flight of stairs to the entrance. Casinos had lost all of their magic, he reflected, when people started gambling in hopes of actually winning. In the old days of exiled royalty, fugitive embezzlers, and dissolute playboys, you gambled in order to lose. You won a queer sort of reverse status if you threw away a fortune. Now people gambled to make money. Tacky.

He spun his cigarette out the open door of the limo, and followed it into the cool night air. It was midnight, too early for the high rollers, too late for the tourists from the cruise ships. Eady was relieved. He seemed to have an uncanny knack for standing next to American widows who kept telling one another, "I've budgeted forty dollars for this casino, and I don't care if I win or lose."

The gossip columnist walked up the stairs and was strolling indolently beneath a chandelier when he saw three people sitting at a table in the bar, looking as if they had missed a train. Ivan Bloom sat staring at nothing. On his left, Ashley St. Ives examined her nails as if they held crossword clues. On his right, Raven Charles sipped a Perrier. Eady smelled an item.

"I say!" he boomed, striding across to them. "Happy coincidence! What will it be? Roulette?"

Ivan looked straight ahead. "Snake eyes," he said tonelessly.

Eady didn't understand. Ashley filled him in. Takeuchi had bought

Realistic Pictures. Ivan was deposed as studio chief—promoted sideways to a new division, developing electronic gizmos. The new job was obviously a P.R. ploy. Ivan would be expected to resign.

"He's out?" said Eady, glad for a scoop on a silver platter, but not believing his ears. "Who's in?"

"Whoever takes over, he's got his work cut out for him," Ivan said.

Raven Charles remained silent. What could she say? Takeuchi had thrown her a real curve, bringing her along on the boat, breaking the bad news to Ivan, but not telling Ivan that he'd already chosen Raven as his successor.

Maybe Takeuchi hadn't been able to find the right opening. Ivan had taken the news badly, had left the table to stand by himself at the bow of the yacht, and had refused to speak to Takeuchi at the Monte Carlo hotel pier. Imperiously sweeping Ashley and Raven off the ship along with him, he had pushed them into a taxi and marched them into the casino. Now Raven found herself psychologically incapable of telling Ivan what she already knew.

"Cheer up, Ivan!" Eady said. "Hollywood is the only place in the world where your success is measured by how many places you've been sacked. Let's roll a few!"

Ivan stood up and meekly followed Eady into the salon, like a pallbearer. Without his presence between them, the two women automatically moved just a little farther apart.

ONCE again Sheila Chesham was in the darkness that she hated and feared. Blindfolded with a silk scarf, handcuffed to Billy and Mason, she had been led off the ship and down what sounded like a long, damp passageway in a cave. Pontoon and Gold Tooth were apparently using electric torches to light the way, but she could see nothing. Slipping on wet mud and tearing her ankles against the sharp edges of rocks, she pictured invisible tentacles reaching out for her.

For Mason Devereaux, their stumbling journey was like a nightmare revisited—like that endless time he had been lost in the pitch darkness of the underwater ballroom at Thorn Hill. That time, his deliverance had come from following the way upward until it led to a passageway and finally to freedom. This time, again, their steps seemed to be leading upward. Mason did not feel well. He was light-headed, and running a temperature that made the inside of the mask feel like a clammy steam room.

Billy Baxter, manhandled roughly by one of the kidnappers, fell heavily over the first step of a staircase, and then began to climb uncertainly into a void. From the sounds around him, he judged they had left the unfinished cavern and were climbing in-side some kind of staircase of stone, wood, and iron. A heavy door moved creakingly open somewhere ahead, and their handcuffed parade jerked uncertainly into another invisible passageway. This time there was a louder sound underfoot—steel, probably. They walked for what seemed an eternity. He tried to measure their progress by picturing football fields, but couldn't keep track of the yard lines.

"One word, one sound, one squeak, and you are all dead," Pontoon said under his breath.

"He means it," said the voice of Gold Tooth.

"Believe me, old man, I haven't the slightest doubt," said Mason, just before he blacked out and pitched forward into a void. The oth-ers heard the sickening sound of structural supports giving away, the crack of wood and the tortured squeal of dislodged nails, before they were pulled down after him, one by one, chained together and falling through a void toward a fate they could not imagine.

THE man who called himself Excaliber Pontoon had formed his kidnap plan with an evil brilliance. Studying every crime book in the YMCA library in Bucharest, he had discovered that all kidnappings failed in one of two crucial points: The delivery of the money, or the handing over of the hostages. The money could always be traced. Or the kidnappers could always be snatched when they were releasing their victims. At last, in the small print of *Nash's En-cyclopedia of World Crime,* he discovered the solution to both hazards: Electronic transfer of funds to a phony destination, and the hiding of hostages in plain view.

His plan, he was convinced, was foolproof. Sheila Chesham's

father would transfer the funds by wire, so that there would be no paper currency to be traced. They would be payable to the national bank of Romania, earmarked for the national debt account. Since that account always showed a deficit of billions, a bump of a few million pounds would go unnoticed, particularly since no one was likely to check the Romanian national debt to see if it had received unsolicited donations from overseas. Pontoon would transfer the ransom out again, to a Swiss bank account he had established in the name of the government of Romania, but without its knowledge, when he was an accountant for the central committee. He was the only person who knew the account number.

Meanwhile, Sheila Chesham and the others—the pathetic Mason Devereaux, the ridiculous Billy Baxter—would be handcuffed, blindfolded, and led through a labyrinth of passages from a private boat-mooring in a cave beneath the cliffs of Monte Carlo. The passages led to the casino, and had been built by Rainier to provide a quick getaway in case the casino were ever assaulted by terrorists. Pontoon had learned of their existence when he was head of security for Ceaușescu's state visit to Monaco.

In the gloom of a secret corner beneath the casino ceiling, the captives could be locked up for hours or days, while Pontoon and Gold Tooth returned to their boat and disappeared from the sight of the world. Pontoon knew his captives expected to be shot dead, but there he would have to disappoint them. He believed small one-on-one crimes of violence were not cost-effective compared to the fortunes that could be moved by fraud, and they inspired too much police enthusiasm. By the time he informed the authorities about where Sheila and the others could be found, he and Gold Tooth would have long since gone their separate and secret ways— Pontoon, of course, with all of the money, but Gold Tooth with memories of a job well done.

In a split second, Pontoon's plan was undone. Devereaux had stumbled and fallen heavily to one side, toppling off the catwalk that the captives were being led along. The others had followed him, dragged by their chains into a terrifying fall they could not see or imagine.

I N the great room of the Casino at Monte Carlo, Ivan Bloom had just bet one thousand dollars on the black and Fontaine Eady had put down his own twenty-dollar chip, when Mason Devereaux landed with a sickening thud on the roulette table. Two other bodies fell in a heap on top of the actor, and then, as the horrified gamblers looked up at a gaping hole in the casino ceiling, they saw a rat-faced little man desperately windmilling his arms, trying to keep his balance, until he pitched forward and fell after them, impaling himself through the heart on the tall brass spike in the center of the roulette wheel. As he was skewered, his revolver discharged, and another man tumbled out of the ceiling and landed, dead, on the red.

There was a moment of stunned silence. And then an Iron Mask, which had caught on a nail in the ceiling, fell to the inlaid floor, bounced at an angle, and rolled noisily down the marble stairs.

L I G H T. Blessed, healing, warming sunlight, falling onto Mason's face from the open terrace window of his suite at the Voile d'Or, an exclusive little hotel on Cap Ferrat. Light, falling on the breakfast tray in front of him, as he selected a ripe spring berry and popped it into his mouth. Light, falling on his china cup, as he drank hot, strong English breakfast tea. Light, falling on his chin, as he fingered the stubble that had grown while his head was trapped inside the antique Iron Mask. Light, falling on the Mask itself, which he held in the crook of his arm while Fontaine Eady gave instructions to photographers for the *Sketch*.

"I think I'll keep the beard, now that it has established itself," Mason said to Eady. "What do you think? Distinguished? Too rakish?"

"It's the perfect touch, old man, if you plan to star in the remake of *The Lost Weekend*. Otherwise, call the barber. Some men look bearded. Others merely look unkempt."

Eady dismissed the photographers. Devereaux sighed. His fingers probed the large purple bruise on his chin, caused when the Iron Mask was jerked from his head as he fell through the casino ceiling. It had all happened in an instant. One moment he was being led blindfolded and handcuffed. The next he had pitched forward terrifyingly into empty space. Then he'd been looking up into the star-

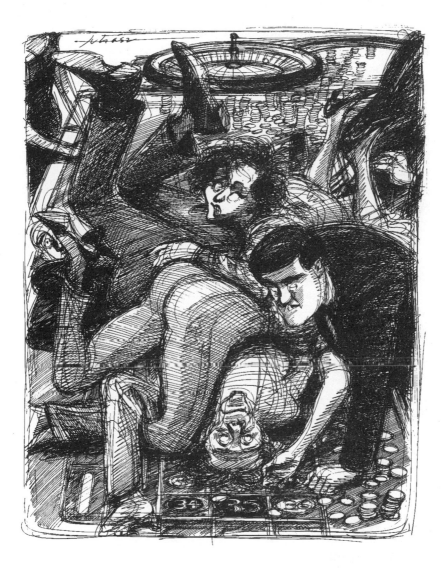

tled eyes of Fontaine Eady, who had said: "Good lord! Mason Devereaux! Afraid they require jacket and tie, old man."

A casino handyman used a hacksaw to cut through the handcuff chains joining holding Mason, Sheila, and Billy. After disjointed interviews with top police officials, who had been obsessed with damage to the casino's image, Billy and Sheila had been hurried into limousines hired by Ashley St. Ives. Mason was taken to a hospital for treatment of pneumonia. It had been dicey for a day or two—they'd hooked him up again to those hateful IV drips—but now, a few days later, weak but resting, he was enjoying the view over the little yacht harbor of Cap Ferrat, a view that Winston Churchill had painted, and Graham Greene had often admired over his afternoon drinks.

There was no happy ending for Gold Tooth and Pontoon, who had been transferred to the police morgue. The rat-faced little man was removed with the roulette wheel still nailed through his body. Even with the corpse covered by a large white sheet, it made a macabre sight as it was carried down the front steps of the casino, the table used as if it were a stretcher, with the shrouded outline of a wicked brass spike sticking up in the center.

Eady had arrived at Cap Ferrat with an armful of back issues of the London papers. Mason read all the accounts of the shooting death of Harold Gasper in his flat at the Albany. Mason's mind had instantly flashed to Douglas Brown, and he had picked up the telephone to call Inspector Rowley, before replacing it thoughtfully and reaching for a drink instead. How could he account for his knowledge of a connection between Gasper and Brown, without incriminating himself? Mason had been delivered from one captivity, and had no desire to talk himself into another.

Eady, who had formed his own theory about the *Phantom* murder, watched carefully as Mason read the papers. But when Mason volunteered nothing other than a conventional sigh of pity for poor Harold, Eady did not pursue the subject. He had a notion that Mason's role in the case, if not precisely criminal, would not stand up under scrutiny.

"It's true, isn't it, that nobody knows where we are?" Mason asked, troubled by the possibility that Brown might somehow endanger them. Sheila had gone for a walk by the harbor, and suddenly he wished she were back in the room.

"The *Sketch* is paying a great deal of money to maintain you incommunicado," Eady said. "Our treat. Of course we've told the people in California where you are. They can keep a secret."

"I must confess I feel safer in hiding," Mason said.

"The jackals will inevitably descend one of these days," Eady told him, looking out over the water. "Once you're on the mend, you'll be deluged with offers. Do me a favor. Take some advice from me. I've covered show business for years. I've seen what happens. You are temporarily the most famous man in the world. What that means is that you have the potential to become a notorious has-been. You were already a has-been before all of this publicity began. Don't repeat yourself. It's a bore."

"What would you advise, apart from a drink?" Mason asked his friend.

Eady sighted on Monte Carlo in the distance.

"That's precisely what I wouldn't advise, old man. There comes a time in the life of every drinking man when he has to admit that he has done enough drinking for a lifetime, and if his lifetime has not ended as a result, he had best surrender gracefully."

"Stop drinking?" asked Mason. "Just when I'll have enough money to buy my own?"

"Two men became famous playing King Arthur in Camelot," Eady told him. "Both were named Richard. Burton and Harris. You knew them. I knew them. What was the difference between them?"

"I'm sure you'll tell me."

"The one who stopped drinking," Eady said, "is still playing King Arthur."

Mason cleared his throat uncomfortably and turned the pages of one of the newspapers.

"What inspires this sudden outburst of frankness, Fontaine?"

Eady remained with his back to the room. "Let's change the subject, shall we?" he asked. "This black woman. Raven Charles. The producer. What do you know about her?"

"She is considering me for the film version of *Phantom of the Opera*," Mason said. "She claims she wanted me from the first, even before poor Bradleigh Court was killed. She said she saw me at Stratford. Back during my days of promise."

"And what about the other woman?" Eady said. He had something on his mind. "Ashley St. Ives. The agent. What do you know about her?"

"She signed me to a personal contract," Mason said. "It was in London, the day I left the hospital. Bringing me to Cannes was her idea. And then she entrapped me in the press conference that led to the Iron Mask. For that I do not thank her. She has returned to Los Angeles, I believe."

"What does she have in mind for you, old boy?"

"*The Mason Devereaux Saga*," Mason said. "Originally she had a made-for-TV movie in mind, but this morning her fax referred to a miniseries."

"I should think so," Eady said. He lit a cigarette and blew smoke out the veranda window. "There's no way to cover all that's happened to you in a movie lasting two hours, less commercials. Plus a romantic subplot, of course."

"You must admit it's box office," Mason said proudly. "The shooting, the underwater ballroom, the Iron Mask . . ."

Fontaine Eady sent his cigarette spinning to the ocean far below.

"It's a comedy, Mason," he said. "Slapstick. Farce. Appear in that story and you'll be a laughingstock for the rest of your life."

"Ashley St. Ives is talking in terms of a small fortune," Mason said.

"There is always that," Eady admitted. "After all, Devereaux, you've spent years selling out for nothing. Why not sell out for a large amount this time?"

"Are those my only choices?"

"Who knows what your choices are, Mason? You should be dead five times over. Do what you want. I'm flying back to London this afternoon. All I can provide is a suggestion or two, based on my experience as the most insightful entertainment reporter on the globe."

"I know what you're going to tell me," Mason said. "I should wash my hands of the St. Ives woman, and trust Raven Charles."

"Did I say that?" asked Fontaine Eady. "I believe you thought it before me, old man." And he was gone.

Left alone in his room, Mason Devereaux thoughtfully turned the Iron Mask over in his hands. It was a wickedly beautiful thing. A delegation from Paris was on its way to reclaim it. Mason would be happy never to see it again, and yet he was the only man alive who knew what it felt like to be the Man in the Iron Mask. The original man in the mask, Mason reflected, inspired plays, movies, novels, and even comic books. Yet nobody knew who he really was. Mason had the opposite dilemma. Everybody knew who he was. But he had inspired nothing.

T O lose yourself in a city of seven million people, you begin by growing a beard. Douglas Brown knew that from the movies. And you start to wear a hat. He had found an American baseball cap in a stall at Camden Lock. And you wear dark glasses. He put on his Ray-Bans. The irony was that nobody seemed to be looking for him. He felt like the Invisible Man. Was he really so inconsequential without his job and friends?

After adopting the disguise, the next thing you do is move house. Brown had found a room under the flyover at the foot of Portobello Road, near the Jamaican market. Reggae boomed in through his window half the night, but nobody bothered him and he could sprawl on the bed all day long, with his hands clasped behind his head and his eyes staring at the ceiling. Occasionally he went out for a sandwich, or a hot meal at the corner pub.

He had all the money he needed for the time being. But time crawled past with agonizing slowness. He thought of going to the midnight shows at the Electric Cinema but was afraid someone would recognize him; it drew a audience that included the fringe theater crowd, relaxing after work. He thought of getting drunk but had never done much drinking. He tried reading but had to read the same passages over and over again, while the bloodless face of Harold Gasper swam in the air above the page, a small round hole between his eyes.

He had no plan. He did not particularly want to be arrested by the police and charged with murder, but up until the day of his disappearance the police had shown no interest in him. He reflected, staring at his ceiling, that disappearing had been the most suspicious thing he had done. And now he was afraid to reappear, because he had no idea what the police had concluded in his absence. He had killed two men because he wanted to marry Sheila Chesham, and now he was nobody and nowhere and they were dead and she could not have found him on the telephone even if she had wanted to talk with him, which was not likely.

He waited. Sometimes just before closing time he walked up Portobello to the Sun in Splendour and danced furiously all by himself. He drew little attention. He was not the only desperate solo dancer.

I VAN BLOOM was miserable. He sat listlessly in his electronic den, surrounded by thousands of dollars of video gear, but there was no joy to be found this morning. He picked up a remote controller, thinking that perhaps he could poach the satellite feed of the Oprah Winfrey program, but then his eyes fell on the Sony trademark, and the device dropped from his fingers. First the Japanese sold you all this stuff, and then they used the money to buy you out.

Ivan had flown to the Cannes Film Festival in a private jet, as one of the most powerful men in Hollywood. He had returned to America by commercial airline as an unemployed ex-executive. It had been humiliating, lining up in the departure lounge at the airport in Nice, clutching his boarding pass, being herded with such lower orders as agents and critics. Thank God Ashley was sitting next to him on the plane, blocking conversation with some impudent stranger who might already have read of his firing in *Screen International*.

Ashley, who by nature never stopped talking, had been unusually quiet during the endless flight to Los Angeles. At the time Ivan welcomed the silence, but now he wondered if she had lost interest in him when he was fired. Was it was possible she had been attracted to his power rather than to himself? He honestly did not know. He had been so powerful for so long he no longer knew instinctively how it felt when a woman really loved you.

His pocket telephone rang. He took the call on a speakerphone next to his armchair. It was Raven Charles. He had been expecting the call.

"You know that Takeuchi has asked me to run the studio," Raven said.

"That's what I already heard. I expect the news is gonna be in *Variety* by tomorrow."

"I'm accepting his offer."

"I would if I were you."

"Ivan, I'll always be grateful for what you've done for me."

Ivan sighed and cut the end off a cigar. "Raven, honey," he said, "I take it personally that the son of a bitch sneaked in and bought the studio and stabbed me in the back. What happens to you, I don't take personally. If a guy in this town got mad at everybody who got what he wanted, he'd end up in a rubber room. Good luck, baby. Enjoy it."

There was a silence at the other end. Ivan almost imagined he heard a sniff of emotion.

"Thank you, Ivan."

"Hey, maybe you'll return the favor someday."

He hung up and lit his cigar and walked out onto the deck of his pool. He had lost the studio and he was probably going to lose Ashley St. Ives. Why did he feel—not cheerful, perhaps, but serene?

The studio, he would miss.

SHEILA CHESHAM liked to look in at the Bar du Port in the late afternoons. It was a five-minute stroll from the hotel. She had heard that in the last decades of his life Graham Greene had stopped at the little bistro every day. Now he was dead, and she felt in a elegiac mood. She had almost died herself. She sat at a table that Greene had perhaps used, ordered a café au lait, and looked out at the sailing craft. Her thoughts drifted to the Voile d'Or, where Mason Devereaux was no doubt happily installed at the bar.

Sheila did not know what to do about Mason, or about her own life. They were staying in separate rooms at the Voile d'Or. Was that how she preferred it? What did Mason think? After the escapes that had made him the most famous man in the world, Mason stood poised on the brink of a new career. He was going to Los Angeles. Should Sheila go, too?

In London nobody had known who Mason was, or cared much about the young woman who roamed through used bookstores at his side and listened to his stories in pubs. Mason had been grateful for the companionship, she knew, but did he think of her as—a woman? He had kept her so much at arm's length that she suspected a deep fear was buried inside of him, a fear that he was not prepared to conduct a proper relationship and so preferred not to begin one.

Sheila sipped her coffee and watched as the seabirds hung motionless in the air. Of course Mason had a drinking problem. Perhaps he thought that as a drunk he had nothing to offer her. Well, did he? Sheila's mother had often suggested she find a friend her own age, but the problem with men in their twenties, she found, was that they were obsessed with their own careers and saw women only as support systems.

An old man nodded to Sheila, interrupting her reverie. He stood at the side of her table.

"You are the young woman who was involved in that fracas at the casino," he said. It was a statement, not a question. She nodded.

"Then you are Sheila Chesham. The friend of Mason Devereaux." She nodded again, and forced herself to smile. She did not approve of personal questions from strangers, but the man was so old and so soft-spoken that it was a courtesy for her to answer.

"Once, many years ago," the old man said, "I saw Devereaux play Hamlet. He was the finest Hamlet I ever saw." He turned to the door. "I often wondered what had happened to him," he said. "He must be getting on toward his Lear, I imagine."

The old man was gone. Sheila sipped her coffee and found that it had gone cold. She got up to leave, and looked around for the proprietor, who was sitting outside the door, his chair propped against the wall, savoring a cigarette. She paid her check and stood for a moment, looking up and down the quay. It was empty.

"Which way did the old man walk?" she asked.

"What old man?"

"The old man I was speaking to just now, who left before me."

The owner shrugged. "No one has come in or out," he said. "You must have been dreaming."

T ROUBLE , " said Billy (Silver Dollar) Baxter. "We got trouble." He was sitting behind a big desk in his new office, in his new capacity as special assistant to the president of Realistic Pictures, and he was talking on the speakerphone with Raven Charles. "Big trouble."

"What about?" Raven asked. She was in the executive suite at Realistic, which was still furnished as Ivan had left it when he flew to the Riviera.

"Remember that business about who pulled the trigger when the Phantom was shot?"

"I thought it was all settled," Raven said. "Harold Gasper pulled the trigger. After Gasper was murdered, Scotland Yard revealed he was their prime suspect. He was going to be charged with reckless something, wasn't he?"

"Yeah, and remember, the guy that got shot was Sir Bradleigh Court, because Mason, who was supposed to be on stage, was too drunk," Baxter said.

"Tell me something new," Raven said.

"Did Mason know, or did Mason not know, what Gasper was going to do?" Billy asked. "In other words, should he have been shot instead of Sir Bradleigh? Or, for that matter, charged along with Harold Gasper?"

Raven was very alert. "Why are you asking me this?" she said.

"Because Ashley St. Ives tells me she knows the answer," Billy said, "and that unless you make her the producer of the *Phantom* movie, she's going to have to say some things about Mason that nobody wants to hear."

PART SEVEN

New World

MASON DEVEREAUX sat and brooded in the piano bar of the great ocean liner *Norway.* He was alone. Sheila Chesham had returned to Thorn Hill, to regain her bearings, she'd told him, after the confusing events of the last few weeks. He wondered frankly if they would ever meet again. What future could a girl in her twenties actually look forward to with an aging drunk who drew trouble like a magnet? Perhaps it would be best to set her free, now that he was going to work in Hollywood for a year or more.

His face, which he tried to avoid in the clouded mirror behind the bar, was drawn and haggard, even beneath the tan he'd acquired by taking his hangovers to the sun deck. Mason had sailed out of Southampton for Miami on one of the *Norway*'s rare Atlantic crossings, hoping to revive himself after the kidnapping. Ocean liners had always symbolized peace and escape to him, but his rest had been disturbed by the arrival of a fax from Billy Baxter: "St. Ives knows what happened to the Phantom."

If Ashley St. Ives knew the true story of the *Phantom* shooting, there was only one place she could have learned it—from the man who had supplied Gasper with the gun. Gasper was dead, and Mason believed he had died without revealing their secret. That meant that only Douglas Brown could have told Ashley; for blackmail purposes, probably.

But Ashley was on his side—wasn't she? Then why had she told Baxter, who would tell Raven Charles, a secret that could destroy Mason's modest little comeback? Mason thought of himself as a man sailing toward triumph, who looked back and saw the stark specter of ruin gaining on him. He lifted a finger to the bartender, who brought him another whiskey and soda, and then he tried to coax his thoughts into order.

WHEN the doctors at Monte Carlo had finished working him over, they'd told him he was undernourished, dehydrated, and probably experiencing withdrawal symptoms from alcohol. As soon as he was strong enough to drink, he'd taken Sheila with him for a week at the little hotel perched on the edge of the yacht harbor. There he had treated his withdrawal symptoms in the most direct way possible, in the charming little bar whose French doors opened onto a view of the boats. Sheila had looked at him sadly—no doubt the dear girl thought he was killing himself—but she had bitten her tongue. Perhaps she didn't feel close enough to offer criticism. Mason himself was at a loss to define their relationship, except to admit that he would have felt incomplete if she hadn't been there. They took separate rooms and maintained a certain cordial courtesy that stood in place of a riskier relationship. Mason didn't have to be told he should cut down on the booze—but he'd earned a few, after the ordeal he had been through. Besides, everybody at the bar insisted on sending him rounds.

The telephone and fax machine had poured out messages and offers for Mason, and one morning after breakfast on the lawn overlooking the Mediterranean he had told Sheila: "Looks like we might be able to trade this in for sunny Southern California. Ashley says I can take my pick of the networks for *the Mason Devereaux Saga,* and Raven Charles wants to test me for the *Phantom.*"

Sheila heard the "we" but did not respond to it. "What do you think about Ashley?" she asked, her voice carefully neutral.

"I know what you're thinking," Mason sighed. "A predator. Fontaine warned me off her when he was here. He said the miniseries would make me a laughingstock. At the end of the day I'd be better off, he said, just listening to Raven Charles. But the thing is, I'm under contract to St. Ives. I signed up in that moment of weakness when she dangled the Cannes Film Festival before my eyes. Once we're actually out there in la-la land, I imagine things will sort themselves out."

There was a silence, punctuated by the cries of seabirds. "Mason . . ." said Sheila, quietly, "I think I'll go back to Thorn Hill and spend a few weeks with my family."

"Of course you should do whatever you want," Mason said.

"You know I'm very fond of you."

"There, there, old girl." He wanted to embrace her, but gave her a chaste pat on the hand instead.

"I'm sure everything will work out wonderfully, Mason."

He had been moved. He had even wanted to urge her to come along with him. She was the closest friend of a lonely man. But he put on a brave actor's face and shuffled through the stack of offers in front of him.

"I've always wanted to travel in the States," he said, making small talk to cover his embarrassment. "I was as far as Broadway once. Never got any farther. Here's an offer from Disney World in Florida—they want me to be grand marshal of their Fourth of July parade. I have half a mind to sail to the States by ocean liner, and take them up on it. That would give me time to build up my strength and collect my thoughts. The Americans do amusement parks frightfully well, so they say."

Sheila said that sounded like enormous fun. The next morning they had packed and flown back to England together. He had spent some time in London, settling his affairs, subletting his rooms at the Eyrie Mansion, saying good-bye to old friends, and being interviewed in the Coach and Horses, where he now arrived by taxi, after receiving an advance from Ashley. Sheila had called several times and left messages with the hall porter, and he had called back and left messages with the butler. It had all been a haze of ready drink and celebrity, and then he had sailed, finding in his stateroom a dozen roses with no card attached.

Then the ominous fax had come from Billy Baxter. Now he sat in a bar of the *Norway*, surrounded by a crowd of boozy travelers who were singing "Twilight Time," and deepening shades of night were falling.

DURING long hours staring at the ceiling of his room, Douglas Brown had created pipe dreams in which a powerful Hollywood agent somehow pulled strings and spirited him out of the country, or covered for him, or—here the details grew blurred. In his dreams he clung to the notion that if Mason could somehow be discredited in Sheila's eyes, then the whole chain of events would reverse itself, and he would find himself back on the grassy lawns of Thorn Hill, chatting with Lord Chesham.

He had finally decided to call Ashley. He had discovered in his wallet the card she had handed him at Thorn Hill, and walked up to the Sun in Splendour to place the call. She had come on the line immediately. Brown had not identified himself—had tried to disguise his voice even though he doubted she could recognize it.

"Who is this?" Ashley asked sharply.

"A friend."

"Don't be tiresome. What exactly is your purpose in calling me?"

"I guess I just wanted to talk to somebody."

"Say what's on your mind."

He had, telling her Mason Devereaux had been a party to the scheme that killed Bradleigh Court. Ashley had listened with elation leaping in her heart, but she kept her voice brittle.

"This information is useful only if the source remains my personal secret. Do you understand?"

Douglas Brown listened to Ashley St. Ives with one ear while trying to block out the pub jukebox in the other.

"Of course I do," he said. "That's why I called you. If I had wanted to make my information into public knowledge, I would have called Fontaine Eady, instead."

RAVEN CHARLES told her secretary to hold all calls. She closed the door of her office and turned to face Ashley St. Ives and Billy Baxter. Ashley had lit a cigarette without asking, and now crossed her legs as if she felt right at home in the executive suite—as indeed she should, Billy thought to himself, since for years this room had been Ivan Bloom's office.

"This whole business could actually be handled very simply, very easily, with everyone happy," Ashley said. "I'm sure we all love Mason Devereaux and we want only the best for him. But what would the very best be? The networks are in a bidding war for *The Mason Devereaux Saga*. He would also be the perfect choice to play the Phantom. We could work out all the agreements right here in fifteen minutes, verbally, and leave it to the lawyers to fill in the details."

"Such details as . . . ?" Raven said.

"Raven, we've known each other for a long time. You know how much I want to leave the agent business and start producing. This is my moment. I feel it. I want to make the miniseries, and as Mason's agent I can do that with or without you. But I also want to produce the *Phantom*. That was your project, but you're running the studio now. You have your hands full. I'd like to see you assign it to me." She paused. "To Ivan and me."

Raven waited until she was sure Ashley had finished. Then she turned. "Billy?" she said.

Billy let out a long, low whistle. "What you have not mentioned yet, Miss St. Ives, is your telephone call to me yesterday, during which you said you had the goods on Mason in the *Phantom* murder case. You said the news could destroy his career. Assuming you're right—why, as Mason's agent, would you want to destroy his career?"

"That's the last thing I'd want to do to the poor, dear man," Ashley said smoothly. Raven, seated behind her desk, allowed Billy to ask the obvious questions, while she marveled at the icy calm of the woman. "As Mason's agent, I want only the best for him. That means the miniseries, and the *Phantom* film project. As the producers of the film, Ivan and I would make an incredible box office and critical success."

"You're talking like a press release," Billy said. "Let's talk turkey. If you get the job, you keep quiet. If you don't, you blackmail us. You know Miss Charles wants Mason for the *Phantom*. You'd destroy him to stop her."

"Billy, Billy, Billy," Ashley said with sad reproach. "What a way to talk to an old friend! How long have we known each other?"

"Less than two months," Billy said.

Raven stood up behind her desk. "I think we have all the information we need at this point, Ashley," she said. "Thanks for dropping by. The studio will get back to you as soon as possible, one way or the other."

Ashley seemed surprised that the meeting was over. "There isn't a lot of time," she said, stubbing out her cigarette. "Mason will never be bigger than he is right now."

"Unless the *Norway* sinks," Billy said.

B U T Ivan, darling, you always loved your electronic gadgets," Ashley was telling her lover. It was the evening of the same day, at an hour when they were usually in a fashionable restaurant, spending and being seen to spend. Tonight Ashley had suggested they stay in and eat carryout from Mr. Chow. Ivan had thought it was a good idea until he remembered he no longer had a chauffeur to pick up the food, and then he had been embarrassed to tell Ashley what he was thinking, and so he had bitten the bullet and sent a taxi for it. Now they talked about his future.

"This is not a real job they wanna give me, baby," he said. "This is a public humiliation. Takeuchi only put me in charge of the gizmo division so he would have something to say in the press release. I'm a high-powered executive. I was ninth on that list in *Entertainment Weekly* about the hundred most influential men in the business. That was only three weeks ago. As fast as I'm slipping, I'm probably still above seventy-five. I make movies. I take this job, I can't show my face in this town. What am I gonna say when I run into Rich Frank at Morton's? That I can get him a deal on a big-screen TV?"

"Ivan, honey, hang in there. Your Ashley is going to take good care of you. We'll be producing the *Phantom*. Just you wait and see."

"We?" said Ivan.

Ashley ran her fingers through what remained of his hair and nibbled on an earlobe. "I'd be the producer, baby dumpling, and you would be right there with me. Wouldn't that be wonderful, us working together all day long?"

Ivan Bloom was stunned. "*You* would be the producer?" he asked her. "*I* would help you? Ashley, you don't know the first thing about producing a movie."

"That's where you would come in. I'm setting this whole thing up for the two of us, Ivan. Don't spoil it. Ivan?"

"Don't bother me. I'm watching something important."

"You have the sound turned off."

"Muted," he said. "The correct term is muted."

FOR Sheila Chesham, these days were spent in a willful return to childhood. She moved back into her old room at Thorn Hill and picked up the book on her bedside table, which was *Pride and Prejudice*. Jane Austen's calm prose was like an antidote.

Her parents knew enough to stay away. Peter and Beverly Chesham followed their daily routine: The morning newspapers, lunch on the veranda, Lord Chesham's daily inspections of the spiders. Sometimes they would see their daughter sitting in one of the chairs down under the trees on the lawn, but they respected her privacy. When she joined them for dinner, the conversation was stilted, but then at Thorn Hill, dinner conversations had been stilted for centuries. Lady Chesham watched closely and kept her own counsel.

Sheila was telephoned three or four times by people looking for Douglas Brown, and she told them the truth, that she hadn't seen him since that angry afternoon in May. Fontaine Eady sympathized: "He doesn't phone, he doesn't write. What about Mason? Any word from him?"

"He doesn't telephone either," Sheila said.

"Are you worried?"

"Worried is the given state of any friend of Mason's."

FROM his chair in a sheltered corner of the *Norway*'s aft deck, Mason Devereaux watched the great ship's wake as it formed in the dawn. He must have passed out and slept in the chair all night. He reached mechanically to the table beside him and found the remains of one of those jolly drinks with an umbrella and a cherry in it. He extracted the umbrella and let it flutter away in the wind, and then he drank what dregs of rum and melted ice remained.

This is finally it, old boy, he thought to himself. The end of the line. You're sailing to America. It's the break you've been dreaming of for a lifetime. And it's all to be snatched away, replaced by shame and humiliation. The world sees you as a hero. You know better. Soon the world will know better—will know that you conspired with Harold Gasper in that idiotic shooting, and would have been killed yourself, if you hadn't been too drunk to crawl on stage.

He walked creakingly to the ship's railing. It was so early no one else was about. Accusing thoughts whirled in his mind. Sheila was spending some time with her family. He knew what that meant. Fontaine Eady had lectured him to stop drinking, and had warned that the proposed TV miniseries would make him a laughingstock. Now, if Billy's telegram could be believed, Douglas Brown was about to retail his shameful secret.

When an actor dies, it is sometimes said he has gone to study a long silence. Mason braced himself on the rail and judged the distance to the sea below. Perhaps it was time to begin his studies.

"Mr. Devereaux?"

He turned to find himself addressed by a young black man in a uniform of navy blazer, gray slacks, starched shirt, checkered vest, tie, and a Mickey Mouse lapel pin.

"My name is Jay Smith, sir. I've been looking for you all over the ship. The steward said you didn't sleep in your cabin last night."

"I was wakeful," said Mason, who looked as if he had been living under bridges.

"I'm with Disney public relations. I hitched a ride out here on the tugboat. We'll be docking in Miami in half an hour, and then we'll take you by limousine to Orlando for the big parade."

"Parade?"

"The Fourth of July parade, sir. Day after tomorrow. You're the grand marshal."

"Of course. That parade. Yes. Very kind of you. Have you, by any chance, something to drink? I find myself a bit unsteady on the old pins this morning."

Smith looked at him closely. "I don't think they serve at this hour, sir. It's not even six A.M. We dock early. I asked the steward to pack for you, so all you'll have to do is present your passport and go straight into the limousine."

"Splendid."

W E ' V E had some laughs together. There were even times when Ashley and I thought we loved each other. But damn it all, Raven—this time the woman's gone too far."

Ivan Bloom instinctively lowered his voice. They were having a late lunch in the little dining room off the lobby of the Sunset Marquis, a rendezvous he had suggested because it was quiet and discreet. Ivan, who was rarely quiet, had great need to be discreet.

"It's blackmail, Ivan," Raven said. "The studio puts Ashley in charge of the *Phantom,* or she destroys Mason's career."

"Is she only bluffing?"

"If she can't make the picture herself, she'd do anything to keep me from making it. She plays for keeps."

Ivan knew that Raven was telling the truth. He also knew—had known for days—that his relationship with Ashley St. Ives was over. Ashley was blackmailing not only Raven, but him. She had offered him the coproducer credit on the *Phantom*—itself an insult—as a way of buying his silence as she pulled her dirty little trick. Ivan didn't do business that way.

"Did she put her threat in so many words?"

"Not really. Billy Baxter accused her of blackmail, but she smiled that sweet little smile and asked if we didn't want what was best for Mason."

"Where was this?"

"Your office, Ivan. My office, now."

"Bingo!" said Ivan Bloom. The clouds lifted from his face for the first time in days. "My old office! I've got it so wired, it makes the Nixon White House look like ham radio."

T R E E S attacked him. Vines swooped dizzyingly from the ceiling. Parrots shouted angry warnings. Mason stood in the lobby of the Polynesian Resort on the grounds at Disney World, his white-knuckled hands gripping the back of a wicker chair, and fought his way through an alarming hangover. He had arrived in Orlando the day before, been taken directly to his suite, and discovered that the tiny key they had given him would open the little refrigerator he found under the sink. That was more or less the last thing he could remember, except for jamming his left big toe on a chair at some point in the middle of the night. Now he was down in the lobby, preparing to go somewhere and do something.

Jay Smith, the Disney host in charge of Mason, had left him anchored to the chair for a moment, and was whispering into a telephone at the front desk.

"He seems to be in pretty bad shape," he said. "He was hung over when I got him off the ship in Miami, and he made a detour through the airport bar before I could get him in the limo to Orlando. Now he looks even worse than when I dropped him off yesterday. When I phoned him from the lobby, he wanted to know if land had been sighted."

Smith listened, hung up, and strolled back over to where Mason was engaged in a stare-down with a parrot.

"Is there anything you'd like to see today?" he asked. "Any attractions you'd like to visit? There are a lot of interesting attractions over at Epcot, like Goofy's World of Healthful Living . . ."

"See?" Mason croaked.

"Or perhaps the Disney/MGM Studio Tour? Behind the scenes in the world of movies and television?"

The parrot was chained to its perch, Mason observed carefully. It was probably unable to leap at him and eat his eyeballs. That was good. He vaguely heard the youth say something about a movie studio. Was he expected to appear in some sort of scene? There had been memos in his suite, which he had forgotten to read. The safest strategy was to agree with everything.

"Studio? Excellent!" Mason attempted to sound cheerful and alert. Smith guided him toward the front door of the resort, but Mason veered off to the right, and stopped at the bar of the Alona Moana Room, where he pointed speechlessly at one of the pictures on the menu, and was served a coconut shell filled with shaved ice and rum. Mason had another before Smith was able to guide him to the limousine.

I VAN BLOOM adjusted his tie and ran his fingers over his clean-shaven chin, inspecting his image in the mirror. He looked, he decided, like a man with plans. Visions. Deals in the works. He did not look like what he was, a former Hollywood mogul who was now reduced to chairing meetings where graduate students lectured him on advances in chip miniaturization. He walked out of his dressing room and into the boudoir of Ashley St. Ives, who was enveloping herself in a cloud of expensive perfume.

"I hope I'm doing the right thing," Ivan said.

"Of course you are, sweetie. I've explained it a hundred times." She ran her finger around the inside of his collar. "He's wearing a tie! That's the first time I've seen a tie on my Bloomy Bunny in five years!"

"When you're the boss," Ivan said, "you let the Suits wear the ties. I'm not the boss anymore."

Ashley shrugged. "Now remember. Your presence will be more important than anything you can say. Let me do the talking. Here's the story. We'll start out by hinting that Mason Devereaux was involved in the conspiracy to shoot that man dead onstage in London. We'll imply that Raven Charles had to have known about the conspiracy, but she kept quiet about it, because she wanted to star Mason in the movie of the *Phantom*. Right now Mason is in no shape to star in anybody's movie, but Raven is still planning to film the *Phantom*. Our pitch is very simple. She assigns the *Phantom* to us, and lets us produce the movie, with our company, in our way, with our casting, at our price—or we expose her as a conspirator."

"You do the talking," said Ivan.

W HERE is Mason now?" asked Ashley St. Ives, taking a seat across from Raven Charles and smoothing her skintight skirt.

"I think in Disney World," Raven said. "They've invited him to lead the Fourth of July parade. Then he'll come out here a day or two later."

"The Disney people are always particularly paranoid about the reputations of the people they use at their amusement parks," Ashley said. "Isn't that what you've heard?"

"Meaning what?" asked Billy Baxter, as Raven sat in noncommittal silence.

"Meaning that a man implicated in a murder would not be their first choice to wave the Stars and Stripes and party with Pluto."

"Pluto's a dog," Ivan said. "He doesn't party. It's Goofy."

"It's worse than goofy," Ashley said. "It's scandalous. Mason can never hope to be taken seriously in the business again—if he ever was."

"Ivan," said Raven, ignoring Ashley, "why don't you just make yourself comfortable right here behind your old desk? I'd feel funny sitting here, with you in the office."

"It's your desk now, Raven," Ivan said morosely, but he allowed himself to be coaxed into his old chair, and seemed to brighten slightly as he looked out over the office and adjusted the telephone. Billy Baxter materialized at his side with a cup of coffee, and then went to stand behind Raven at the window.

The phony small talk only underlined the excitement that filled the room. They all knew they were there to contemplate the commission of a crime, and the feeling was vaguely exhilarating. Ivan had been in rooms like this many times over the years, rooms where top executives met behind closed doors to bend the law. It was a macho exercise, he thought; grown men acting like kids in a game of chicken, sitting around a table waiting to see who would be the first to wimp out and start whining about the law. The difference was, today the executives were women.

Raven willed herself to look calm, to seem unconcerned about the bombshell they knew Ashley was about to drop. She turned and looked out the window, allowing Ashley to quite deliberately dominate the room, sleek and brazen in the spotlight.

"Let's cut to the chase," Ashley said. "Getting drunk and falling down a well is not quite the worst thing Mason Devereaux has ever done."

"It's not even the worst thing I've ever done," Billy said.

Ashley ignored him. She paused for dramatic effect, looking directly at Raven Charles. "Mason is also a conspirator to murder. And I think you know all about it."

"Know all about what?" Raven said calmly.

"When Sir Bradleigh Court was shot dead onstage during *Phantom of the Opera*, the trigger was pulled by Harold Gasper. Everybody seems to agree about that. But why was Sir Bradleigh on the stage in the first place? Mason was scheduled to understudy that performance."

"He was drunk as usual," Billy Baxter said. "It was all covered in the papers at the time. He started the play but he fell by the wayside. His lordship went on in his place. Professional courtesy."

"And got murdered in cold blood before a full house," Ashley said. She tapped her sharpened red nails against the arm of her chair. "I have some information about that. Harold Gasper was a fool, but he is not entirely to blame. The fact is, Gasper thought the gun was loaded with blanks. Mason Devereaux knew it wasn't. He faked getting drunk, set up Bradleigh Court to die, and framed Gasper to take the rap for him."

She lit a cigarette. "Two birds with one stone," she said. "Not bad. His rival was dead, and Mason was an international celebrity."

Ashley paused for her words to sink in. She had fabricated her version from what Brown had incoherently hinted over the telephone. That was one of her skills—taking a good story and making it better. She had little interest in the exact facts anyway—because she didn't intend her version ever to leave this room. She hadn't even bothered to call Brown back in that grotty pub where she pictured him still waiting for her call. She had a vague suspicion, which she did not like to dwell on, that it was against the law to talk with him.

Raven had listed to Ashley with an immobile face. "Those are serious charges," she said at last. "I hope you've taken them to Scotland Yard."

"I'm taking them to you," Ashley said, the cold in her voice like steel. She blew out smoke. "Ivan and I are both taking them to you. Right, Ivan?"

Ivan, toying idly with the console of electronic controls on his desk, nodded absently. "And the reason we're taking them to you," Ashley said, "is because these are things you already know." She stabbed out her cigarette. "The bottom line is this, Raven. It would be extremely timely for you to assign the *Phantom* to Ivan and me."

"And if I do not?"

"I'll blackmail you. I'll expose Mason Devereaux as the criminal fraud that he is, and you for covering up for him."

"Blackmail?" said Raven. "Can't you find a more diplomatic word?"

"We both know what we're talking about here," Ashley said savagely.

"Do you think that's enough, Ivan?" asked Raven.

"That should be more than enough," Ivan said.

"More than enough what?" asked Ashley, looking from one to the other.

"More than enough for our studio archives," Billy Baxter said. "Congratulations, baby! You've just starred in Hollywood's funniest home video."

Ashley's eyes darted from Billy to Ivan, who was pressing buttons on the console built into his former desk.

"Ashley, sweetie, you really shoulda paid better attention," Ivan said. "This joint is wired for sight and sound."

Ashley looked Ivan straight in the eye. He looked straight back at her. "You double-crossed me," she said. "You sneaking, lying rat."

Ivan shrugged. He took a videotape from a machine under the desk and handed it to Billy Baxter, who slipped it into a big brown envelope.

"The day you made your big mistake," Ivan told her, "was when you assumed I'd go along with your stinking little extortion. Your second mistake was to tell me I'd get second billing. Your third mistake was, you forgot I'm really a pretty good guy." He stood up. "I mighta been able to overlook one and three, but number two was pushing your luck."

"This is blackmail!" Ashley cried. It wasn't a bad line. It got her the biggest laugh of her career.

THE car brought them around the back way, avoiding the crowds. Smith led him down a private passage into the studio tour, which was jammed with happy tourists. Mason had been picturing a drab soundstage of the sort he had worked on in England, and was startled to find himself apparently on Hollywood Boulevard, looking up at the Chinese Theater. How could this be? Had he not been paying attention? Had the boat sailed to California instead of Florida?

Mason struggled to remember his school geography, and a chill crept down his back. Was it possible that he had blacked out during the entire passage through the Panama Canal? He looked around unsteadily, trying to regain his bearings. There was something called the Brown Derby—restaurant probably—with a bar, no doubt—and another spot—Backstage Grill—no doubt a bar there—and . . . a roar like thunder crashed through the air, and Mason turned to see a ball of fire appear above a stand of palm trees.

Cold sweat dripped inside his shirt. Was this real, or a hallucination? God knows Hollywood was said to be insane. But this was incredible. He was surrounded by carnage. How did people live here? He yearned to be back at the Coach and Horses, where life was orderly and sane.

"Is there . . . anyplace cool, and dark, where one could sit down for a moment?" he asked his guide.

Smith looked around. They were standing in front of the Great Movie Ride, which took patrons on a boat trip down dark rivers where famous movie scenes played out on the banks. Better there than in a place where Mason could order a drink. He took Mason's arm and steered him through a side door. Inside, the Disney employees recognized Mason and helped usher the actor into the backseat of one of the boats.

Mason fell gratefully across the entire bench, and Smith took the bench in front of him. The boat floated silently around to the waiting area, where tourists filled the other seats, and then it cruised into darkness while loudspeakers played "Hooray for Hollywood!"

On either side of them, animatronic figures danced and sang. Smith had taken the ride many times, and knew it well: The munchkins from *The Wizard of Oz,* Tarzan swinging on his jungle vine, Rhett Butler sweeping Scarlett O'Hara into his arms. The tourists were having a great time, ducking when Jimmy Cagney fired his machine gun across the bow of the boat, and singing along with Gene Kelly in *Singin' in the Rain.*

At last the ride was over and the pier came back into view. Smith waved at the Disney guide in charge of unloading the boats. But there was a strange look on her face.

"What have you done with Mr. Devereaux?" she asked. Smith turned. The rear bench was empty.

W H A T do you think, Billy?" Raven Charles was feeling strangely depressed, now that she had faced Ashley and defeated her. The woman had almost fled from her office, half an hour ago. Ivan Bloom had looked after her with mixed emotions, which gradually brightened into relief. Now Raven, left alone with Baxter, fell back on an office couch and kicked off her shoes.

"Think? About this? We won. St. Ives is history."

"About Mason. Do you think Ashley knew what she was talking about? Did Mason know the gun was going to be fired? Did he arrange the death of Bradleigh Court?"

"When you got a drunk like Mason," Billy said, "you don't go looking for complications, because he couldn't keep them straight. I thought about that *Phantom* shooting backwards and forwards—and remember, I was out drinking with Mason later the same night it happened. The whole Bradleigh Court murder theory falls down on two simple points. Nobody knew Court was gonna even be at the theater that day—so how could they plan to shoot him? And, two, what bang do they get for their buck? Why jeopardize the run of the play by killing the star?"

Raven sighed and wriggled her toes. Tension had been building in her for weeks. "Can Mason play the *Phantom?*" she asked. "Is he too far gone?"

"Could he ever?"

"The Mason I remember could have."

"Then he still can. Of course, I may not remember the same Mason."

THE wind blew strong off the ocean at Malibu, and Ashley St. Ives stood at the water's edge and screamed at it. There was no one close enough to hear. She had driven to the beach immediately after her meeting with Raven Charles—the meeting that was supposed to have ended with Ashley producing the *Phantom,* but ended instead in defeat when Ivan, the rat, revealed that he had videotaped everything.

That tape, she knew, destroyed her hopes of making the film. It also neatly ended her run as Mason Devereaux's agent. When Mason saw the tape—and she was sure he would—he would see her accusing her own client of murder, and blackmailing his friends with the information.

Ashley turned and walked back up the sand to the house for one last time. Ivan had kicked her out. The movers were packing her things. What a traitor! His betrayal went against Ashley's sacred law of Hollywood relationships, which said that if you slept with a guy, he should at least stand behind you if you were trying to screw someone else.

Now what could she do? She no longer had Mason as a client. All her plans were destroyed. Even her fallback position, a palimony suit, was out of the question because of the videotape, on which she had not behaved like a pal.

THE security arrangements at Disney World are crafted for discreet efficiency. The script says guests should never be aware of a guard nearby, and yet guards are everywhere—the innocuous tourist with the camera around his neck, the jolly redhead in the Mickey Mouse T-shirt, the bald guy fanning himself outside the Indiana Jones show. Sometimes even the familiar figures of Donald Duck or Pluto conceal eagle-eyed security men, scanning the crowds for potential trouble.

Early in the afternoon of July 3, an unusual all-points alert went out to every beeper on the property. Mason Devereaux, the famous

British actor who was to lead the Fourth of July parade, had wandered off drunk and was lost somewhere on the 23,000 acres.

Jay Smith, the Disney host in charge of Devereaux, was standing in the control booth at the Great Movie Ride, telling his story over the phone to the park security chief: "He wanted to go somewhere cool and dark, so I took him in here, and he collapsed across the backseat of the tourist boat. I sat immediately in front of him. He was all right when the ride began. When we got back to the boarding dock, he had disappeared."

No, Smith had not spoken to Mason during the ride. No, he had not heard an outcry, or a splash. Yes, he now realized he should have sat next to Devereaux—but the actor had sprawled sideways across the entire bench, and Smith had thought it tactful to leave him that way.

M ASON was under fire. A gangster had jumped out from behind a doorway and was blazing at him with a machine gun. Two men in an old car had drawn up and were returning the fire with their own weapons. Somewhere a woman was screaming. There seemed to be a small stream running down the center of the street, and Mason jumped into it, heedless of the current, and began to run, awkwardly bent over, to get out of the line of fire. Sirens wailed. The gangster screamed "Take that, you lousy copper!" and sprayed the car with bullets.

Mason escaped being hit, and ducked into a tunnel that led behind the gangster's hideout. Where was he, in some kind of sewer? Soaking wet, he walked through the waist-high water toward a light ahead, and suddenly found himself in a jungle. He clambered up onto the bank.

"*Aaaiiieee!*" A figure clad in a loincloth swept down out of the trees, his foot slamming Mason on the side of his head. Mason toppled forward, unconscious, into the jungle foliage. Five minutes later, as a team of security guards waded past with flashlights, his form was invisible in the tall grasses. He had no idea how long he was out, before another savage scream brought him back to his senses. Tarzan was swinging once again above his head. Mason crept forward on his hands and knees, slipping through the thick growth on the riverbank, until he emerged dripping at what seemed to be another tunnel.

What was going on here? Was he dreaming? Dead? In the midst of some monstrous alcoholic hallucination? He splashed water on his face, and it felt wet and cold—not like a dream. There was only one thing to do: Keep going forward, and hope that somehow he would muddle through to the other side of the nightmare. The knot on his head, where he had been kicked by Tarzan, was throbbing now. He was dizzy, reaching for handholds, when an evil witch appeared in an explosion of smoke and pointed her broomstick at him, cackling. He turned to run but fell over a munchkin at his feet.

In a sheer panic, he ran blindly ahead, until—Good God, was that Judy Garland? Surely she was dead? And yet she sang: "Somewhere, over the rainbow . . ." Mason laughed maniacally, and sloshed ahead through the cold water, muttering under his breath: "Why, oh why, can't I?"

"Just singin', and dancin', in the rain . . ."

Now it was Gene Kelly in his slick yellow overcoat. Mason was growing annoyed. He did not like to be toyed with, not even by hallucinations. He stood next to a lamppost and watched Kelly splashing through puddles of water, until a sudden rain shower burst over his head. Anger flared within him. He would see whether these were the bloody DTs! Mason ran forward and tried to snatch the umbrella from Kelly's fingers, but it was held in a tight grip, and as he wrestled with the dancing figure, he became vaguely aware that a boat full of people was passing a few feet behind him.

"Look!" a voice screamed. "It's Mason Devereaux—the guy on TV!"

He turned to see a dozen tourists training their cameras on him. Flashes burst, and the bright lights exploded in his head. With a desperate heave he tore the umbrella from Gene Kelly's hands and used it as a shield against the invaders. Then Kelly, who was holding onto the lamppost with one hand, swung around and caught Mason full in the jaw with an elbow. Mason, who remembered a thing or two from his early days in a rugby scrum, planted a foot

behind Kelly's leg while pushing forward with his shoulder, Kelly went down in a wet heap, his arms and legs waving mechanically in the air, his head jerking from side to side as he continued to sing: "What a glorious feelin', I'm happy again!"

Mason crouched over his victim, a heavy hand planted on Kelly's chest, and looked up, snarling, as more flashbulbs detonated. Who were these people, and why wouldn't they leave him alone? From the corner of his eye, he could see a guide in a blue blazer climb out of the boat and creep cautiously toward him. He wouldn't lay a hand on Mason. This was war. Mason whirled and ran into a shop front on the wet sidewalk. It opened onto a darkened area. He slammed into another wall. His fingers found a push-bar, he threw his body against it, and a second later he was in blinding sunshine.

He kept on running. He could hear voices calling behind him, but he paid no heed, running until his lungs were burning, up a staircase, the pursuers close behind, and into a train, the doors closing before they could catch him. The monorail glided away, and he was safe for the moment, gulping great lungsful of air, until the doors opened again and he hurled himself through them, tumbling down a flight of stairs. At the bottom he leapt to his feet, wild-eyed, teeth bared, and pushed blindly through a crowd until a big black shoe tripped him, and he fell crashing to the ground.

"Mason Devereaux," a voice said sadly. It sounded like the voice of his fate. "Look at you. Don't you think it's time to clean up your act? Just because you're an alcoholic doesn't mean you have to be a drunk."

Mason rolled over with a groan. His eyes were blinded by the glare, but then a large friendly face blocked out the sun, and he found himself looking up into the warm brown eyes of Goofy.

T HE still photos stink bad enough. But that's not all. Now it turns out one of the tourists had a video camera, and is trying to sell the footage to 'Geraldo.'"

It was the next morning. Billy (Silver Dollar) Baxter was pacing restlessly on the expensive rug in his new office at Realistic Pictures, talking to Raven Charles.

"Damage control? Don't make me laugh. Mason gets plastered, falls off a boat during the Great Movie Ride, and ends up in a wrestling match with Gene Kelly—who wins. The next time we see him, he's passed out cold and being carried to an ambulance in the arms of Goofy."

Baxter picked up a copy of *Daily Variety.* "Have you seen the trades? They got a real cute headline: 'Mason Jarred.' This isn't a miniseries, Raven. It's a stand-up routine. Forget about Mason for the *Phantom.* The fat lady just sang."

He reached in his pocket for a silver dollar and absentmindedly began to walk it across the backs of his fingers. "Hello?" He looked at the receiver and hung it up. A second later his door opened and Raven Charles appeared in person.

"I hung up, Billy. The walls in my office have ears." She walked over to the window and drew the blinds. Then she stood with her eyes closed, and it seemed to him that she was trembling.

"I know it's rough on you, kiddo," Billy said. "You were counting on Mason to make his big comeback in the *Phantom*. Me too. But he's a bad pony and I ain't gonna bet on him. The papers are filled with all the snapshots the tourists took, showing Mason out of his mind, swinging from the vines with Tarzan. What do you think the actuaries are saying right now? Is this the guy they want to insure as the lead in a fifty million–dollar musical?"

Raven had a solemn face. "Maybe he really is a lost cause," she said.

"Maybe?" Billy spread out the morning papers on his desk. "Take a look at this. The tourists had their Brownies out when Mason took the Great Movie Ride."

Raven looked at the photos that had been flashed all over the world, showing Mason kicking a munchkin and grabbing an umbrella away from the Gene Kelly robot.

"After this caper," Billy said, "there's only one role for Mason that the public is gonna believe: Spokesmodel for the Betty Ford Center."

"They say you have to hit bottom before you want to get better," Raven mused. "Maybe when Mason sees these pictures . . ."

"Raven, sweetie! You ain't seriously still considering this lush for the *Phantom*? There goes your career."

"I'm flying to the hospital in Florida," Raven said. "I want to see Mason face-to-face. And call Sheila Chesham in England. He needs to talk to someone he can trust."

"M Y name is Goofy, and I'm an alcoholic."
Mason Devereaux was buried inside a nightmare. He thrashed between hospital sheets that were soaked with his sweat, and groaned aloud, hallucinating that he was at an AA meeting at Disney World.

"Hello, Goofy!" The room was filled with famous faces—rabbits and mice, dogs and dwarfs, a pig wearing a cap with red plaid ear-muffs, and an old duck with dollar signs for eyeballs. At the front of the room, Goofy lit a cigarette and sipped from a cup of coffee. "Are there any newcomers? Anyone attending a meeting for the first time? Out-of-towners?"

Mason raised his arm. It felt made of stone. "My . . . my name is Mason," he said. "I'm from London."

There was a long pause.

"And???" Goofy said, encouragingly. "*And???*"

But Mason had forgotten his lines. The old flop sweat was back again. All of the eyes in the room were on him—even the mermaid in the corner. A rabbit with buck teeth turned around and prompted him in a stage whisper: "And you're an alcoholic."

"And I may . . . possibly . . . have a slight drinking problem . . ." Mason said, forcing the words between clenched teeth. One of the dwarfs snickered, but he saw that a single tear ran down the mermaid's cheek.

I T ' S a fairly serious case of withdrawal hallucinations, but prob-ably not the classic DTs," the cheerful woman in the red cardi-gan told Raven and Sheila, late the next day. "Let's put it this way. He's seeing mice, but they're wearing red suspenders."

"How long will this go on?" Sheila asked. She had not slept since she got on the direct flight to Orlando, and there were dark tired circles under her eyes. Raven Charles had met her at the airport and briefed her on Mason's condition.

"He should begin to come around by tomorrow morning."

"And then?"

"He shouldn't even think about making plans until he does some-thing about his drinking. Someplace like Betty Ford might be good for him. They're used to celebrities and people who think they're the exception to the rule."

"He's that bad?"

"We never use words like good or bad," she said. "But he's bad."

Raven took Sheila's arm. "Let's go for a little walk," she said. The two women left the hospital detox ward and walked out into the July Florida heat. Sprinklers were making lazy circles in the air.

"Is there any hope?" Sheila asked. "What do you think?"

Raven smiled. "Of course there's hope," she said. "Alcoholism is the only disease you can decide to get well from."

"But what a choice for Mason to make!"

"Between life and death? You're right. A lot of drunks puzzle over that one for years."

PART EIGHT
─────

La La

T HE big seagoing yacht lazily turned the corner into the Newport Beach harbor and came to rest. Takeuchi, sipping coffee
on the aft deck, nodded with approval. The crew had safely
brought the ship from the French Riviera, down through the Canal,
and now up here for his use in Southern California, where he had
boarded only today. He had flown ahead to Hollywood immediately
after the Cannes Festival, of course—after the upheaval when he
bought Realistic Pictures, and the sensation when that rat-faced little man had skewered himself on the roulette wheel, and Mason
Devereaux had been saved.

Takeuchi threw the morning paper to another man sitting with
him on the deck.

"Look at this," he said. "Sensational. If you can get stories like this,
circulation will take care of itself."

The other man picked up the paper with one hand and looked
lazily at the shots of Mason in drunkland. Then he threw it back on
the table. The man's name was Spike
Murphy. At the age of thirty he had a
hard-boiled reputation as a swashbuck-
ling scandalmonger whose only gods
were the circulation figures. Takeuchi
had hired him to launch *Fact Digest*, a
supermarket sleaze sheet.

"It needs a new twist," Murphy said.

Takeuchi raised an eyebrow and
glanced down again at the shots of Devereaux in combat with a munchkin.

"This isn't good enough for you?"

SPIKE MURPHY

1 6 8

"It's old news," Murphy said. "Weekly papers like ours have to develop exclusives, not reprint the mainstream sheets. Handled properly, this story could be brought along, developed, enhanced, until it put your paper on the map. We'd be making news, not reporting it. Just fill me in on one thing. Do you have Devereaux under contract to Realistic?"

"Raven Charles thought at one time he might be a good choice to play the Phantom. Now . . ."

Takeuchi looked at the papers and shrugged.

"He might be a good choice to play a much larger role than that," Murphy mused. "One that I would personally write for him. One that he could play in this world, and the next."

"You're not thinking of harming Mason?"

"If I have my way, he'll live forever."

MASON had not seen a blanket so neatly folded since his Army service. He stood back and admired his handiwork. Each of the corners was square and tight. You could bounce a silver dollar off the top of the bed—and Mason did, using a dollar Billy Baxter had given him. This was definitely a shipshape bed. Mason sat down on it, buried his head in his hands, and groaned.

The flight from Orlando to Palm Springs had been agony, even with Raven and Sheila to hold his hands. He had been without drink for three days—his longest dry spell since that time in the 1960s he'd made the movie in the Tibetan monastery. Every nerve in his body had vibrated independently, and his voice was a croak. But that wasn't the worst. The worst was that everyone on the airplane had recognized him, and he was sure they were snickering at him behind their in-flight magazines.

Now here he was at the Betty Ford Center, living in what looked like a college dormitory room, encouraged to drink all the fruit juice he wanted. Mason hated fruit. It drew flies and spoiled the taste of alcohol. The center's routine had been explained to him. There would be group therapy meetings morning and afternoon, sessions with his counselor in between, AA meetings once a day, and opportunities to participate in mild exercise. Mason regarded the exercise with a particular loathing. There was something profoundly un-dignified about standing outdoors with a group of strangers, flapping one's arms. Presumably through this process he would grow sober, a condition he could barely imagine.

There was a knock at his door, and Mason creaked to his feet and opened it. It was his counselor, a round-faced man known to everyone as Humble Howard.

"Time for afternoon group," Howard said. He stepped aside and let Mason precede him down the hallway into a central area where a dozen recovering alcoholics were waiting. Mason vaguely recognized one of them, a woman who wrote best-selling sex novels. Every one of them knows me, he reflected bitterly, even though they may pretend they don't. Why do they call it Alcoholics Anonymous, when I am the least anonymous drunk in the world? Maybe I could become an anonymous sober person. It would be a change.

"Mason, darling." It was the novelist, a loud woman with a mane of streaked blond hair. They had met yesterday. She'd said they'd met once before, at a Buckingham Palace garden party, or perhaps backstage at an Elton John concert. He said he doubted he had ever attended any such event. She said he could hardly forget a royal garden party. He chuckled dryly to himself. She had no idea what he was capable of forgetting. Today, seeing her, Mason's thoughts were in a muddle. Her name was either Victoria or Regina, of that he was certain. Perhaps it was Trudy. Her anonymity, Mason reflected, is safe with me.

WEEKS passed. Forbidden the newspapers, not allowed to watch TV, safe from the outside world, Mason Devereaux lay on his back in the sun with his hands cradled behind his head and listened to the wind blow in the palms overhead. And he thought.

He meditated on a lifetime spent in the close company of drink, which had become his friend when he was sixteen years old and had stood by him, through thick and thin, for more than thirty years. In those early days the booze had worked to give him confidence, when he went out after work with the older actors he idolized so much— O'Toole and Warner, Finney and Courtenay. He had been the kid, but after a few pints of strong bitter, he was holding his own in the shoptalk.

Bradleigh Court had been a friend as well as a rival in those days. Poor Bradleigh, now dead, but compensated somewhat (Mason consoled himself) by becoming forever immortal as a hero of macabre stage folklore. Bradleigh, who went back to his hotel room on those provincial tours, and read Shakespeare into the mirror while Mason drank with the older actors. Bradleigh, whose voice had never matched Mason's unforgettable sound, but who soldiered away until finally, in his thirties, he was getting the roles that Mason would once have taken, while Mason was closing pubs instead of opening in plays.

But now I have a second chance, Mason thought. Bradleigh is dead. But I am alive and breathing and stretched out full-length on the grass and the birds are singing and the sky is blue. And perhaps if I do not drink again, I need no longer be a laughingstock.

He rolled on his side and opened his eyes to look over the lawn of the Betty Ford Center. Of course, thought Mason, I may never act again. I may grow sober, but the public will always remember me as a silly buffoon, falling down wells and blundering about with a mask stuck over my face. But there are other things I can do besides act. I can direct. Produce. Do the voices on airline commercials. The ad agencies have been without the voice of God ever since Orson Welles died. Or perhaps I could move to Thorn Hill with dear Sheila, and chat with her father about his spiders. If she would have me, an unemployed actor with every shred of dignity removed.

F IRST, we would use a tranquilizer, to calm the sleeper," the Sandman explained to Murphy. "We would allow the body to complete any digestive housekeeping that might be in progress. Then we would lower the temperature to a deep coma state. We would massage it carefully with oils, to preserve skin tone, and then lower the body temperature still further, until the central organs ceased to function. To a layman, this state resembles death, but of course we know better."

"Of course we do," said Spike Murphy. The two men were parked in a car overlooking the Pacific Ocean, safe from eavesdroppers. The real name of the man Murphy was talking to was Dr. Joseph Coyne, but in the chilly little world of cryogenics, the Sandman had won his nickname because he actually believed he was only putting his clients to sleep.

"We flush the bloodstream and replace it with an organic antifreeze. It's based on oil of peppermint, which we obtain from the finest health food stores. Then, very quickly, we drop the body close to absolute zero. It's all routine."

"What about waking him up?" Murphy asked. "How routine is that?"

"Until now, the cryogenics industry has never had occasion to awaken anyone," the Sandman explained patiently. "All of our clients are still asleep."

Murphy sent a cigarette spinning out the car window. "What if you can't wake him up?"

"The key word is *yet*," said the Sandman carefully. "In the industry, we believe that eventually science will develop procedures for awakening all of our clients. If we can't awaken a sleeper now, we'll do it later."

"How much later?"

"As much later as it takes."

THE part of the AA meeting that Mason liked the best came right at the end, when they all linked hands and said the Serenity Prayer: "God, grant me the serenity to accept the things I cannot change, the courage to change the things I can, and the wisdom to know the difference."

When Mason had heard the prayer on his first day at the Betty Ford Center, he had almost gagged: It struck him as the sort of sentiment one might find on a cheaply printed card, pressed into one's palm at the bus station. Strange how the words had lately started to appeal to him.

The little group in the conference room dropped their hands when the meeting was over, and went wandering their separate ways. Mason lingered behind, drifting in the direction of Marjorie

Whittaker, the trash novelist. Discouraged from smoking during the meeting, Marjorie Whittaker had pulled a Marlboro out of her purse and was lighting it even before Mason could spring forward with his Zippo.

Mason was developing warm feelings toward Marjorie. Over the last month they had found themselves increasingly thrown together, perhaps because they were both British exiles in California, perhaps because they were about the same age, perhaps because, as Mason reflected, they both had a deep tidal longing for some sort of mooring post, after the confused years of alcoholism.

They went out walking in the early desert dusk, the sky a deep violet, the air already chilly with the approach of evening. Mason asked Marjorie the one question that was always safe at the center: "How's your program?"

"Fair. I can hardly get to sleep at night, my mind is racing so quickly with scenes from my past life. When I was drinking, I had all these alibis. All these explanations about why I was right and the world was wrong. I always thought I was the victim, and everybody else was stupid or cruel if they didn't understand why I needed to drink every day. The things I put my husbands through!"

"Quite," said Mason, determined not to be topped in self-abnegation. "I sat in a pub for years cherishing the myth that I was a great actor whose roles had been stolen away by ambitious social climbers and greedy agents. But when I sat down and forced myself to tick off those lost roles, I discovered that in most cases I had been too hung over to show up for the auditions."

"Oh, Mason, what's to happen to us?"

"It is rather frightening, isn't it? When I was drinking, life was predictable. I would get up, I would get drunk, I would go to bed. In between I would earn a living, to the degree that it didn't interfere with my drinking. Now I wake up and I have absolutely no idea what will happen to me all day long. Rather stimulating."

Marjorie nodded and began to stroll, and as he matched her pace their hands somehow found each other's. Mason quickly withdrew his hand, a guilty impulse, because romantic attachments among the patients were frowned upon. His eyes stole sideways to look at

Whittaker, who had been gaudy with makeup in her early days at the Center but had scrubbed up quite nicely into a handsome woman. Then he felt a little tug in his heart, wondering how Sheila Chesham might have felt, to see that quick furtive moment of their hands.

As Mason's stay in the center drew to a close, Murphy began making daily visits to the anonymous brick building in the Valley that held the Sandman's laboratories. He had developed a skewered respect for the cryogenicist. It was safe enough to take people's money with the assurance that they would awaken long after they, and you, were dead. But to take their money and promise short-term results: Now that took balls. The Sandman was even rumored to work with clients who were not yet quite dead at the time of his services, a practice frowned upon in the cryogenics industry.

One afternoon Murphy met with the scientist in what was known as the Refrigeration Room. He swung open the big insulated door, and found the Sandman sitting in an aluminum lawn chair and reading some papers.

"Comfy?" Murphy asked.

"Quite. The metabolism slows down in the cold, and so one lives longer by sitting in such a room as this."

"How much of a difference does it make in a lifetime?"

"Perhaps as much as twenty minutes."

"Is it worth the trouble?"

The Sandman shrugged. "Would you make me a gift of twenty minutes of your life, this moment?"

"No way."

The Sandman smiled and looked at a clipboard he was holding. "I have some progress to report."

"Great!" said Murphy, wrapping his arms around himself to keep warm.

"I think we can talk in terms of two years. Or twenty months, to be on the safe side."

"We're talking about, you freeze him, you bring him back, good as new?"

The Sandman winced. "Approximately as good as new, Mr. Murphy. We're using a process that's on the cutting edge, you know. New methods, new technology. Approximately, would be the best word."

Murphy nodded. "How much?" he said.

"For Mr. Devereaux," the Sandman said, "I could make you a price of $200,000. That's cash, of course. You save a little because we're not talking about long-term storage."

HUMBLE HOWARD, the counselor in charge of Mason's group, did not like to hug people, and he did not like to be hugged. In his opinion, hugging had taken on far too much prominence in the recovery business. "I spent twenty years in bars, hugging drunks every time the Dodgers won a game," he liked to say. "I didn't sober up in order to hug former drunks."

Graduation day at the Ford Center was therefore a difficult time for Howard, who had to deflect the newly sober clients as they came trotting toward him with their arms outstretched. He was grateful for someone like Mason Devereaux, for whom a handshake was embarrassingly intimate, and so Mason and Howard lurked together in a corner, shaded by a potted plant, and watched the hugging from a safe distance.

"How many of them do you imagine will stay sober?" Mason asked.

"Of those who want to be sober, and go to their AA meetings, almost all," said Howard. "The others will have their work cut out for them."

"I must tell you that I feel like a new man," said Mason, who found such words painful but felt he had to say them anyway. "I've emerged from a fog of thirty years' duration."

"Yeah, well, don't get all carried away," Howard cautioned him. "Some people, they leave here, they have a relapse because they get depressed. Other people, they have a relapse because they're so happy to be sober they decide to have a drink to celebrate."

"Mason!" cried Marjorie Whittaker, spotting him from across the room. The trash novelist was wearing a red summer frock, cut low in the front, as a costume for her entry into the sober world, and had a matching straw hat with a wide floppy brim. She swept across the room toward him, her arms wide for a hug, but Mason was able to position himself subtly behind the potted palm.

"Dinner tonight, back in the world of the civilians?" she asked. "Morton's? Spago? My treat! Now that we're sober they're actually going to be happy to see us!"

Humble Howard looked concerned. "It might be wise," he said, "to stay out of some of the old places until you're comfortable with sobriety . . ."

"Darling Howard!" Marjorie said. "Those places know all about people who don't drink. Wolfgang has even added a water steward, to go along with the wine man."

Mason allowed himself a chuckle. "When you and I were drinking," he said, "we would have had nothing to do with one another. You at Morton's and me at my pub in London."

"And now you're my favorite sweetie pie," said Marjorie, throwing her arms around him at last and planting a large red kiss on his nose.

"Hello, Mason."

The voice was quiet, but he could not mistake it. He looked over Marjorie's shoulder, past the wide-brimmed hat, and saw the soft eyes of Sheila Chesham. She held a bouquet of flowers for him. Mason freed himself from Marjorie and moved back a step.

"Hello, Sheila," he said. "I didn't expect to see you here today."

"I'm so happy for you," she said simply. "This is the best thing you have ever done for yourself."

"Yes," he said. "Yes, I think it is."

Marjorie turned to look at the newcomer and then fished in her purse for a mirror and lipstick.

"Sheila Chesham . . . Marjorie Whittaker . . ."

The two women looked at each other, and knew in a glance that they were rivals. They exchanged a cold handshake. Mason discovered that in sobriety he had not forgotten how to be a coward. He escaped the tension between them by awkwardly excusing himself and actually crossing the room toward the big coffeepot.

As he fled, Devereaux felt his heart pounding. He had carried on a flirtation with Marjorie, it was true, despite the lectures by the staff against the dangers of romance to the newly sober. They had held hands and even actually kissed one night in the moonlight, but now Mason found himself suddenly caught up in an enormous new emotion, stronger and more pure than anything he had experienced during thirty years dulled by drinking.

He was in love. Most helplessly in love, with Sheila Chesham. The moment he had seen her, he had been blindsided by emotion. He was tremendously moved that she had flown out from England to be with him on this day. Suddenly it all became clear: All of those long months when she had stood by his side, all of her patience, all of her empathy, all of her quiet beauty, her strength, her humor, her intelligence, and the way she had seen him make a public fool of himself and yet had not lost faith.

Mason felt his eyes misting. He turned to tell Sheila what he had just discovered, but saw her still trapped in some kind of stilted conversation with Marjorie. A sob welled up in his throat, and he walked blindly out the door.

S HEILA, looking across the room, saw Mason leave. She listened impatiently to Marjorie's litany about the miracle of Mason's recovery, and was finally able to break off the conversation. She turned quickly to follow him. But Raven Charles had just arrived—another guest at Mason's graduation—and she smiled warmly at Sheila.

"I'm surprised to find you still here," Raven said. "I thought you would have left with Mason."

"Mason hasn't left yet," Sheila said. "He's just outside."

"But I could swear I saw him leave," Raven said. "Just a second ago. In a car with two men."

"It couldn't have been Mason," Sheila said. "He would never have left without saying good-bye."

She ran out into the parking lot, but there was nobody there. She looked around the lawn, and then back inside the Center. Raven joined her quietly.

"You're sure it was Mason?"

"It was Mason," Raven said. "He didn't seem to see me. He seemed to be having some sort of argument with the two men."

"I don't know what this means," Sheila said, "but whatever it means, it's not good."

Raven saw the fear in Sheila's eyes. She took the cellular phone from her purse and dialed 911.

I N the darkness on board the *Rashomon,* two cigars glowed and faded, and then one of them was flung over the side, spinning through the dark like a falling star. The night was so still that Spike Murphy could hear the hiss when it hit the water.

"If I don't have your full backing on this, of course I won't go ahead," he said at last.

Takeuchi's cigar illuminated his eyes, which were regarding Murphy intently.

"We are talking about life and death, Mr. Murphy," he said at last.

"Life, and death . . . and then life again," Murphy said.

"Does this man know what he is talking about? This Sandman? What is his name?"

"Joe Coyne. They call him the Sandman because he sincerely believes he is merely putting his clients to sleep, only to reawaken them at a later date."

"He freezes them?"

"Yes. He brings them down close to absolute zero. The theory is that they can be revived years from now. For example, if a client is dying of a disease with no cure, the Sandman can freeze him until a cure is found."

"Ah, yes. Like Walt Disney."

"According to the Sandman, that's an urban legend. Walt was never frozen."

Takeuchi nodded. "Walt wanted it that way." He studied the end of his cigar. "Has anyone ever been awakened from such a sleep?"

"No, but the Sandman has an answer for that. He says that under the terms of the typical contract in the cryogenics industry, nobody who has ever been frozen is due to be awakened yet."

"But now you want him to freeze Mason Devereaux."

Murphy shifted in his deck chair. His mouth felt dry, and he was impressed by the enormity of his plan.

"What if . . ." he began. "What if . . . you only froze a guy for a couple of years? And thawed him out before the tissues broke down? What if you didn't freeze him solid, but only slowed him down? The Sandman thinks it would work."

It was strange, how giving voice to such unthinkable actions made them seem possible.

"And if it does work, Mr. Murphy? What are your plans?"

"We'd leave Mason Devereaux in the cooler for, say, twenty

months. After all of his weird adventures, he's probably the most famous man alive. Certainly the easiest to get our hands on. And yet there isn't anyone to protect him, or come looking for him, or give a damn if he disappears. There wouldn't be any messy diplomatic incidents, like if we froze the pope."

"Then what?"

"We fake his death. He's gone. But there are all these rumors that he's been sighted. Our papers feed the rumors. Mason is sighted in a shopping mall in Sandusky, Ohio. At a Chicago Bulls game. His ghost haunts the opera. Then, just when the rumors get completely ridiculous—we produce him! *Fact Digest* scoops the world by producing Mason Devereaux, alive and well, from beyond the grave."

"But Mason will testify against you?"

"How can he? He has absolutely no idea what happened to him." Murphy's voice quickened with enthusiasm. "He's in love with us, because we saved his life. When we thaw him out, we implant hypnotic suggestions about where he's been. While he was dead, see, Mason left his material body and was welcomed onto the next level by a superior being who took him on a tour of the universe. Mason holds a press conference and announces that he has all the answers. He's been down a black hole. He knows what caused the big bang, and how it could have been prevented. And he has a personal message from Elvis to his fans. We get a dozen covers out of him, and then it's all recycled on TV."

Takeuchi allowed himself a gravelly chuckle.

"But why go to the bother of freezing him? Why not simply hold him prisoner somewhere?"

"One, if he's conscious, he causes trouble. Two, he can testify against us. Three, we produce papers showing that he had a deadly disease and requested that he be cryogenically frozen. We tell him he signed them, and that we cured him. Four, even if we can't thaw him out, at least we have a great scoop about his present whereabouts. The Sandman is utterly trustworthy because he's a mad genius who cares only about funding for his experiments. Fifth . . ."

Takeuchi held up a hand to silence him. Then he stood and

walked to the rail, and when he spun around, his face was a mask of anger. "This entire scheme is criminal, illegal, and utterly foolhardy," he said.

Murphy said nothing.

"I categorically forbid you to go ahead with it," Takeuchi said. "What do you take me for, a fool? Building circulation is one thing, Mr. Murphy. A man's life is something else."

Takeuchi pushed a call button, and a crew member came to take Murphy ashore. As the *Rashomon* fell behind and the tender chopped toward the dock, Murphy turned Takeuchi's instructions over in his mind. There was one detail he had not shared with the press lord. Devereaux's temperature was around ninety degrees, and falling.

SHEILA CHESHAM had driven back to Los Angeles with Raven Charles in her limousine. She had Raven drop her off at the Bel Air, and now she sat in the hotel garden, looking sightlessly at a cup of tea. Raven had asked to stay, but Sheila had told her she wanted to be alone. It had been such an ordeal, talking to the police, hearing Raven tell her story over and over, listening to the tiresome Marjorie Whittaker testify that Mason had experienced a complete recovery and would "never never never" have gone off for a drink.

Sheila realized this was the end of the road. She had flown to California to support Mason on the day of his reentry into normal life. But Mason, it appeared, was not ready for normality. Who else could disappear in broad daylight with friends all around him? He wasn't an actor, he was a magician. She still cared deeply for Mason, but Sheila realized it was time to get on with her life. She could not spend forever waiting for Mason Devereaux to put together twenty-four sane hours in a row.

THIS was the part of the job Spike Murphy enjoyed the most: The deadline rush before the last pages of *Fact Digest* were sent to the printers. He loved to play with the headlines, to search for the perfect word that would spring out from the supermarket display rack and force readers to pick up his newspaper, even against their will. Tonight, with a scoop on one of the biggest celebrity stories of the year, he admired his latest masterpiece:

DRUNK TANK SPRINGS LEAK!

MASON DRIES OUT, EVAPORATES

The story, written mostly in boldface capitals and breathless italics, told of Mason Devereaux's mysterious disappearance from the Betty Ford Center, where he had just completed treatment for his "world-famous drinking problem."

"Fruit juice was served at a closed-door reception," it said, "as Mason was congratulated by celebrity friends including curvaceous British heiress Sheila Chesham and Raven Charles, the glamorous Hollywood studio chief—BEFORE HE DISAPPEARED INTO THIN AIR!"

Photographs showed Sheila and Raven as they emerged from the Palm Desert Police Department after filing a missing-persons report, and a sidebar story quoted "Russia's leading expert on spontaneous human combustion," who speculated, "decades of vodka and cigarettes may have turned Mason into a HUMAN TIME BOMB primed to EXPLODE in the SCORCHING DESERT SUN."

It was, Murphy congratulated himself, a fabulous front page. How Takeuchi would like it was another matter. He handed the proof to a copyboy, and picked up a hot line to double the print order. The paper was ordinarily printed a week in advance, but for this story Murphy hadn't even blinked at the printer's overtime bill. This was the story that would put his paper on the map—and blow the *National Examiner* out of the water.

The copy kid looked at the page and said, "Jeez, where do you think this guy could have disappeared to?"

"Thin air," said Murphy. "Don't you read the paper?"

MASON floated in and out of consciousness. The sensation was like emerging from anesthesia after major surgery—or waking up with a hangover. He was vaguely aware that he was on a bed in a darkened and silent room. A blanket covered him, and rails on either side of the bed kept him from falling to the floor. He would painfully begin to form a thought—What happened?

Where did everybody go?—and then he would slip into unconscious-ness again.

Once he was awakened by the impression that a shadowy figure was standing by the side of his bed, but Mason slipped away again before he could look for its face. Another time, jerking his hand spontaneously, he became aware that an intravenous tube was taped to it.

In his hallucinatory dreams, Sheila and Raven swam in and out of focus, congratulating him for having sobered up at last. Then their faces would turn into sorrowful masks, and he would think to himself, I got drunk again! But when, and how? I know I'm drunk, but I can't remember taking the first drink! Then Sheila would walk away from him, down a dark tunnel, her face turned away after a last reproachful look. In his dream, he would reach out a hand toward her, and then a sharp pain would remind him of the tube dripping into his vein.

THROUGH the locked, soundproofed door of Mason's room, and down a long corridor, in a cheerful office filled with green plants, Spike Murphy and the Sandman drank coffee. On the table in front of them, half a dozen daily papers were spread out, all of them headlining Devereaux's disappearance. Murphy scanned the *Los Angeles Daily News*, smiled, and threw it onto the top of the stack.

"It's the first time in history," he said, "that a supermarket paper has scooped the mainstream dailies. The ink wasn't dry on our pressrun when my phone started ringing with reporters trying to find out what my sources are. Every TV network in the world is camped outside of our offices.

"And only we know the secret," said the Sandman, making a lit-tle tent with his fingers.

"How is he?" Murphy asked.

"In excellent shape. The stay at the Ford Center was good for him. Healthy nutrition, rest, regular hours, no drinking—you might say they prepped him for us very nicely."

"And . . . he's strictly incognito?" Murphy said, tilting his head in the direction of the door.

"Nobody knows," the Sandman said. "I am the only person with the key to the Slumber Rooms."

"Good," said Murphy. "Then you and I are the only people alive who know what happened to Mason Devereaux."

"It went amazingly smoothly," the Sandman said.

"The way to kidnap your typical actor," Murphy pontificated, "is, just tell him his limousine is waiting. He gets in the backseat like he's on automatic pilot." He sipped his coffee, and then leaned closer to the Sandman, unconsciously lowering his voice. "I don't want you to put Mason completely under—not yet. Cool him down, keep him breathing, sedate him a little, put him where nobody will find him. But don't put him into a cryogenic state until we find out exactly how this story develops. I want to keep my options open."

"Of course I will do whatever you say," the Sandman said. "The extra delay will actually be good for Mason. It is the first time we have been allowed to work on a living subject. Freezing people after they are already dead is an example of unnecessary procrastination, don't you think?"

BILLY (SILVER DOLLAR) BAXTER scowled at the same front page that Murphy had earlier been admiring, and then threw it down on the desk of Raven Charles.

"Something stinks," the press agent said. He had been on the phone for hours, telling the press he could neither confirm nor deny that Mason had even been in the Betty Ford Center, and that Raven Charles had no comment on reports of his disappearance.

Raven was studying the latest issue of *Fact Digest*. "You do a lot of work with these trashy gossip sheets, don't you Billy?"

"Yeah. In the PR game, you spend half your time trying to keep your successful clients out of them, and the other half trying to get your unsuccessful clients into them."

"Do they have the same kind of deadlines as a real newspaper?"

"Naw. They make up half the stuff, so for that they don't have deadlines at all. The rest, they write it kinda vague, so you never know exactly when something happened. Or even in what country, half of the time."

"Mason disappeared on Saturday," Raven said. "It's Monday, and this paper has the story. How could they move so quickly?"

Billy took the paper from her and regarded it silently.

"They coulda printed it yesterday," he said. "This is an advance copy. But you've put your finger right on something. How did they get the story so fast?"

Their eyes met.

"There's only one possible explanation," Raven said. "They knew it was going to happen."

PART NINE

Afterdeath

I T was the Monday after Mason Devereaux's disappearance. A council of war gathered at noon in Raven Charles's offices at Realistic Pictures. Raven and Billy Baxter had called Sheila Chesham at the Bel Air and asked her to join them, and now they sat and listened to an FBI agent called John Kratz.

"You make a good case," Kratz told them. "From what we know about the deadlines of the weekly scandal sheets, there's no way *Fact Digest* could have printed the story about Mason unless they had some kind of advance knowledge. But these trash papers are tricky to go after. They have teams of expensive lawyers on twenty-four-hour call, ready to sue anyone who accuses them of anything. If you're going to charge them with kidnapping, you need some sort of proof."

"But it's right here in black and white," Billy said, waving a battered copy of *Fact Digest*. "Mason disappears on Saturday, and the presses roll on Sunday morning. How did they know so fast?"

"There's one possibility you may not have thought about," Kratz said. "They may have discovered Mason was in the recovery center, and staked it out. Sometimes they do that with celebrities. When he disappeared, they may have been the first to know. Maybe they had an informer on their payroll."

Raven picked up the sensational front page and then threw it down again. "You think they may know more than they're reporting?"

"They'll take a single fact and string it out for weeks."

"What do you recommend?"

"The paper is edited by a man named Spike Murphy," Kratz said. "I'm going to ask him to come in for an interview."

Billy Baxter picked up the paper. "Murphy," he said. "The name rings a bell." He squinted as he read the tiny type at the bottom of page two, which supplied the ownership and publishing information.

"Holy God!" he said. "You know who publishes this piece of crap? Takeuchi!"

Raven's hand flew to her phone, punching the code that would direct-dial the man who owned, not only the piece of crap, but also Realistic Pictures. As the others waited in silence, Sheila Chesham walked over unnoticed to the desk and picked up the paper. Down there in the same small type, she noticed, was the office address of *Fact Digest*.

DAY passed unnoticed into night in the twilight world of Mason Devereaux, whose mind surfaced occasionally into moments of awareness before drifting off again into troubled dreams. He had no idea how much time had passed, or where he was, or why he had been left alone in a room. If he were in a hospital, surely there would be doctors and nurses around? Other patients? Someone to bring him his meals? He could not remember eating anything since . . . before. That was the problem. When was then, and when was now? He had been in the Center, of that he was dimly certain, and now he was here. But how had he come from there to here?

During one period of consciousness, it occurred to him that perhaps this was death. Perhaps the mind took the immensity of death and converted it into images that it could understand, like a silent limbo in a darkened room. Then what about the man who came to see him sometimes? Was he an angel? A devil? He did not think it was God. Not with the face of a mad scientist.

Mason smiled for the first time in an eternity. Then he noticed that he smiled. Then he noticed that he noticed. He seemed more aware than he had been before. More conscious. He turned his head and looked around, and vaguely realized that he was in a hospital bed in an ordinary room with no windows and no other furniture except for a large steel storage cabinet. The fact that I am aware of this, he thought, shows that I am alive, not dead. He looked down at his hand, which was still attached to an intravenous drip. They do not have hospital equipment in heaven, he thought. No need for it, I hope.

His mind struggled to make sense of nonsense. He counted off the things he knew: He was alive. He was in a room. He was not in a hospital. If his friends knew where he was, they would come to see him—ergo, they did not know. The room was probably locked. He was probably a prisoner. He had been sober when he last remembered anything. Therefore, he was not hung over and not drunk. Therefore, he was drugged. Therefore, he had been drugged and was being held against his will. But now for some reason the effect of the drug was weakening, and so he could begin to figure all of this out. The logical mind, Mason thought, is a most wonderful possession.

The door opened and the man came in again. The mad scientist, as Mason thought of him, with his scrawny goatee, wearing a white lab coat and with a stethoscope around his neck. Mason closed his eyes and breathed slowly, as if he were still unconscious.

The Sandman took Mason's pulse and glanced at the intravenous drip. "Still sleeping soundly, my friend?" he said. "Dream on! For soon you will dream forever!"

Mason heard footsteps as the man walked across to the steel cabinet, and the sound of a key in a lock, and a door opening. Then he heard the man talking to himself. He had that peculiar note of unmistakable madness in his voice, and Mason envied him for it— he had been trying to find such a note for years on the stage.

" 'Take good care of him,' " the Sandman was saying, quoting Spike Murphy's instructions. " 'But don't put him under quite yet.' Not quite yet! What does he take me for? A criminal? I have no interest in his puerile newspaper story. All I care about is the conquest of time."

The footsteps came back across the floor toward Mason. He felt a cool alcohol swab on the inside of his left arm, and then the prick of a needle.

"Just to relax you, my friend," the voice said. "And soon we will drain you of your mortal blood, that allows you to live but dooms you to die. And then to sleep. How long would you like to slumber? One century? Two? A thousand years?"

The needle was removed, and the swab passed briefly over Mason's arm again. Then the footsteps went away.

I want to get out of this place, Mason thought. He opened his mouth to scream, but while he was trying to decide if screaming was wise, sleep crashed down upon him like a wet jungle rain.

IT was a looking-glass world for Sheila Chesham, who for the first time in her life was driving a car with the wheel on the left-hand side. The traffic in Los Angeles was frightening enough, she thought, without the illusion that every oncoming car was in her own lane.

Her first impulse, during a long dark night of doubt at the Bel

Air, had been to fly back to London. She could not put her life on hold, waiting for Mason to heal the chaos of his existence. Then she had thought again about the mystery of Mason's disappearance, and it had struck her with a deep conviction that Mason had not just wandered off in search of a drink. Something evil had happened. When Raven had invited her to attend the meeting with the FBI man, Sheila had resolved to stay in Los Angeles until Mason's twisted destiny resolved itself in one way or another. Now the garish headlines in *Fact Digest* only underlined that conviction. Perhaps the paper knew more than it was telling.

She nudged her rental car into a space near the nondescript brick building that bore the address of *Fact Digest*. It was on one of those side streets in West Hollywood that was otherwise occupied with tanning salons and foreign car mechanics. No sign on the outside of the building betrayed its occupants, but in a parking lot behind the structure she could see an old Studebaker Golden Hawk with a vanity license plate that read: FACT. It must belong to someone on the staff, she thought. She looked again at a publicity photograph she'd asked for from the Realistic Pictures PR department. Then she slumped down in her seat so she could not easily be seen.

She tried to make her mind a blank, to blot out the possibility that Mason had fallen for Marjorie Whittaker, the trash novelist he'd met in the center. She knew that Mason was in a period of upheaval—that he was reeling under the unfamiliar pressures of notoriety and sobriety—and she forgave him if he temporarily fell under the spell of a man-eater like Marjorie. In time, she felt, he would see the light. And the light, she hoped, was that despite all of the differences that seemed to separate them—of age, of class, of lifetimes spent in different worlds—they belonged together.

The back door of the brick building opened, and a man with curly hair and a gold earring walked out and got into the old sports car. As the Studebaker wheeled into the street, she crept up smoothly behind it, threading her way through the unfamiliar traffic that all seemed on the wrong side of the road, following him down La Cienega and onto the Santa Monica Freeway, where her rental car had all it could do to keep up with the supercharged Hawk.

Spike Murphy looked in his rearview mirror and slowed slightly, to make it easier for Sheila to follow him.

MUST think. Must think. Mason Devereaux repeated the command to himself over and over, trying to will his drugged mind to haul itself up into wakefulness. He had no idea how long he had been in the darkened chamber. No idea, indeed, where he was, or why, or the identity of the mysterious man who had promised to drain his blood and let him sleep for a thousand years.

Every time his mind crawled back to consciousness, it seemed that the man was there with another hypodermic, to plunge him back into the shadows of confused dreams. What Mason was able to retain, between periods of oblivion, was that he was in desperate danger—that this man planned to practice the most alarming experiments on him. Mason felt as if he were the victim of the mother of hangovers, and yet there was hope in that feeling. An ordinary person, feeling the way Mason felt, would simply curl up and die. But Mason had felt just as bad on most mornings for the last thirty years, and was able to plan. In his drinking days, he had plotted how to get his next drink. Now he plotted how to save his life.

The door opened, and the sinister man reappeared, a smile on his face. He walked over to the bed, peered down into Mason's face, and took his pulse.

"Pretending to sleep, my friend? But your brain waves betray you. You are conscious, and thinking, and so I will tell you what to look forward to. Open your eyes. I know you're there."

Mason opened his eyes and saw the smiling face of a fanatic.

"My name is Dr. Coyne. But I am known as the Sandman, because I put people to sleep—for a very long time. I believe in the future, Mr. Devereaux. Someday I plan to freeze my own body, so that I can be reawakened in hundreds or thousands of years, after science has made man immortal. I want to live forever! I want to be able to speak French someday! Doesn't everybody? That is the gift I am granting you. In a few moments you will go to sleep. The blood will drain from your body, to be replaced by a fluid of vitamins and organic antifreeze. The next voice you hear will be that of a man or woman not even yet conceived—a scientist from the future. And if all goes well, you and I will meet again, perhaps in the next century."

A wave of adrenal fear crashed through Devereaux, giving him the strength to struggle weakly against his bonds. The Sandman shook his head sadly and attached a tube to the needle embedded in Mason's arm. The actor could see the rich red life-force of his blood, spilling into a plastic bag. And then the world seemed to flicker out of focus, like a bad television signal, before the screen went black.

I N London, a young man with a sad face sat alone in a room. Douglas Brown found himself thinking a great deal lately about Harold Gasper. Before he had murdered the theater investor, he had thought about him hardly at all, except as an inconvenience. It had seemed fundamental to him that if he killed Gasper, there would be no possible link to connect him with the death of Bradleigh Court—except for the suspicions of Mason Devereaux, who had his own secrets to keep. Brown's knowledge of crime methods came from the newspapers and a few true-crime books he had read, and he knew that in such situations the murderer usually eliminated the witnesses.

He had gone over to Gasper's rooms on that day without any sort of thought-out plan. He would see what happened, he told himself, refusing to let his mind admit the enormity of what he was likely to do. He was almost in a trance, just as he'd been the day he'd handed Gasper the gun that killed Bradleigh Court. Something had come over him. He could not think clearly, and seemed compelled to follow a course of action whether or not it seemed wise. Certainly if he had stopped for a drink or a smoke his resolve would have evaporated, and he would have gone back home.

But no. Gasper had spoken condescendingly to him, and all night long the sarcastic words had whirled in his brain, until they seemed to rearrange themselves into a sentence of murder. The next day he had walked up to Gasper's door, surprised to see that the man from Scotland Yard was not at his post. Gasper had let him in. There had been countless things he had planned to say to Gasper, but instead he had taken out the gun and shot him, once, through the forehead. Then he had walked away.

Now he had endless conversations with Gasper in his dreams. Sometimes Gasper screamed out in fright at him, but more often they held civilized conversations about the morality of murder, and one night Gasper had even advised him to read *Crime and Punishment* for insights into his own condition. The next day Brown had actually walked into a bookstore on the Charing Cross Road and taken the book down from the shelf before it struck him as odd that he should take reading suggestions from a dead man in a nightmare.

SHEILA CHESHAM followed Spike Murphy's Studebaker down the off-ramp into an anonymous neighborhood in the San Fernando Valley. Lucky for her, she thought, that the old car was so easy to follow; it stood out from all the aerodynamic clones on the highway. The Golden Hawk was moving slowly, down to an intersection, then left into a street of strip malls, then right into the parking lot of an anonymous office building.

She pulled her car to the curb and watched as Spike Murphy got out and went into a back entrance of the building. If she was right and Murphy knew where Mason was, then perhaps he had led her straight to him. She thought briefly of looking for a telephone, but she was afraid of losing the trail—and besides, who could she call? The police? To tell them she had followed a man she'd never met to an address she did not know?

She slipped out of her rented car and walked quickly across the parking lot to the door. It opened easily, and inside she saw the air-conditioned gloom of a modern office building. There was a directory next to the door, and she started to read it, before a hand grasped her tightly around the upper arm.

"Sheila Chesham, I believe?"

She twisted, saw that she was being held by Spike Murphy, and struggled to be free.

"Don't be afraid," he said, releasing her. "We're on the same side. I need your help to rescue Mason."

I N the penthouse of the Century Plaza hotel, FBI agent John Kratz was shown into the presence of Takeuchi. Raven Charles was with him, along with Billy Baxter.

"I'm going to get right down to brass tacks," Kratz told the media lord. "Mason Devereaux is missing. We don't know how your newspaper could have printed the story so fast unless there was some kind of inside knowledge. We can't find this guy Murphy who edits the thing for you. Where is he, what does he know, and what do you know?"

"I was afraid this would happen," Takeuchi said. "I was going to call the police myself. This man Murphy is so ambitious that he will apparently stop at nothing to build his circulation. He ran that story about Devereaux disappearing from the Betty Ford Center against my personal instructions. Celebrities in a position like that should have a certain amount of privacy."

"It ain't privacy we're talking about," Kratz said. "It's kidnapping. We think Murphy had a hand in it."

"Impossible."

"Where is he now?"

"I have no idea."

The tall, fierce-eyed FBI man and the handsome press lord locked eyes in a stare-down. Silence grew in the room. The telephone rang. Takeuchi lifted the receiver and listened. Then he handed the telephone to Kratz.

"Here is Mr. Murphy for you now."

M U R P H Y towered over a terrified security guard, who ran the outer lobby of the Sandman's clandestine laboratory. He and Sheila Chesham had burst in through the glass doors, demanding to see the Sandman immediately. There had been no answer to the guard's page on the office intercom, and then Murphy had grabbed the telephone and dialed Takeuchi's private number.

"We need help here!" he shouted into the phone. "Mason Devereaux is being held behind locked doors by some kind of wacko scientist. God knows what's happening in there!"

He paused. "Who? The FBI? Get over here right away!" He covered the mouth of the receiver. "The FBI is already at my boss's office," he told them. He handed the phone to the guard. "Give them the address."

He turned again to the heavy steel door leading to the inner rooms of the office complex, finding it locked. The guard gave the address over the phone, promised to hold on, and turned quickly toward them:

"Mason Devereaux? He's in there?"

Murphy looked at him. "I don't know. But I have a hunch he might be. And if he is, we've got to rescue him from that lunatic."

The guard looked confused. "But I recognize you! You've been coming to this office for more than a week."

Murphy instructed his face to look sad.

"I was interviewing this lunatic for an exposé. He was telling me about some cockamamy hypothetical experiment he'd like to do on someone like Mason—to put a drunk to sleep, and wake him up after they cured alcoholism. Then Mason was kidnapped, and this morning it hit me like a thunderbolt that the Sandman was crazy enough to actually do it. He's probably freezing the poor sap right now."

The three of them stood looking at the impassive gray face of the steel door. On the wall behind them, the second hand went around and around on the clock, measuring out time, of which the Sandman had promised Mason Devereaux an eternity.

F ROM the muffled sounds echoing down the long corridor, the Sandman judged that he did not have long to work. The laboratory door was steel and it was strong, but eventually the fools would break in and try to interrupt his experiment. There might, however, just barely be enough time. He did not want to rush. It took precise calculations to rewrite the destiny of the human race.

He monitored the tube that was slowly draining the blood from Mason's body, and another that contained a solution of vitamins and a plasma substitute that could sustain low temperatures—the fluid he had told Mason was antifreeze. Then he began to wrap the clammy body in clinging plastic and aluminum foil, beginning at the feet, moving steadily and carefully, working his way up toward the centers of Mason's life and memory.

From somewhere inside his deepening coma, from a place below the level of conscious thought, a word formed itself and then forced its way up to Mason's lips. The Sandman looked up momentarily, then resumed his work. Funny, he thought, how speech persists with a will of its own. That had almost sounded like a name.

S HEILA was filled with an overwhelming need to act. She could not wait one more second inside the sterile office with its plastic plants and fluorescent lighting, outside the steel door that would not yield. Spike Murphy, who had seemed cool at first, was growing increasingly alarmed. He had given up badgering the security guard for a key to the door, and was hammering on it with a wastebasket. The FBI and the police were allegedly on their way—but where were they?

Sheila had to move, to do something—anything! Moving on automatic pilot, she ran outside and flagged down what looked like an emergency vehicle on the street in front of the building. It was a tow truck from the freeway road service.

"Help me!" she screamed. "A man is trapped inside that building and the door won't open! He may be dead in a few minutes! He's being tortured and we can't stop it!"

She was weeping uncontrollably as she cried out, and the truck driver instinctively believed her story. He followed her inside the building, saw Murphy still pounding at the door, and turned to the guard.

"He's inside?"

"Down a long corridor," the security man said. He seemed a little dazed by the flurry of activity around him.

"There must be a window on the room?"

"It's locked, with steel shutters."

"Show me."

They ran outside the building and the driver plowed his truck through shrubbery and across the lawn to where a blank steel plate covered what should have been a window. Swinging down from the driver's seat, he jumped into the back of his truck and came out with the torch end of an acetylene device used to free drivers from the twisted steel of freeway crashes. The white-hot flame cut through the plate steel like a spoon through gravy.

Sheila looked up. A helicopter had appeared out of nowhere, and was circling overhead. She could hear sirens approaching down the empty side streets. The tow-truck driver, who somehow assumed the law was on his side, continued to attack the steel plate with his torch. A second helicopter arrived and landed on the roof of the building. A SWAT team materialized out of nowhere. Sheila realized that Raven Charles was standing at her side.

"He's in there!" she shouted. "Something terrible is happening to him!"

Raven saw that the girl was on the dangerous edge of shock, and wrapped her arms around her, to calm her.

The police pulled a ram from their emergency vehicle and slammed it against the plate steel, already weakened by the flame of the torch. They rammed it again and again, until finally the plate tore loose and fell inside the building. The SWAT team was over the sill in a second. Sheila and Raven rushed to the window of the sealed room. Their eyes, accustomed to sunlight, were blinded for a second, but then the strong beams of electric torches illuminated the scene. Sheila screamed in despair.

W HAT she saw was a frantic little man in a laboratory coat, struggling to free himself from the arms of the police. And on the table in front of them, wrapped in aluminum foil all the way up to its neck, was a body with the gray, cold, colorless face of Mason Devereaux.

A moment later, Spike Murphy materialized in the room. Somehow he had broken through the hallway door. It seemed to Sheila that for a second the entire scene was frozen in time and space, as everybody stood still, paralyzed by the evil scenario they had interrupted.

"You son of a bitch!" Murphy cried out theatrically, leaping toward the Sandman. "What have you done with Mason Devereaux?"

"I have given him immortal life!" the Sandman shouted back proudly. The SWAT cops held him and looked down at the foil-wrapped body and waited for orders. It was not clear to anyone exactly what had happened.

"Well, now you must take immortality away from him," Murphy commanded, "and give him his own life back again. Reverse the process! You are the only one who knows how to do it. Come on, Sandman. Give him back his blood!"

"Just one doggone second here," said Kratz, the FBI man, who had just climbed in through the window.

"There's literally not a second to lose," Murphy said. "A murder is in the process of taking place right here before our eyes. This man can stop the process. No one else can. There's no time."

Kratz looked from the Sandman to the lifeless body of Mason Devereaux and back again.

"Release him," he said to the cops.

The Sandman shook himself free and tried to recapture the zeal of a moment earlier, but it was no use. Now he looked tired and defeated, as if the sunlight streaming into his private world had awakened him.

"Can you do it?" Kratz asked him.

The Sandman shrugged. "I can try. The process is at a midway point. We can flush out the slumber solution with his own blood— and fresh plasma, if you have any."

"We have a lot of it," said one of the cops, calling for blood units on his shoulder radio.

"Do it," Kratz said. He looked around the room. "I don't want anyone leaving this room," he said. "Line up and shut up."

HOW many times, thought Sheila, had she waited like this, with Mason's life in the balance? Wasn't it time for fate to give the poor guy a break—to allow him peace and happiness, especially now that he had finally sobered up?

She sat with Raven and Billy in the police command tent, set up in the parking lot of the Sandman's building. Inside the building, the mad cryogenicist at last achieved his dream of working at the top level of medical research. He had been joined by a team of specialists from Cedars-Sinai Medical Center, who were trying to bring Mason back from the jaws of death. There was no way and no time to move the comatose actor; helicopters had airlifted equipment and experts from the hospital. On the sidewalk in front of the building, the heroic tow-truck driver told his story over and over for the TV cameras.

Raven handed Sheila a cup of hot tea and then touched her lightly on the arm. "I've seen you here and there with Mason," she said quietly, "but I've never been quite sure what your relationship is. Of course I don't want to invade your privacy . . ."

"I love him," Sheila said simply, aware that this was the first time she had used those words about Mason, to herself or anyone else. She bit her lip to hold back the tears. "Oh, I love him so very much. But . . . but . . . I never told him that, you know—never, never, and now I never will."

I T was like the golden hour at the end of a long summer day, when the light comes from everywhere and nowhere, and the colors of the flowers seem saturated. Somewhere in the center of this light was Mason, who could not quite remember who or what he was. Everything seemed elusive. Music played, without notes. Faces appeared, without identities. There were volumes without shape, spaces without dimensions, warmth without temperature. This was not the "next" world, because it did not exist in a series with anything else. It was.

Everything that existed in this world was something he understood, without understanding. He could have composed the music, he felt, because it seemed to spill from within him. The light also came from within him, and the warmth. The faces were neither inside him or outside, and although he could not see their features, he felt that he recognized one of them.

Richard? he said. It was his brother Richard, who had died in a fall from a pony at the age of eleven. But not that Richard. Richard not as a boy, but as a man. But not a man. Richard as an essence. He tried to focus on the face, to see why he thought the face was

Richard, but he found that there was no face there. It was every face. Yet it had the essence of Richard.

Richard?

The not-Richard non-face smiled, and it seemed that they were holding hands, although neither had a body.

Mason, not-Richard said, although he did not seem to speak. And then Mason knew that he was Mason. It was not something he really wanted to know. He tried to turn to look around, but found he was already looking in all directions—or, rather, that he had no eyes and simply knew what was to be seen. Where was this?

Now that was curious. The formation of the thought—where is this?—was painful, somehow: a thought that did not belong in wherever this was. Mason instinctively knew that in this place there was no other place, and so one did not ask where this place was. It was bad manners. And like all bad manners, his question deserved to be punished.

It was. He felt. Until he felt, he had been unaware that he could not feel. Even now, he did not know where he felt—because he had no body. Nor what he felt. Then he knew. He felt pain. Then he knew where. Behind his eyes. Then he knew he had eyes. Then his body returned to him. Then he called out again, Richard? but the nonface of the not-Richard was gone.

"Mason?"

He was Mason. He had not spoken. Therefore someone else had spoken. Remembering that he had eyes, he opened them, and saw a face that was a real face, and looked only in one direction, toward him. It was strange, he thought, to be in a world where faces could look in only one direction at a time.

He knew this face. "Sheila," he said. He was aware of a flash of excitement all around him—somehow he could still sense the feelings of others—and he saw Sheila's eyes fill with tears.

"Mason," she said. "You're going to be all right. It's so good to have you back. We love you."

"I was . . ." he began.

"Yes, Mason?"

"Hello, love," he said, and she bent down and kissed him on the lips. He had been meaning to tell her that he had been in heaven, but then again, he thought, as he felt the warmth of her kiss, how could that have been heaven, and not have Sheila's lips?

I F we can keep Mason's recovery a secret, we can get to the bottom of the whole story," the FBI agent John Kratz told the small group that clustered in a private room at Cedars-Sinai Hospital, down the corridor from where Mason was in the intensive care unit. "As far as anyone on the outside knows, Mason is still deep in a coma. Spike Murphy is giving interviews about how he stumbled onto the Sandman's scheme and rescued Mason. There has to be more to it than that."

"When I followed Murphy there to the Sandman's laboratory, and we broke inside, the security guard said a strange thing," Sheila said. "He said he recognized Murphy. He said Murphy had been coming to the office for more than a week."

"What did Murphy say?" Kratz asked.

"He said he'd been working on an exposé. The Sandman had talked to him about putting someone like Mason to sleep, and when Mason disappeared, that's when Murphy figured out the Sandman had him."

"Yeah, and my aunt has nuts," Billy Baxter said.

I N the presidential suite of the Century Plaza hotel, Spike Murphy and Takeuchi sat regarding one another. Takeuchi had chosen the venue because he knew it was swept every week by the Secret Service, and was not likely to be bugged. In an hour, Murphy was scheduled to meet the press.

"I need to know the real truth," Takeuchi said at last.

"I have told you the real truth," said Murphy.

Takeuchi sighed and poured himself mineral water from a crystal decanter.

"I am a man with many investments in the United States," he said. "If it appeared that one of my employees had kidnapped someone and arranged to have him frozen . . ."

His voice trailed away.

"My original plan," Murphy said, "was simply to develop a story that would put *Fact Digest* on the map. I stumbled across the Sandman, and learned that he wanted to freeze a living person, as an experiment. Of course I knew the guy was nuts. But I suggested Mason Devereaux for his experiment, because I knew that Mason would generate twenty times the publicity of anybody else. Of course I was always gonna stop things before they went too far."

"When you brought the idea to me," Takeuchi said, "you proposed to kidnap Mason yourself. You planned to thaw him out in two years, as I recall, to provide another scoop for the newspaper."

"With all due respect, sir," said Murphy, "perhaps you heard me wrong. I wasn't gonna do anything myself. I was telling you what could happen to Mason—if we did not prevent it."

"Don't toy with me," Takeuchi said. "I know what you said, and I absolutely forbade you to have anything to do with the scheme."

"Of course that's your version," Murphy said. He was aware that he was fighting for his freedom; if his own story about the Sandman was believed, he would escape criminal prosecution. "Let's put all of our cards on the table. Mason disappeared, and you read about it in your own paper when the advance copies were sent over on Sunday, and yet you said absolutely nothing to the law for almost twenty-four hours after that. If this case goes to trial, any jury will see that you could have moved more quickly to save him. If the jury knows about what I told you. Of course, the only way a jury is gonna find out about our conversation is if you tell them. Or if I tell them."

Murphy's threat was there in the air between them, a palpable thing. Takeuchi could not take action against Murphy without incriminating himself.

Takeuchi reflected. "The Sandman is not talking?" he said finally.

"The guy's completely around the bend. He told the cops he would tell them everything—in two thousand years."

"Mason?"

"In a coma, rehearsing to be a test case in a life-support controversy."

Takeuchi arose. "Then I must congratulate you, Mr. Murphy, on having acted so quickly and courageously to save Mr. Devereaux."

He bowed slightly, from the waist. The two men looked at each other with cold, hard eyes.

"Thank you, sir," said Murphy. "Now let's go have that press conference."

SILENCES had always been difficult for Mason to play on a stage. He was most at home when he was speaking and moving—drawing attention toward himself. In those plays where he had to remain quiet and motionless for long periods of time, he grew uncertain and self-conscious. He had fled from the opportunity to open in a play by Beckett for fear that the silences would drive him mad.

But now, returned from the very brink of the long silence of death, Mason bathed in the quiet of his hospital room. A very short list of visitors was allowed to see him for five minutes every hour, and sometimes even those visits were replaced by the attentions of a team of psychiatrists and neural experts, who tested his memory and mental reflexes. By all the odds, he should have sustained brain damage during his mistreatment at the hands of the Sandman, but oddly enough, he had emerged from the ordeal feeling refreshed. It was as if the deep sleep and the gradual cooling of his body had cleaned out some of the noise of a disorderly lifetime. Now he seemed to think with a new clarity. He was pleased with himself.

"Do you know, old girl," he told Sheila during one of their brief visits, "I actually wonder if the Sandman was on to something. I haven't felt this clearheaded in decades."

"The Sandman had nothing to do with it," she said, tenderly taking his hand, for at last they had permitted themselves to touch one another. "This is what it feels like to be sober, Mason. You've awakened every morning of your life for the last thirty years with a hangover. Welcome to the human race."

"Perhaps you're right," Mason mused. "I always wondered how people could walk down the street looking so bloody unconcerned, when my head was throbbing and my attention span was down to five seconds. I wanted to walk right up and ask them what their secret was."

Blanketed in his newfound serenity, Mason actually enjoyed the long silences in his room, as the California sunlight walked across the walls, and nurses came in with vitamins, fruit juices, and the newspapers. He was pleased to see that the press was paying full due to his latest escapades, and indeed one paper had started a series on the phenomenon of Super Celebrity. Mason read that while other celebrities—Elvis, Madonna, Churchill, Napoleon—had actually done things to make themselves famous, he was the first person to reach that stratosphere simply by bad luck.

Of course all of the articles reported that he was still deep in a coma. That was the FBI strategy; the bureau believed its investigation would go better if no one knew Mason was competent to be a witness.

Mason also knew, by reading the papers, that a man called Spike Murphy was about to hold a press conference. He had never heard the name before, but a photograph of Murphy stirred a vague memory. Had he seen him once before—a shadowy, vague figure at the corner of his consciousness?

M ASON'S rather awed guest, during one visiting period, was Ivan Bloom. Mason had asked for him. The former head of Realistic Pictures had found an unexpected happiness as head of the home electronics division.

"Have we met before?" Mason asked, frowning.

"Casually," Bloom said. "I had a bet on the roulette table when you landed."

They laughed. Raven had told Mason how Ivan masterminded the bugging operation when Ashley St. Ives had tried to blackmail them. Now Mason had another assignment for him.

"I read in the papers that there's going to be a press conference this afternoon," Mason told him. "A man called Takeuchi is going to appear with another man called Murphy."

"Yeah, the guy who claims he saved you from the Sandman," Ivan said.

"You're an electronics expert, Mr. Bloom. Can you rig me a two-way hookup so I can eavesdrop on the press conference?"

"You can do that just by watching it on the tube," Bloom said.

"Two-way, Mr. Bloom," Mason said firmly.

Their eyes met, and an unspoken message was communicated. "I'll have the guys in my department get right on it," Ivan said.

TAKEUCHI, who had spent a lifetime operating in the background of his many enterprises, was acutely uncomfortable as he walked to the table with all the microphones on it. The ballroom of the Century Plaza was packed with reporters and television cameras, and there was high voltage in the air; the journalists congratulated themselves on being part of the biggest human interest story since Lindbergh. The media lord took his seat next to Spike Murphy, who had cleaned up nicely in a suit and tie. Seated to one side was Raven Charles, in her role as head of Takeuchi's movie studio.

Murphy began by reading a statement explaining that *Fact Digest*, having been on top of the Devereaux story right from the beginning, was now ready to help close the case.

"Through a lucky chance, I stumbled across the Sandman only a few days before he put his twisted plan into motion," Murphy read, his voice a flat monotone. "He mentioned the notion of experimenting with someone like Mason. Of course I thought he was insane— but madmen like the Sandman make good copy for papers like *Fact Digest*. I never dreamed he would act on his delusions, until Mason disappeared. Then I put two and two together and was lucky enough to bring help to Mason just in the nick of time."

He paused to look out over the room, his eyebrows pulled down into an ominous frown.

"Thank you very much, Mr. Murphy," said a voice that seemed to come at once from every corner of the room. It was the same voice that had once been described as the sound of a bartender in hell. The room was hushed and time seemed frozen.

"Excuse me for interrupting," the voice continued. "Yes, this is Mason Devereaux. The studio has been kind enough to supply me with an audio link from my digs here at the hospital. And I can see you all splendidly on Cable News. I just wanted to make a brief

statement. Of course it was you, Mr. Murphy, along with the person known as the Sandman, who kidnapped me away from the Betty Ford Center. I will be pleased to repeat that statement in court."

Murphy sat stone still at the table as pandemonium broke out in the room. Takeuchi, at his side, seemed to shrink from him as if he were contagious. Ivan Bloom stood at the back of the room, his arms folded across his chest in satisfaction, and when he caught Raven's eyes, he smiled. In the days when he ran the studio, he'd been a sucker for surprise endings.

PART TEN

Chicago

NOBODY would find them here. Mason and Sheila sat on a lawn overlooking Lake Michigan and drank tea in the rosy light of the late afternoon. Ancient sand dunes ran down to the water's edge, where children built castles in the sand. Behind them, a massive old stone house offered them protection from the outcry that followed the affair of the Sandman.

The house belonged to Raven Charles, who had loaned it to them as a refuge, and here they had fallen into a comforting routine. They rose early, had strong black cups of coffee, and then walked down a wooded lane to the country market to buy the newspapers. Then toast and orange juice, over the papers, and then Mason went out to a table under a tree to work on his memoirs. Sheila had presented him with a Macintosh, but he was afraid of the machine and wrote in longhand on yellow legal pads. Raven was handling the auction on the book rights to his adventures, which were expected to fetch well into seven figures.

Then of course there would be the TV miniseries, *The Mason Devereaux Saga,* which had been on the back burner as long ago as Cannes. "It's the only project in Hollywood history," Billy Baxter had observed, "that the longer it's on the back burner, the bigger the pot gets." And on the wicker table at Mason's elbow, as he looked out over the great lake, was the screenplay for *Phantom of the Opera.* Raven hoped to go into production in the new year, after the special effects had been ironed out.

Mason was tempted to say that he had never been more successful, professionally. But then of course he had hardly ever been successful at all, professionally, so the savour was new to him. Yet there were hours at a time when he hardly thought of his fame, his coming fortune, or his prospects of finding his name above the title of a major motion picture. His hand moved out confidently across the table and took Sheila's, and as he felt the pressure of her hand against his own, his heart sighed. It had been such a long, confusing ordeal, his life, and now the pain seemed to be at an end.

"Sheila," he said, deliberately placing his teacup back on its saucer. "There is something I have to tell you."

She turned away from the lake, disturbed by a note in his voice.

"The shooting of Bradleigh Court," Mason said. "Do you recall all of the circumstances surrounding it?"

"What do you imagine, Mason darling? That was me, remember, hanging from my hair twenty feet in the air over the stage, right after Bradleigh was shot dead."

"Yes," said Mason. "And now here we are with the whole future laid out before us, and I hold your hand, and we love one another."

"Yes, Mason."

"What I must say to you, dear girl, is that there was more to the shooting of Bradleigh Court than anyone knows. I must begin by being completely honest with you."

Sheila's fingers tightened on his hand. "You know you can tell me anything."

"I will try to make the story as concise as possible," Mason said. His eyes seemed to be focused on painful memories. "You know that Harold Gasper got me the job as Bradleigh Court's understudy?"

"Of course."

"There was more to it than that. He came to me one day with a proposition. He suggested that I substitute for Bradleigh at a matinee. He would be in the Royal Box with a revolver that shot blank rounds. I would be prepared with a charge of stage blood. At the end of the second act he would shoot me, I would fall over and bleed, and be spirited to a private hospital where, in due course, I could emerge fully recovered. There would be enormous publicity. I would become famous, and his shares in the play would leap in value, because of the ironic parallels between the legend of the Phantom and the tragedy."

"In other words," Sheila said quietly, "you knew a shot was going to be fired at that performance."

"Yes. That was the real reason I didn't want you to be present."

She sat silently. The implications were enormous. The whole legend of Mason Devereaux was based on his image as an innocent bystander to whom a series of bizarre misadventures had occurred. If it were known that he had been a conspirator involved in the first one . . .

"You can easily piece together what went wrong," Mason said. "Harold Gasper told me the whole story before he was killed. He foolishly went to Douglas Brown to obtain a weapon. He was going to pay Brown for his role. But Brown, of course, had his eye on you. He could see that we were drawn toward each other—although why you were attracted to a shambling wreck like myself, I cannot imagine.

"Brown wanted your family's money. He wanted me dead but didn't have the nerve to kill me. So, toying with fate, he placed one real bullet in the chamber, along with the blank rounds, before he gave it to Gasper. I had one chance in six of being hit. But on the day of the performance, I was taken quite drunk. Bradleigh Court was backstage in costume for some publicity photos. He walked out in my place, and was shot dead. Bad luck."

"Poor Bradleigh," Sheila said.

"Yes. I shall take the memory of his body with me to the grave."

"But, Mason, I'm glad it was Bradleigh and not you."

He gave a wry smile. "What happened next is unclear to me," he said, musing. "Harold of course knew that Douglas Brown had put the fatal round in the chamber. Rowley, the man from Scotland Yard, suspected Gasper. One day Harold came to me and said he would keep the whole thing as his secret—he would take the rap. Then, a few days later, while we were at Cannes, Gasper was murdered."

"Douglas Brown?" Sheila asked.

"He had the motive, and I haven't been able to think of anyone else who did. I've been waiting for Scotland Yard to twig to the whole thing, and arrest Brown. And me. But they haven't stumbled over the connection. The *Phantom* case was put on hold after Gasper was killed. They're still looking for his killer, I suppose . . ."

"Why didn't you call the police and tell them your suspicions about Douglas?"

"I should have. But I was disoriented at the time—it was right after the kidnapping—and I was drinking. You remember. We were at the Voile d'Or. And how could I name Brown without implicating myself?"

"Where is Douglas now?"

"According to Eady, nobody has seen him for ages. At first I was rather concerned he might try to finish the job by coming after us, but I was too drunk to get anything organized on that subject, and now we're in a place where nobody could possibly find us."

Sheila thought for a moment about Mason's confession. "Then that's the whole story as far as anyone need be concerned," she said finally. "Let's leave it that way. When you conspired with Harold Gasper, you were drunk and confused. You're a different person now. Why can't we simply agree, between ourselves, to forget the past, and move on?"

"It isn't quite that simple, dear girl."

"It would be the truth," Sheila said.

"It would be . . . a form of the truth," Mason said at last. "When I was at the Betty Ford Center, wringing the alcohol out of my system, there was a man named Humble Howard who was my counselor. He kept talking all the time about honesty. Rigorous honesty. Until we were prepared to be painstakingly honest with ourselves, he said, it was likely we would drink again."

"I'm sure that's true," Sheila said.

"Then you can understand, dear girl, why I must step forward and tell the truth."

The sun had almost disappeared into the waters of the lake.

"All you stand to gain, you could destroy," Sheila said quietly.

"But I will be able to look you in the eye as an honest man," Mason said. "And I do not want to drink again. Not that. I find I rather enjoy being in touch with my emotions—even if, in this case, they are shame, and abject terror."

THE first thing Fredson Rowley liked to do, when he was searching a suspect's flat, was to simply sit down in a chair and exist in the space for a time. He let himself into Douglas Brown's abandoned rooms in Covent Garden, threw some old papers onto the floor, and took an armchair. The atmosphere smelled of rot and mold. Rowley looked through an open door into the kitchenette and saw that Brown had departed without doing his dishes. He stretched out his legs and scrutinized the flat, which had the look of a lonely man's retreat. Ties were thrown over lampshades. Books were left facedown to mark a page. There was not a single picture on the wall.

It was yet another bachelor flat he had entered as part of his work on the *Phantom* murder case. The first had been Mason Devereaux's. To a bloke like himself, Rowley reflected, these theater chaps seemed to live a life of glamour. You read about their romances in the gossip columns—how Brown was engaged to a beautiful young heiress, how Devereaux had been linked romantically with her— and you pictured them living in a world of champagne and chocolates. Yet both of those men had come home every night to ill-lighted, untidy rooms full of stale air and old cigarette ends. He wondered if the Chesham girl had ever seen where either one of her beaus lived.

Rowley had been one step behind Douglas Brown for weeks, and then the trail had gone dry. The stage manager's disappearance, right after the murder of Harold Gasper, had been an arrow of guilt pointing straight at him. Acting on a tip from a regular at the Sun in Splendour, he had ordered the pub staked out after Brown was seen there. But Brown had not returned. An informer in the Jamaican street market at the bottom of Portobello Road had taken the police to a furnished room, but Brown never returned to it. The most audacious stunt Brown had pulled was checking into the Savoy for the night. He had apparently been all over the West End, but without anyone seeing him.

It went one, two, three, thought Rowley. Bradleigh was shot dead. Harold Gasper held the gun. Someone had put a real round in among the blanks. Brown had disappeared. Therefore, Brown had knowledge of the shooting—and became the obvious suspect in the murder of Harold Gasper. And that led to the inescapable conclusion that Mason Devereaux, the everyman who had become a hero, must have known Gasper was going to fire the shot.

Rowley shifted uncomfortably and lit a cigarette. There was something that did not fit, some nagging detail at the back of his mind that would not fall into place. Something wrong with Gasper's version of the story. Rowley remembered his interview with Gasper at La Caprice, the restaurant where they had talked the day after the first shooting. Gasper had not supplied the scenario of the shooting; Rowley himself had, while Gasper merely agreed.

Stubbing out his cigarette in one of Brown's overflowing ashtrays, Rowley went digging through the briefcase at his feet. He finally produced a transcript of his conversation with Gasper, which he had dictated to a secretary within an hour of their visit.

> Rowley: I discovered a curious thing about the murder weapon when I examined it.
> Gasper: Yes. The other rounds were blanks.
> Rowley: Perhaps you thought the gun contained all blanks. How unlucky for you that one chamber contained a real bullet.
> Gasper: How unlucky for Bradleigh Court.

Rowley returned the transcript to the briefcase and lit another cigarette. He sat smoking quietly, trying to reconstruct the sequence of events on the afternoon of the *Phantom* shooting. Mason Devereaux had testified that while he was beneath the stage, trying to free Sheila Chesham, a shot had rung out, and then he had been hit on the head with a revolver. Obviously the same revolver Gasper had just fired, then thrown down an air shaft. Gasper had therefore not examined the gun before firing it, or he would have discovered it contained a real round. If he had thrown the gun away immediately after firing it, how had he known the other chambers contained only blanks?

IT took a special edition of "America's Most Wanted" to deal with the fugitives from justice in the two cases involving Mason Devereaux. In Los Angeles, after the press conference so unexpectedly interrupted by Mason's disembodied voice, Spike Murphy had walked off to the men's room and disappeared before anyone had the foresight to arrest him. In London, Fredson Rowley had appealed to the public for information leading to the arrest of Douglas Brown, who was required, in the ancient formula of British law enforcement, "to assist the police in their inquiries."

Rowley's call came too late for Brown. There had been a period when the former stage manager had been keenly offended by the indifference of the police toward him, but after he had checked out of the Savoy without being arrested, something had broken inside of him, and he fell into a deep and shapeless depression. He no longer read the papers—not even those wind-blown rags that drifted near his pallet of cardboard, underneath the arches behind Charing Cross Station. In late August the nights were still warm enough to make it halfway tolerable, sleeping rough, if one did not mind such nuisances as lice, noisy drunks, or the occasional episodes of homeless-bashing.

The nights Brown spent in deep and dreamless sleep. Daytimes, he wandered the Queen Victoria Embankment or walked into the gardens to listen to the rousing martial music of the military bands that gave public concerts in the afternoon. He fed himself from the pickings behind the Wendy's store on the Strand, and found that begging in the streets made him invisible to the police—who ordered him to move on, but never really looked at him.

Brown's thoughts were filled with a single unanswerable question: How had he come to this? How had a few lines of gossip in a newspaper column transformed him from the fiancé of the richest girl in England to a faceless drifter on the London streets?

I need to know what you knew, and when you knew it," Raven Charles told Takeuchi. "Did Spike Murphy tell you he was involved in the plan to kidnap Mason Devereaux?"

Her voice was quiet but firm. They were on board the *Rashomon*, at anchor off Newport Beach. As he looked across at her, Takeuchi reflected that she was sitting in the very place where Spike Murphy had sat when he had first outlined the mad scheme to freeze Devereaux alive. Takeuchi put a match to a cigar and sighed heavily as he exhaled.

"Miss Charles," he said at last, "I know a refreshing directness is part of your style, but is it really your place to issue me with an ultimatum?"

"There is nothing else I can possibly do," she told him, with a stern strength. "My credibility is at stake. I am the person who brought Mason to America, to work for Realistic Pictures. You own the studio. You also own *Fact Digest*. Mason has testified that Murphy and the Sandman kidnapped him from the Betty Ford Center. If you knew about it, then it might look as if I knew about it. And then I could never work in this town again."

"In Hollywood?" Takeuchi said, playing for time. "A reputation as a kidnapper would only enhance your stature, Miss Charles."

Raven looked away. Takeuchi had never met anyone quite like this strong black woman. He tried to remember why in God's name he had ever put her in charge of the studio in the first place. Certainly Ivan Bloom would have been more reasonable in a situation like this. Takeuchi remembered the night he and Raven had dined together on his yacht off Cap d'Antibes, during the Cannes Film Festival. She had been so fragrant, so elusive. Had she seduced him into giving her the job? Takeuchi blew out smoke. No, he concluded, he had seduced himself.

"Do you know my first name, Miss Charles?"

"No," she said, surprised.

"Nobody does. Most people, I imagine, believe I have only one name—like Liberace, or Madonna." He allowed himself a dry chuckle. "I am going to tell you something that very few people know. My full name is Robert Mitchum Takeuchi."

He spoke as if conveying a profound secret. Raven was aware that for Takeuchi this revelation was an appeal to her—a plea to see him as a fallible man, and not simply as a media icon. "I am not sure what that has to do with Mason Devereaux," she said, gently.

"I was raised in the Napa Valley," he said. "My parents were great movie fans. Robert Mitchum was their favorite star. I think I bought Realistic Pictures because I believed the movies were part of my destiny. Mr. Murphy's newspaper, on the other hand, was started almost absentmindedly, because I knew how much money it could make. When Murphy came to me with his insane plan to kidnap Mason Devereaux, I sat right here in this chair and listened quietly. He said the Sandman could freeze people while they were still alive, and then revive them later. Murphy wanted to put *Fact Digest* on the map by making Devereaux disappear—and then sensationally producing him again, a few years from now. He said it would be like finding Elvis still alive."

"It's the sickest thing I've ever heard of," Raven said.

"Oh, yes. Unbelievably sick." Takeuchi smiled. "I categorically forbade him to do it. Those were my very words. It's all on tape, if you care to listen. I had already made up my mind to replace Murphy as editor, when I learned that Devereaux had, in fact, been kidnapped."

"He did it in defiance of your orders."

Takeuchi spread his hands. "Who knows what he will say in court? In my opinion, he never intended for the Sandman to freeze Mason at all. The Sandman was a demented crazy man who suited his convenience. Murphy was not a killer, only unprincipled and devious. His plan was to set up the Sandman as the kidnapper, and then cash in the publicity by rescuing Mason. But Murphy did not make a very good criminal. He let Mason get a look at him during the kidnapping. Perhaps he thought Mason would keep quiet, in return for his freedom. In the meantime the Sandman took the experiment into his own hands, and began the process of freezing Mason. What could Murphy do? He was no murderer, but it must have occurred to him that with Mason frozen, there were no witnesses except the Sandman, who could easily be framed."

"But Mason survived," Raven said.

"He does seem to have nine lives, doesn't he? And now he's able to testify against Murphy."

"But Murphy can testify against you?"

Takeuchi shrugged. "My tape proves I told Murphy not to do it," he said. "It's not admissible as evidence, but the authorities will be interested to hear it. Still, when I saw the story that Sunday in *Fact Digest*, I should have gone straight to the FBI." He rotated his cigar. "I didn't."

"Why didn't you, Mr. Takeuchi?"

"I was afraid, Miss Charles. I don't like the FBI. It's really very simple. All of my citizenship papers are forgeries. I was raised in this country, but for various reasons I am not a citizen and cannot legally own most of my media properties."

"But Rupert Murdoch became an American citizen. That's how he bought all of his properties."

"A wise move. I got it the wrong way around," said Robert Mitchum Takeuchi. He blew out smoke in the quiet evening air.

THERE had been a storm the night before, and the waves had roared against the beach all day, but now, at twilight, Lake Michigan was calm again. On the eastern shore, Mason and Sheila strolled along the beach, right at the water's edge where the sand was damp and easier to walk on. They held hands. Such simple gestures still filled Mason with awe and gratitude. His romantic adventures had all been rough and tumble, fleeting and meaningless. If you spent your life in a pub, you tended to meet women who drank too much.

"It has been ages," Mason said, "since I passed this much time so quietly. I was always a city person. My idea of relaxation was ten minutes in a taxicab."

"Chicago is fifty-one miles that way," Sheila said, pointing at the far horizon. "We could go in for dinner."

"Can you see it across the lake?"

"It's too far."

"Chicago," Mason mused. "That's where that woman does her television program. The one they show in London. We would watch it sometimes in the Coach and Horses."

"Her name is Oprah Winfrey," Sheila said.

"I rather liked her," Mason said. "What would you say, dear girl, to the notion that we drive around the lake to Chicago, and I tell my story on her program?"

"Do you mean, tell the truth about what happened during that last performance of the *Phantom*?"

"That's what I mean."

MASON DEVEREAUX sat backstage in the greenroom of the Oprah Winfrey program and drank hot tea. He hoped it would dissolve the large lump of fear that had lodged itself halfway down his throat. Sheila Chesham sat at his side, looking through the morning paper, trying to appear unconcerned, her heart pounding in sympathy for Mason. There was a telephone in the room, and at last Mason got up and placed a call.

"I'm going to tell Raven Charles," he told Sheila. "I don't want her to hear about this from anyone else." He spoke quietly into the phone and then returned to his tea.

"What did she say?"

"She said she would watch. I told her I was going to tell the truth and she told me to do what I had to do."

He sat and looked miserably at a monitor on the wall, where a promo for his appearance was already running.

"Do you know, I've never had the slightest luck with live television," he said suddenly. "The stage was my home, and I did films when I was lucky enough, and the odd TV commercial. But on live TV I've always been acutely aware of the camera peering impertinently down my throat."

"Imagine a friend at the other end," Sheila said. "Imagine me."

A producer came in to fetch Mason, and he was led through a bewildering maze of passages and staircases until suddenly he was backstage and could hear Oprah Winfrey introducing him as the luckiest man alive. He smiled grimly, his lips twitching, and tried to look confident as he marched out and took his seat in front of the audience. They were all dressed in jolly bright colors, and he was acutely aware of his shabby gray suit from Moss Brothers.

There was a glass of water close to his hand, and he sipped from it, his fingers shaking. As he looked up he was astonished to see that the audience had risen in a standing ovation. He stood up and applauded them back, a reliable bit of British stagecraft, and as he settled down again he found that the applause had actually put him in a fairly good mood. He was almost beaming, until he remembered what he had to say.

O N board the *Rashomon*, Robert Mitchum Takeuchi viewed the Oprah Winfrey program along with millions of others. The media lord was simply one more viewer, sunk in his captain's chair, watching fascinated, as Devereaux stated simply and clearly that he had a confession to make. That he had known blank shots would be fired at the fateful *Phantom* matinee when Sir Bradleigh Court had been killed. That it was all part of a silly and criminal publicity stunt dreamed up by the late Harold Gasper. That he was ready to accept responsibility. That after a lifetime of alcoholism and a series of showdowns with terror, he wanted to make a fresh start and try to get things right this time.

"But one of the bullets was real?" Oprah asked him.

"Tragically so."

"Who loaded that bullet in the gun?"

"Harold Gasper told me it was Douglas Brown, the stage manager, who had supplied him with the revolver. Brown, I believe, had a romantic attachment to my fiancée, and preferred me to be out of the picture."

Winfrey aimed her microphone at the mouth of a bubbly blond woman who was sitting on the aisle. The woman's friends all giggled in the background as she said, "Mr. Devereaux, I just want to say that we all love you so much!" The audience burst into applause. "My friends and I came here all the way from Milwaukee to see you. And we don't see how you could possibly be guilty of anything."

"But . . ." Mason began, interrupted by cheers. Now Oprah was sharing the mike with an earnest young black woman.

"You're not a criminal, you're a victim! What harm would have been done if a few tourists had seen a fake shooting during the play? It would have given them something to talk about for years. I saw

Phantom of the Opera, in New York, and I didn't think it was all that great. If you ask me, a shooting would have improved it."

Now a man was on his feet in the next row, shouting into the microphone: "It wasn't your fault!" The audience burst into more cheers. A grandmotherly woman across the aisle got slowly to her feet, boosted by old ladies on either side of her. Oprah whipped the microphone around to her. "We love you, Mason!" she shrieked.

T AKEUCHI watched until the final credits of the program rolled, and then he picked up a telephone to get Raven Charles's opinion.

"It was a love feast," she told him. "Five standing ovations. Oprah hugged him at the end of the program. He obviously went on that show expecting to attend his own execution, and the audience forgave him on the spot."

"Will the courts do the same?"

"Neither Mason Devereaux nor Harold Gasper put the real bullet into the chamber. Douglas Brown did. It was bad luck for Bradleigh Court that he was standing on the stage when the bullet hit. But who has had worse luck than Mason, in the months since then? People will say he's paid his dues. Our legal people say if the case ever goes to trial, he'll be bound over, but he'll never go to jail."

"How does this affect our own projects?"

"His confessions on 'Oprah' won't destroy his image because he has never been viewed as a hero—more as a survivor. The public expects celebrities to confess their sins on television. He's still the right actor to play the Phantom. The public can't imagine anyone else. As for the TV miniseries based on his life, it just makes the story better. All during those incredible adventures, Mason is torn by his guilty secret."

"Yes, I suppose you're right," Takeuchi said. "Ah . . . Miss Charles, there's one other thing. About our conversation the other day, regarding my citizenship . . ."

"It will remain confidential."

"Even though I could have . . ."

"Sometimes we act as heroes, and sometimes we do not. At least you were honest with me, Mr. Takeuchi."

"Bob," he said. "Please call me Bob. Nobody has called me that since my mother died."

D OUGLAS BROWN watched the Winfrey program on the screens of thirty television sets in the window of the Granada store on Oxford Street. As Oprah hugged Mason at the end, he turned away and walked blindly in the direction of Hyde Park. The irony was too painful to contemplate: He had enhanced Mason's career and turned him into a popular hero. There had been reaction shots of Sheila Chesham, sitting in the audience, and each one had pierced Brown's heart like a spear.

He kept walking, diagonally across Hyde Park and then down the Brompton Road. Hour after hour he walked, until he found himself at a motorway. He stuck out his thumb.

M ISS CHARLES? Devereaux here." Mason was lunching in booth number one of the Pump Room, calling long distance to Los Angeles. Sheila, next to him, held his hand under the table. He asked Raven for her impressions of the Winfrey program, and his face brightened as he listened. He looked cheerful when he hung up.

"It seems that honesty is the best policy," he told Sheila. "Nothing has changed. She still wants me for the *Phantom*. She says the program will only enhance my popularity."

"Then you actually didn't even need to confess on television," Sheila said.

"Oh, yes, I did," Mason said. "It has cheered me up enormously. I never could keep guilty secrets."

Devereaux ordered a flaming steak served up on sword-point, and was dismayed to find the Pump Room no longer offered the specialty, which Robert Morley had once described to him as most entertainingly vulgar.

"It's just as well," Sheila told him. "With your luck, the waiter would stumble and set the table on fire."

A busboy materialized and refilled their glasses with ice water. Mason drank deeply from his glass and had put it down again before he realized that it tasted strange.

"Did we order some sort of mineral water?" he asked Sheila. And then, before she could answer, he leaped to his feet, overturning their table with a great crash, and raced toward the bar area. Sheila twisted in her seat and crawled over the back of the booth in an attempt to stop him, before she saw what Mason saw: The busboy, who had shed his white coat and was now struggling with the bartender and a security guard, had the twisted face of Spike Murphy.

"What are you doing to me?" Mason shouted into his face.

"It's all over for me now," Murphy said, ending his struggle, suddenly deflated. "I thought perhaps if I could discredit you, to keep you from testifying against me . . ."

Two more plainclothesmen arrived from hotel security. The police were called.

"How did you know where I was?" Mason asked.

Murphy looked behind him for a chair and sat down, completely drained of strength and resolve. "Finding celebrities is what I do best, Mr. Devereaux," he said wearily. "I simply followed your limousine from the television station."

Sheila had arrived at Mason's side and protectively touched his cheek. "Did you taste something in the water, darling?"

"Did I?" Mason asked Murphy pointedly.

"A sort of bitter taste?" Murphy asked.

"That's right."

"It would be a variant of LSD."

Mason started to lunge at the man, but a security guard put out a restraining arm.

"Oh my God!" Sheila cried. "Mason is a recovering alcoholic! After what he's been through, how could you drug him?"

"I've done worse," Murphy said.

Two Chicago policeman came importantly into the restaurant, pushed through the crowd that had gathered, and handcuffed Murphy.

"Make him tell you what he gave to Mason!" Sheila cried out.

"He put LSD in his drinking water! He needs to be taken to a hospital immediately! Mason, darling, tell me how you feel right now!"

Her eyes wildly searched the room. Mason Devereaux was no longer there.

W A L K straight, Mason told himself. Nod to the left. Nod to the right. That was how the Queen did it. A hand to the crowd, then touch the neck, then wave to the crowd on the other side. Shake the hand of the man standing on the sidewalk. Man in a uniform. Bus driver. Get on the bus. Red bus. Same color as in London. Red bus. London.

His mind in the grip of the drug, Mason found himself in a totally objective universe. He had no opinions about anything. Nothing had a nuance. All was surface. Red bus. Staircase. He climbed the stairs of the red bus. Seat empty. Sat down.

"Look, it's Mason Devereaux!" A large woman in the front of the bus was pointing to him. Woman. White pants. Blue blouse. Others on the bus turned around, and Mason catalogued their clothing: Baseball cap. T-shirt. Running shoes.

"We saw you on Oprah's show this morning!" the woman cried out, and then she and her friends crowded down the aisle to surround him. "Don't tell me you're a Cubs fan!" she said. "Get outta here! Go Cubbies! Can we take a picture with you?"

Several of the women clustered around Mason, while the large woman gave her camera to a fellow passenger. They all said "cheese!" After a moment, Mason also said "cheese!" Then he said it again: "Cheese! Cheese! Cheese!" It was a word with a certain eerie quality to it. Cheese. T-shirt. Baseball cap. He almost lost his balance as the bus lurched forward and pulled away from the hotel. Cheese. He sat down in the nearest seat. Cheese. Everybody around him started to sing.

"Na na na na, na na na na, hey hey, good-bye!"

Song. Mason had no idea if it was a good song or a bad song. He sang: "Na na na na, na na na na . . ." Strangers slapped him on the back. "Cubs rule the world!" a man shouted in his ear. "Britannia rules the waves," Mason told him. They howled.

SECONDS after the red tourist bus roared away from in front of the hotel, Sheila Chesham burst from the front door, followed by Chicago police officers. The doorman informed them that Mason had looked alert—perhaps too alert—as he had stepped smartly across the sidewalk and marched up the steps of the bus.

"Bus?" cried Sheila. "What bus?"

"The charter to Wrigley Field," the doorman said, and then, seeing that the name did not ring a bell, added, "The baseball field."

Sheila gasped. The police officers put her in the backseat of their squad car, and by the time they arrived at Wrigley Field, Addison Street was jammed with police cars and ambulances. A television traffic copter circled overhead.

MASON was blissfully unaware of the emergency. One of his newfound friends on the tourist bus had slapped a Cubs baseball hat on his head, and stuck a big pennant in his hand. Somebody else had given him a T-shirt. He was wearing a giant pair of dark glasses. The group had produced an extra ticket and swept him along with them to their seats, and none of them found it strange that he continued to sing their favorite song: "Na na na na, na na na na . . . hey, hey . . . good-bye!"

As he reached the top of the stairs leading to the field, Mason was overwhelmed at first by the crowd that filled Wrigley Field. "Na na na na!" he insisted. "You were great on 'Oprah'!" someone told him. "Na na na na?" he asked. A hot dog materialized in his hand, and he ate it, still repeating his mantra, spraying mustard and relish all over his T-shirt. Some of the fans regarded him strangely, as Mason stood up and marched away, waving the banner and chanting, "Na na na na."

Blue. Red. White. People. *Na na na na.* Mason stood tall and walked straight, and was not recognized in his baseball cap and oversized dark glasses. His world had been reduced to logical atoms of shape and color, each with its own innate reality. Square. Circle. *Na na.* Crack! Roar! The crowd stood to its feet and cheered as the first Cub batter hit a home run out of the friendly confines. Forty thou-

sand people sang, "Na na na na, na na na na, hey hey, good-bye!"
Mason sang along.

He had no idea where he was going. Spaces receded in front of
him. Stairs offered themselves. Surfaces guided him. *Na na.*

I N the broadcast booth high above the field, veteran sportscaster
Harry Carey called the game. His molasses voice gurgled with
pleasure as the Cubs surged to an immediate one-to-nothing
lead. "And it's a beautiful day at the ballpark!" he intoned, before
glancing down at a note passed to him by an assistant.

"Enjoying the game today . . . thirty-five members of the Urbana
Rotary Club and their beautiful spouses," Carey read. "They arrived
at Wrigley Field in a chartered London bus. All the way from
London, I suppose!" He chortled at his own wit, and then looked up
as a strange man entered the booth.

"Na na," the man said.

"Who is this guy?" Carey asked, pushing the squelch button on
his microphone.

"Hey hey," said the man, waving his pennant back and forth.
Then Carey recognized his famous guest.

"Strike three, and he's outta there," Carey said into his mike,
calling the game on automatic pilot. Then his voice took on a proud
glow that he hadn't employed since the great day Ronald Reagan
visited the broadcast booth: "Visiting our microphones today, a man
who needs no introduction . . . Mason Devereaux! A big Cubbie welcome!"

"Good-bye," said Mason.

"Yeah, that home run ball was outta here!" Carey said. "Holy cow!"

"Hey hey," said Mason.

"The man knows all the lingo," Carey said proudly. "Ball one, low
and outside."

"Na na na na," said Mason.

"What a pleasure to discover that a man with all the fame and
publicity in the world still has a warm spot in his heart for the great
American pastime! It's a strike over the outside corner," Carey said.
"Fast ball."

"Good-bye!" said Mason.

"Heh, heh," said Carey. "The windup and the pitch—strike two!"

Mason waved his pennant back and forth in front of Carey's field of view, but the veteran broadcaster didn't miss a beat.

"A man who has survived adventures that few people would have lived to tell about, visiting the ball park today. *He* . . . struck him out!"

The crowd roared, and Mason, distracted, looked around. His eye fell on the butterfly net that Carey employed to catch foul balls. He dropped his pennant and grabbed for the net, just as a TV camera swung around to get a shot of Carey in the booth with his famous guest. Mason swung the net aimlessly in the air, and then dropped it down over Carey's head.

"I'm telling ya, folks, whadda sense of humor!" Harry chortled. As he struggled to free himself from the net, Chicago police officers burst into the booth, followed by Sheila Chesham.

"Mason!" she cried. "Don't move! We're here!"

Mason looked up at the sound of his name, and something snapped in his hallucinating brain. The objective nature of the universe—the shapes and colors changed in a second to an ominous subjective abyss of nameless dreads and terrors. He turned toward Harry Carey, who was still waving his arms, trying to free himself from the butterfly net, and it seemed to him that the man was a gorgon from some unknown dimension. Carey's outsize eyeglasses looked to Mason like the staring orbs of a bug-eyed monster.

Struggling desperately to save himself from this terrifying creature, Mason climbed to the edge of the booth and then, still holding tight to the handle of the net that ensnared Carey, jumped over. Sheila and the cops were paralyzed as Mason and the famed broadcaster disappeared from view.

I T was like the world's biggest trampoline. Mason Devereaux and Harry Carey tumbled from the broadcast booth at Wrigley Field and landed on the netting that protected the fans from foul balls. Then they bounced high in the air again, Carey's arms cartwheeling as he struggled to find his equilibrium. On the second bounce the butterfly net came free from around his head, and after the third bounce he was able to hang onto the net and get his bearings.

The net suspended him in midair halfway between the lower and upper decks. Play on the field came to a halt as everyone in the ballpark turned to look at the strange sight. Carey took inventory, found he had survived without injury, and gave a big wave to the fans, who responded with a tumultuous ovation. The broadcaster had lost his famous glasses in the fall, and now squinted in the direction of Mason Devereaux, only to see the actor climbing hand over hand up the net.

"Hey, big fella, take it easy!" Carey shouted at him. Devereaux paused and looked back over his shoulder. Carey tried to remember scenes in movies where hero cops had talked madmen off the ledges of tall buildings. "Ya wanna talk about it, buddy?"

The words seemed to release a trigger in Mason's mind, allowing consciousness to fade back in again. The world came into focus. Words made sense. He knew who he was. He felt the rough rope of the netting in his hands, looked down, and realized his situation

with a shock: He was suspended in midair above thousands of baseball fans, while a silver-haired man in a yellow-check sport jacket was trying to talk sense to him.

BILLY (SILVER DOLLAR) BAXTER grabbed for the intercom and shouted an all-points alert to every extension in Raven Charles's office: "Get in here to the media room—on the double! Mason is at it again!" He stabbed the remote-control device in the direction of the TV set and turned up the volume as Raven appeared in the doorway with Robert Mitchum Takeuchi. They had been working on the budget for the *Phantom*.

"This beats everything," Billy told him. "Mason somehow turned up at the ballpark in Chicago, broke into the broadcast booth, grabbed Harry Carey, and jumped over the edge with him. Now they're bouncing on the foul-ball net like old buddy-boys."

"Has he been drinking again?" Raven asked, her voice filled with dread as she stood in front of the set. Takeuchi moved to her side.

The live television picture showed police and security guards clearing the area beneath the two men. There was pandemonium in Wrigley Field as fans struggled for a better view. Some on the upper decks were in danger of falling off as they leaned forward to see what was happening. From far above Harry Carey's head, an engineer lowered a microphone on a long extension cord, and the veteran broadcaster grabbed it, tapped it twice, and blew into it.

The sound was fed into the public address system, so that everyone could hear Carey's first words: "Holy cow!" The fans roared with approval, sensing that a potential tragedy was now turning into high comedy.

"As I was saying before I was interrupted . . ." Carey began, his rich gurgle returning to normal, and the crowd cheered again. Mason, now only a few feet away from Harry, held onto the netting for dear life and looked down between his legs to the hard concrete far below. Then he saw a familiar face. It was Sheila, waving her scarf at him.

"I say, old man, do you suppose I could say a word or two?" Mason began.

"The man of the hour!" Carey intoned. "Mason Devereaux! I'm still not sure what happened up there in the booth, Mason. Got any more tricks up your sleeve?"

He held the mike out at arm's length and Mason spoke into it. "Hello, Sheila," he said. She waved her scarf again. In front of Raven's screen, Baxter and Takeuchi flanked the studio chief, watching intently as a remote camera picked up Sheila in a closeup. "I'm quite all right now," Mason said, his voice booming through Wrigley Field. A closeup showed him looking only into her eyes, ignoring the tumult all around him.

"Perhaps you can introduce everyone to the lovely young lady," Carey said. "Here comes help, by the way! Hold on tight!"

A fire department hook and ladder truck had driven directly onto the sacred grass of Wrigley Field, and was positioning itself so that rescue workers could try to pick the actor and the sportscaster free from their web in the sky.

"Forgive me, everyone, for this ridiculous disturbance," Mason said into the microphone. "Apparently I was given a drug without my knowledge. I'm quite all right now. I'm sorry to have endangered anyone. It wasn't my doing. I assure you I haven't had a drink in weeks."

"That sure doesn't seem to have slowed you down any," Carey chortled, bouncing on the netting. "Holy cow!"

"My head is quite clear now," Mason said, his words echoing from the Wrigley Field speakers and carrying even across to the rooftops of Waveland Avenue. He saw the long arm of the extension ladder reaching up into the sky for them. "Here comes our rescue now. But if anything should go wrong—there's one thing I want to say."

He turned to Carey, who was still holding the microphone. "If I may?"

"Be my guest!" Carey roared.

"Sheila, will you do me the honor of becoming my wife?"

Sheila bit her lip in surprise and then, in a closeup that would be seen all over the world, she nodded her head in a simple yes.

Watching the scene on television, Raven felt tears welling up in her eyes. As firemen helped Mason Devereaux and Harry Carey to safety on an extension ladder the Wrigley Field organist played "True Love."

LATER that night, Takeuchi's cigar glowed once again on the deck of the *Rashomon*.

"I was rather surprised," he said, "that you took a soft line with me. From your reputation I expected you to be unforgiving."

"I am uncompromising," said Raven Charles, "but not unforgiving."

"Mason was in the hands of the Sandman, and I had a good idea how to find him. I could have wrung it out of Murphy. But I didn't want to get involved. I was a coward."

He drew on his cigar and let the smoke trickle from his lips as he looked across at the beautiful black woman, whose features glowed in the moonlight and the dim lamps from the cabin.

"Perhaps you would have acted—eventually," Raven said. "It all happened in less than twenty-four hours. You didn't have time to think it through."

"I could still be indicted. Murphy could claim he was under my orders."

"They'll never put a finger on you," Raven said. "After the stunt he pulled with Mason, he has totally discredited himself as a witness."

"We exist out here in such a rotten world," Takeuchi said philosophically. "Hollywood considers compromise to be a moral position. Sometimes it takes a Mason Devereaux to remind us of what the human being is capable of. A Mason Devereaux . . . or a Raven Charles."

Raven felt the ocean wind cool against her neck. She'd had a feeling this was coming.

"Raven," said Takeuchi. "Would you mind very much if I kissed you?"

She turned to rest her hands on the deck rail.

"Lay off it, Bob," she said. "This is business."

PART ELEVEN

Rites

EVERYONE in the room recognized the tall, distinguished-
looking man who sat in the back row in the corner, holding the
hand of a young woman. Most of them had seen the replays
on the evening news, showing Mason Devereaux proposing to Sheila
Chesham while he sat on a foul-ball net, suspended halfway between earth and sky. But there was a certain tact at an AA meeting,
a feeling that no matter how famous someone like Devereaux might
be on the outside, in here he was only "Mason."

Sheila could feel Devereaux's hand trembling in her own. "My
name is Mason, and I'm an alcoholic," he said, "and I needed to find
a meeting very badly this evening. I have been without drink for
more than a month, but today I was given a drug by a man who
wished me ill. Earlier, this same man had attempted to kill me, but
what he did today was a far worse thing—because I would rather be
obliterated, than return to the chaos of the days when I was not
sober."

Mason's measured, formal words struck a solemn note in the
meeting room, where slang and shared laughter were more com-
mon. There was a sense that he meant every single word that he
said.

"I came here tonight to say that I have not taken a drink for
thirty days, and that, if necessary, I will sit here on this chair for the
rest of my life rather than go out through that door to a pub."

"Thirty days?" said the cheerful teenage girl who was chairing
the meeting. "Then you qualify for a chip!"

"A what?" Mason asked, but a nun seated next to him was
already urging him to his feet.

"A blue poker chip," the girl said. "We give them out to anyone who makes thirty days. Carry it around in your pocket as a reminder!"

Mason rose slowly to his feet and walked to the front of the meeting room. He took the chip, and was astonished to find tears in his eyes as he turned around again. He held up the cheap bit of plastic, and said, "I had rather have this, than be knighted by the Queen whilst a drunk."

He made his way back to his seat to thunderous applause, and with an actor's keen instincts he was able to turn, nod, brush a tear from his eye, and milk the ovation for a good fifteen seconds after it should have ended.

As Spike Murphy was flown back to Los Angeles handcuffed to an FBI agent, Robert Mitchum Takeuchi paced the deck of the great yacht *Rashomon* and brooded. He did not feel content with the world. He felt positively dissatisfied with himself. After years of building a media empire with little regard for the price he paid or the hostages he took, he now felt diminished and insignificant. And it was all because of that woman Raven Charles.

He lit a cigar and then distractedly threw it into the sea. He walked into the galley and opened a bottle of beer, and then absentmindedly left it on a teak table and walked back up on deck without it. His mind replayed a familiar litany of his holdings: Realistic Pictures, of course, and also daily newspapers, magazines, cable networks, billboard companies, advertising agencies, newsprint mills, radio and television stations, real estate, a silver mine in Nevada— and, of course, Spike Murphy's little supermarket sleaze sheet, *Fact Digest,* which under the circumstances would have to be closed and written off as a total loss.

Takeuchi had a favorite movie of his own. It was *Citizen Kane.* His most-treasured moment in the movie was the shot in the opening newsreel, showing the circles of Kane's growing power as they radiated out to cover a map of America. The most unpleasant moment in *Kane* was the shot where the circles withered, contracted, and died. This morning Takeuchi could feel his circles withering.

Last night, Raven Charles had turned down the opportunity to become Takeuchi's latest takeover—the most prized acquisition in his portfolio. And Takeuchi, like Kane, found that all of his riches and power could not stand up to the tinkle of a woman's laughter. The press lord lit another cigar, and thought. He was one of the richest men in the world. He was single. He was considered by many to be handsome, and he was certainly powerful. Power was the ultimate aphrodisiac, he had read somewhere. But it had been meaningless to the beautiful black woman.

Was she simply not romantically inclined? He didn't believe it. He had seen a tantalizing light in her eyes that was not merely reflected from the candles on the table. His instincts were sound on matters of the heart. Could it possibly be, Takeuchi wondered, that Raven simply did not . . . *approve* of him?

He paced restlessly on the deck and then snatched up a telephone and punched the code that would connect him directly with Raven's desk at Realistic Pictures.

"Miss Charles? Takeuchi. I have decided to fold Murphy's newspaper. I no longer want to associate myself with projects of that nature. I . . . thought you'd like to know."

He listened, nodded, and hung up. Raven had told him it was "not a bad idea." Well, that was something. Takeuchi puckered his lips and tested to see if he still remembered how to whistle.

T H E great manor at Thorn Hill had not seen such activity since 1958, when the Queen had come to visit. A footman, airing out one of the bedrooms in the west wing, found a copy of the *Times* that had not been disturbed in thirty years. Tents were erected on the lawn, and men with stakes roped off part of the grounds as a parking area. There was a queue of trucks from the provisioners, with food, drink, flowers, and folding chairs. Twenty musicians in tuxedos milled unhappily by the kitchen door, emitting experimental blatts and toots, waiting for their bandstand to be erected. They would play for the family tonight and the guests tomorrow.

In her room overlooking the great lawn, Sheila Chesham sat by the window. She had picked up the big black diary from Smythson's that she had written in for years, but put it down again with a sigh.

There was too much to write, too complicated, too incredible. On the distant hill, not far from the old folly that masked the entrance to the underwater ballroom, she could see Lord Chesham walking with Mason Devereaux. The smoke from their cigars streamed from their lips in the fresh breeze. From her father's animation, she judged he was discussing spiders.

Sheila's engagement party was the social event of the early autumn, not only in England, where any heiress to the Chesham fortune was a celebrity, but all over the world. The romance of Mason and Sheila, climaxing with a proposal of marriage before thirty thousand American baseball fans, had made them a storybook couple.

Her mother was sitting on her bed, using the extension phone to talk to the village butcher. Lady Chesham had been driven from her own rooms by a crush of secretaries, social directors, coordinators, and the other functionaries who seemed necessary to coordinate an engagement fete of suitable hilarity.

So many people were moving in and out of Thorn Hill, indeed, that Douglas Brown was not noticed as he took one end of a folding table and helped a laborer lift it off a truck and carry it into the manor. Brown was unshaven and disheveled after days of sleeping rough, but he looked no worse than some of the other men who had been hired as day laborers in the rush for tomorrow's celebration. He helped his partner erect the table in the old library, and then, when the other man had left, Brown walked quickly to the wall and pushed a button that made a bookcase swing aside, revealing the passageway that led, he knew, to the underwater ballroom.

He well remembered the passage from the day they had all been taken on a tour of it, after Mason had stumbled out of the library wall. Now he knew he could use it as a hiding place in the very bosom of the Chesham family. As the bookcase closed behind him, there was pitch darkness at first, but then he could dimly see the outlines of the ancient passageway. A little light leaked in around the edges of the bookcases. Some workmen walked into the library, and he could clearly hear them talking to one another.

He sat down on the floor, braced his back against a stone wall, took out an apple, and ate it.

I really must apologize, old girl," Mason said, "for proposing marriage like that to you in front of the whole world. But when I came to my senses I had absolutely no idea why I was a hundred feet in the air, clinging to that net. I fully expected to die and—I wanted you to know how I felt about you."

"It was the most romantic moment in the world," Sheila said, cuddling closer. Mason stroked her arm, and she turned and kissed him. It was late in the evening, after the twilight concert on the lawn, and they'd found a moment to be by themselves in front of the fire in Thorn Hill's library. "Mason . . . I like it so much that you're able to feel close to me. All during those drinking days I knew that you liked me, but you just couldn't bring yourself to show it. You were always sort of holding me off at arm's length."

"Thought you were engaged to that Douglas Brown, old girl. Besides, why would you be attracted to an old booze hound like me? Richest girl in England, coming home to my bachelor's digs in Jermyn Street? Impossible to contemplate!"

"Douglas was a sick chapter in my life," Sheila said. "I think I was trying to make you jealous. I don't know how I could ever have taken him seriously. He didn't even believe in himself."

RAVEN CHARLES woke at the strange hour of two in the morning, and stepped out through the tall French doors that opened from her room directly onto the lawn of Thorn Hill House. The full moon painted the ancient landscape in dark silver shadows. The new studio chief had arrived a few hours ago, groggy from jet lag after the endless flight from Los Angeles, and had been invited by Lady Chesham to please go to bed immediately so that she would be fresh for the party. A butler had appeared at her door with sandwiches and milk, which she was too sleepy to touch, but now, in the middle of the night, she was wide awake.

There was complete quiet all around her, and it seemed to Raven as if she had not heard the quiet for years. Sometimes, she admit-

ted, she did get tired. Running Realistic Pictures was a job that occupied even her dreams. She had achieved success beyond all ambition, and yet she slept alone and walked alone. Thrusting her hands
deep into the pockets of her running jacket, Raven walked along the
lawn and thought of Takeuchi's telephone call—the one where he
had vowed to shut down Murphy's despicable scandal sheet.

Raven knew why Takeuchi had taken the decision. He suspected—
correctly—that she had little respect for him. He hoped the action
would change his image in her eyes. Had it? She looked out over the
landscape. Not really, she thought. He was a man who was not reliable when the chips were down. He could have pointed the police to
the Sandman's secret laboratory when Mason was missing, but he
had delayed. He was too selfish of his fortune.

Raven turned to walk back to the house, and found a man standing on the lawn a hundred yards behind her. It was Takeuchi, holding a huge bouquet of roses. She smiled and walked toward him,
and he put the roses down on the grass so that he could spread his
arms in supplication.

"I just drove up from London," he said, speaking so quickly she
could have sworn he was nervous. "I have fallen in love with you.
One of the things I believe in life is that we can all change, and
become better people. All I am asking is that you give me the
chance to try."

She walked forward at a measured pace and picked up one of the
roses. He did not move. She held it by the stem and brushed the
flower playfully against his cheek.

"Only you can give yourself that chance," she said.

THAT was not what Takeuchi wanted to hear, but he had to be
content with it. They walked together around the comfortable
bulk of the old house, until they found windows that were still
lighted, even so late at night. Sheila Chesham was standing at one
of them, and when she saw them her eyes brightened and she
pushed it open to call to them.

"I can't sleep!" she said. "I'm too excited! Come indoors and have
a glass of something with Mason and me."

Raven and Takeuchi walked around through the front doors and into the library, where Mason poured them round beakers of port, and an orange juice for himself. The two couples settled down in worn leather sofas on either side of the fire. Mason knew that Takeuchi had until recently been Murphy's employer, but he believed the press lord's story that Murphy had been acting out of his own deluded fantasies. Now Takeuchi was going to make movies with Mason Devereaux. How strangely the world turned.

"It was right here," Sheila said, "that I was sitting with Mommy when Mason burst out of the wall."

"The return of Lazarus from the dead," Mason murmured.

"I saw the program on television," Takeuchi said. "It was astonishing to me that a British aristocrat would conceive of an underwater ballroom."

"They were all in a sort of competition in those days," Sheila said. "There was the Hellfire Club—they met in a cave and tried to shock one another—and Sir John Soane had an Egyptian sarcophagus in his house in town. The ninth earl wasn't to be outdone. It was all the rage to go to dances down there in his ballroom."

"Wasn't there something about his suicidal tendencies?" Raven asked.

"He was nutty as a fruitcake," Sheila said. "His plan was to invite everyone over for New Year's Eve, and then drown them at the stroke of midnight."

"Why drown them?" Takeuchi asked, swirling the port in his glass.

"Why build the blasted thing in the first place?" Mason growled.

Sheila stood up, her face glowing in the light from the fire. "Let's do something absolutely daft!" she said. "None of us can sleep. Let's go down to the underwater ballroom!"

"Not me, old girl," Mason said softly. "I've had the tour."

Raven's eyes were sparkling. "We could have a little private dance of our own," she said. "It's a fun idea."

"Here's my cassette player," Sheila said. "It runs on batteries. Come on, Mason, don't spoil the party! I want to dance with you."

"My memories of that foul hole are not of the fondest," he said, grumbling, but he heaved himself to his feet and took a candelabra from a tabletop.

"Daddy has a flashlight here by his reading chair," Sheila said. "He uses it with a pair of binoculars, to read the titles on the top shelves."

She took the light and walked over to the bookcase, depressing the eyelid on a carved wooden triglyph. The wall of shelves moved out soundlessly, and the smell of ancient, chilled damp blew past them into the room.

"Gonna take, a sentimental journey . . ." Sheila hummed, as she led the way into the gaping darkness. Raven found Takeuchi's hand on her arm, and after descending the first few stone steps found she appreciated it there. Mason stood for a moment looking at the entrance, and then, when the others had disappeared from view, he took a breath and followed them down, the candelabra casting grasping shadows on the walls.

BENEATH the earth, moving through a cold humidity that seeped through their clothing, the party crept down the passage. The ninth earl's Gothic fantasies had been indulged by the architects who built this tunnel from the Thorn Hill library into the chalk substrata of the grounds, and then across to the great depression that he envisioned as an artificial lake. First he had constructed the ballroom beneath it—a chamber topped by two vast quarter-spheres of metal, joined at the top. Then he had flooded the lake and stocked it with fish that his guests could observe through portholes.

As the passageway grew longer, it grew still cooler. Takeuchi took off his blazer and passed it around Sheila's shoulders. They made a bizarre Felliniesque procession, as if through the catacombs of Rome. Sheila picked out the way with the flashlight, followed by Takeuchi and Raven, who stepped fastidiously through the mouldy grunge in her high-heeled Guccis. Mason brought up the rear.

The passageway became a brick tunnel that led straight as an arrow under the earth. A smell of damp and death filled the air. Eventually the sound of their footsteps became hollow, and Sheila pointed the flashlight up to play against a dark ominous steel dome that curved over their heads. The group spread out on either side of the exit from the tunnel and looked around speechlessly. Mason, who had spent two days blundering through this room in pitch darkness, now saw it for the first time. Before them was the ghostly evidence of a celebration that had been abruptly abandoned on a New Year's Eve long years before. There was an elevated platform for an orchestra, bearing wooden music stands, some of them collapsed from rot. Tables still held silver platters and punch bowls. Spider webs spread from the empty candelabra. Faded silk banners fell in tatters from the ceilings.

Sheila felt as if she had interrupted a banquet of the dead. "They never came back after that night," she said.

A S they spread out into the center of the room, the curved metal surfaces of the dome sent their footfalls tapping softly back at them, like echoes from another time. Mason remained near the entranceway with his flickering candles. Sheila used the flashlight to help the others explore.

"Look at this," said Takeuchi.

He stood next to a set of oak and brass levers almost as tall as himself.

"This must be where the butler struggled with the ninth earl, just as he was preparing to pull the levers and open the dome to let in the waters," Sheila said. "The butler saved the day."

"Why did he want to drown all of his guests?" asked Raven, moving closer.

"Why, just for the sheer effrontery of it, I should imagine," she said. "Any man who would build a place like this might easily be insane enough to flood it."

They heard a loud, barking cough, which echoed off the steel walls so that it seemed to come from everywhere, and nowhere.

"Mason?" asked Sheila.

"Not me," he said, his voice sounding strained. The three of them could look over and see him in the candlelight at the foot of the stairs.

Sheila laughed nervously. "I thought I heard somebody cough," she said.

"I think you did," Raven said, instinctively moving closer to Takeuchi. Just then they all felt a strong gust of wind, and Mason's candles guttered and disappeared.

"Stay together!" Sheila said. "Mason! Come over here with the rest of us! Can you see us?"

"I'm on my way," Mason said, just as the beam of Sheila's flashlight turned a dirty yellow.

"I wonder when Daddy replaced these batteries?" she asked, just as the flashlight failed.

Sheila cried out in frustration. Takeuchi put his arm around Raven's shoulders. Mason stooped to place the candelabra on the floor so that he could search in his pockets for matches, and could hear that he had kicked it over in the dark. The cough came again, a tearing, hacking cough that seemed to fill the darkness.

Sheila felt a hand on her arm, pulling her urgently to one side.

"Mason?"

"Not Mason. Douglas."

She tried to scream, but there was a rough hand over her mouth, silencing her. The other hand, on her arm, dug into her flesh, and she was forced to follow where the unseen man was taking her.

"Mason was a fool," the voice whispered in her ear. "He was set up to die. I went to Gasper and offered him money to shoot him dead on the stage. Your money. Gasper agreed."

Sheila struggled to free herself, but Brown was too strong.

"Listen! he whispered. "The revolver I gave him had six bullets in the chambers. He put in the blanks himself—so that if he got caught, he could claim it was only a publicity stunt. Mason fell for it hook, line, and sinker."

"Sheila?" It was Mason's voice. "Call out and I will find my way to you!"

"I've already found her!" Brown shouted defiantly into the darkness.

"Who's there?" Raven called.

Stumbling footsteps echoed off the old damp walls. Sheila was suddenly released, and knocked the flashlight against her palm until the beam sprang back weakly to life. In its dim illumination she could see a gaunt, staring figure whose face was covered with what looked for a startling moment like the Phantom's mask—until she saw it was mud and blood. Douglas Brown stood trembling with his hands on the tall brass and oak levers.

T H E Y probably won't work, Brown thought to himself. It's been two hundred years. They must inevitably be jammed or corroded or disconnected or something. I'll leave it to fate. I'm going to pull them, and if nothing happens, then I'll take that as a sign.

He pulled the levers, which were the work of the most skilled hydraulic engineers the ninth earl had been able to find. The counterbalanced machinery, which had waited so long to do its task, performed it now with awful majesty. Brown looked up as the spheres of the ceiling parted, and just had time to glimpse the stars through the incalculable weight of the falling waters.

His luck was no better than Bradleigh Court's.

L O R D   C H E S H A M sat on his veranda and looked out over the grassy slopes of Thorn Hill House, which looked much the same today as when he had first seen them as a young boy. It had all been so dream-laden and peaceful in those days of childhood, the trees, the lake, the great unchanging presence of the old house. He liked to rise sometimes when the moon was full like this, and look over the ancient landscape, so unchanging and yet so ghostly and insubstantial.

But there was something wrong.

Something . . . new, about the landscape.

He could not put his finger on it. He blinked and looked again, and stepped to the door of the master bedroom, which opened onto the veranda.

"I say, darling, just have a look at the lake, will you?"

"What about it?" his wife asked.

"I would say it is at a lower level than usual."

Just as he turned to look again, a gigantic bubble of air broke through the surface, and with a fearsome roar the water disappeared. From where he stood he could now see the bottom of the lake, where a giant steel eye opened its lids to the moon.

T H E roaring waters crashed and boiled against the old stone walls of the man-made cave, but as the lips of the great spheres began to open, they let in the ghostly light of the moon, as well. Mason understood the situation in a glance, and tore at the arms of Raven and Takeuchi with a fierce urgency.

"Follow me!"

He swept Sheila into his arms as the cascade of water tore at them, and then he ran with her straight at an old oak door, so discolored with mold it almost disappeared into the wall. The door slammed open and they all fell in a heap on a rotting pile of leaves and mud. The water crashed through after them, and Mason struggled to close the door, but could not. Then the water was above their waists and rising so quickly that there was only one choice, and Mason shouted it out: "Ride with the water! Float to the top!"

The rough stonework of the old well tore at their skins, and they used their arms to protect their heads as with a great heave the subterranean tide hurtled them toward the surface and spat them out, limp and gasping, on the parapet of the well. Sheila, bleeding and dazed, struggled to her feet and saw Raven and Takeuchi sprawled on the grass next to the old wellhead. The earth shook as if it were being pounded by an angry giant.

"Mason!" she cried out. "Where are you?"

And then they saw him hauling himself over the edge to safety, soaking wet, covered with mud, and laughing.

"Just as I said, old girl, what a rotten idea for a place to go dancing."

D A Y one, scene one of *The Mason Devereaux Saga* was shot while preparations were already under way for *Phantom of the Opera*. Both productions would be filmed back-to-back on the lot at Realistic, with location work in London. Raven was determined that nothing would go wrong with the two projects bearing her name, and she had promoted Ivan Bloom, her former boss, to the job of line producer on the *Phantom.*

Billy (Silver Dollar) Baxter, who had always dreamed of seeing his name above the title, or anywhere in the titles, was named associate producer and technical consultant on the *Saga,* since he had personally witnessed so many of Mason's adventures. He stood on a set of the Coach and Horses pub that had been built on a soundstage at Realistic, and watched as a stand-in posed on Mason's bar stool for a lighting check. The art directors had done their work so well, Billy could have sworn he was back in the original Coach and Horses—where, one fateful evening, he had been greeted by Mason Devereaux when the world thought the actor was dead.

Fontaine Eady had flown over from London for the first day of shooting. He would stay for Murphy's kidnapping trial. The Sandman had been sent straight to a rubber room.

"Confidentially, just between you and me and your millions of readers," Billy told him, "I'm more of an expert on Mason than Mason is—because he was unconscious or hallucinating half of the time, and I was right there, taking detailed mental notes. When we were locked in the stateroom on that yacht off of Monte Carlo, I thought he was gonna croak any minute. I kept him alive by feeding him olives through the Iron Mask."

"An angel of mercy," Eady said.

"Irving!"

A gofer jumped up from his morning paper and raced across the soundstage. "Yes, Mr. Baxter?"

"On the double. Black coffee for me. Tea for Sir Fontaine. And gimme the trade papers so I can see if I made any more news."

The thick doors of the soundstage opened, and Raven Charles entered with Takeuchi at her side. The exact nature of their relationship was a tantalizing mystery to everyone in Hollywood except for Billy Baxter, who explained, "They're inseparable, but only in public."

Raven shook hands with Fontaine Eady—with reserve, since she remembered he had been a nuisance toward her at Thorn Hill, during the vigil after Mason had fallen down the well. Then she took Billy to one side.

"When is Mason expected on the set?" she asked.

"Not for another couple of hours. The assistant director is drilling the extras now, and they've got a problem with the draft beer. The pump won't work."

"Can't they use bottles?"

"This is supposed to be a pub, not a country club."

Raven nodded. She seemed a little hesitant. "Billy . . . I don't even want to mention this, but you're one of the producers and so I must. In a scene like this, of course, Mason might be tempted. You know, to take a drink."

"Mason?" Billy snorted. "No way! He's on the program."

"I know, but if he starts feeling under tension . . . "

"No problem. I'm right here on the spot. Mason and I are old buddy-boys. We'll take first-class care of one another."

"You are not my first idea of someone to look after Mason," Raven said, smiling.

"Why not? Now he's got me going to the meetings, too."

"You?"

"Keep it under your hat," Billy said. "It's anonymous, you know."

I T was really rather nice, life on what Mason called the expensive account. Especially when one wasn't due at the studio for another two hours. Mason opened the door of their villa at the Sunset Marquis and picked up the morning paper. He walked back inside, where Sheila smiled at him, her hair fanned out against the pillow like a chestnut wave.

"Mason?"

"Yes?"

"That was lovely."

"I think I *am* rather getting the hang of it, old girl," Mason said, almost blushing. He sat on the edge of the bed. "I confess when we first started out I feared I would be altogether too shy."

Sheila trailed a finger across his cheek.

"Look here," Mason said a little later, scanning the front page. "The Murphy kidnapping case has gone to the jury. A quick verdict is expected." He peered more closely at the paper. "The reporter is Fontaine Eady," he said. "What irony. If it hadn't been for Fontaine getting me drunk before that Saturday matinee . . ."

"You would have been dead."

"In that case, I must remember to thank him."